Employment Equity
and
Affirmative Action

ISSUES IN WORK AND HUMAN RESOURCES

Daniel J.B. Mitchell, Series Editor

**BEYOND UNIONS AND
COLLECTIVE BARGAINING**
Leo Troy

CYBERUNION
Empowering Labor Through Computer
Technology
Arthur B. Shostak

**WORKING IN THE TWENTY-
FIRST CENTURY**
Policies for Economic Growth Through
Training, Opportunity, and Education
David I. Levine

**INCOME INEQUALITY IN
AMERICA**
An Analysis of Trends
Paul Ryscavage

HARD LABOR
Poor Women and Work in the Post-
Welfare Era
Joel F. Handler and Lucie White, editors

**NONUNION EMPLOYEE
REPRESENTATION**
History, Contemporary Practice, and
Policy
Bruce E. Kaufman and Daphne Gottlieb
Taras, editors

**LABOR REGULATION
IN A GLOBAL ECONOMY**
George Tsogas

FAMILY LEAVE POLICY
The Political Economy of Work and
Family in America
Steven K. Wisensale

**COLLECTIVE BARGAINING
IN THE PUBLIC SECTOR**
The Experience of Eight States
Joyce M. Najita and James L. Stern, editors

PAYING FOR PERFORMANCE
An International Comparison
Michelle Brown and John S. Heywood,
editors

**THE FUTURE OF PRIVATE
SECTOR UNIONISM
IN THE UNITED STATES**
James T. Bennett and Bruce E. Kaufman,
editors

THE CYBERUNION HANDBOOK
Transforming Labor Through
Computer Technology
Arthur B. Shostak, editor

CHILD LABOR
An American History
Hugh D. Hindman

**INDUSTRIAL RELATIONS TO
HUMAN RESOURCES AND
BEYOND**
The Evolving Process of Employee
Relations Management
Bruce E. Kaufman, Richard A. Beaumont,
and Roy B. Helfgott, editors

**EMPLOYMENT EQUITY AND
AFFIRMATIVE ACTION**
An International Comparison
Harish C. Jain, Peter J. Sloan,
and Frank M. Horwitz
with Simon Taggar and Nan Weiner

Employment Equity and Affirmative Action

and

Affirmative Action

An International Comparison

Harish C. Jain, Peter J. Sloane,
and Frank M. Horwitz

With Simon Taggar and Nan Weiner

M.E.Sharpe
Armonk, New York
London, England

Library of Congress Cataloging-in-Publication Data

Jain, Harish C.
    Employment equity and affirmative action : an international comparison / Harish C.
Jain, Peter J. Sloane, and Frank Horwitz ; with Simon Taggar and Nan Weiner.
        p. cm.
    Includes bibliographical references and index.
    ISBN 0-7656-0452-3 (hardcover : alk. paper) ; ISBN 0-7656-0453-1 (pbk.: alk paper)
        1. Discrimination in employment—Case studies. 4. Discrimination in employment—
Law and legislation. 5. Affirmative action programs—Law and legislation.
    I. Sloane, Peter J. II. Horwitz, Frank M. III. Title.

HD4903 .J335 2003
331.13′3—dc21   2002040873

Table of Contents

List of Tables and Figures   vii
Foreword   ix
Preface   xi

1. Introduction   1

2. Theories of Discrimination   56

3. A Comparative Look at the Impact on Human Resources
    Management of Employment Equity Legislation   70
        Simon Taggar

4. Measuring Employment Equity Effectiveness: Quantitative and
    Qualitative Approaches   108

5. Fair Pay   126
        Nan Weiner

6. Trade Unions and Discrimination   171

7. Public Policy   194

8. Conclusions and Policy Implications   214

Index   223

List of Tables and Figures

Tables

1.1 Ethnic Distribution of Population in Selected Countries 5

1.2 Female and Total Distribution of Population in Selected Countries, 2001 7

1.3 Characteristics of EE/AA Programs in Six Countries 8

1.4 Characteristics of EE/AA Programs in Six Countries 10

1.5 Percentage of Workforce Representation of Women and Racial Minorities in Canada, 1981–1996 20

1.6 Representations of Women and Visible Minorities by Sector and Selected Companies, 1987–1999 25

1.7 Black Representation per Occupational Category 38

1.8 Summary of Occupational Level Representation by Designated Group in South Africa, 2001 39

1.9 Characteristics of EE/AA Programs in Six Countries: Advantages 43

1.10 Characteristics of EE/AA Programs in Six Countries: Disadvantages 46

3.1 Validity Coefficients from Meta-Analytical Studies 87

Appendix 4.1   Scale Categories, Scale Items, and Reliabilities   115

Appendix 4.2   Summary of Narrative Reports by Sector Filed by
               Employers under the Canadian (Federal) Employment
               Equity Act (EEA)   117

Appendix 4.3   Quantitative Approach: A Conceptual Framework   122

5.1   International Conventions Requiring Fair Pay and Status of
      Ratification by Six Countries   130

5.2   Legislation Related to Fair Pay in Six Countries   139

6.1   Role of Women in COSATU Affiliates   187

6.2   COSATU and Affiliates Occupational Positions According to
      Gender   188

Figures

2.1   Labor Market Segmentation and Equilibrium   62

3.1   Legislative Continuum of Structured HR Systems and
      Professional Standards Concerned with Fairness   71

3.2   Relationship between a Predictor and Criterion when a Cut
      Score is Used   82

3.3   Valid Prediction with Adverse Impact   106

3.4   Equal Validity, Unequal Predictor Means   106

3.5   Unfair and not Valid   107

5.1   Female and Male Labor Force Participation   136

5.2   Female-Male Wage Ratio   137

Foreword

Every country has its special social and economic problems—particularly in regard to the labor market and the workplace. And the inhabitants of each can be forgiven for believing that these problems and their solutions are entirely unique. Indeed, the temptation in developing a comparative international volume on concepts such as Affirmative Action and Pay Equity is to commission authors from various countries to write chapters on how each nation has responded. That isolated, one-by-one approach, is decidedly not what readers will find in this volume, however.

Instead, the approach here is to draw on the common lessons and common concepts as they apply in very different circumstances. No one denies the special characteristics of each of the six national systems covered. No one denies the path-dependent evolution of national systems of employment, human resource management, and industrial relations. But at the same time—and true to the ideal of a truly comparative study—the emphasis on the pages that follow is on commonality and cross-border lessons to be drawn.

Ultimately, fairness is a crucial element in any social compact. Societies in which perceived fairness is neglected ultimately can reach tipping points at which massive social unrest occurs. Or increasing repression becomes necessary to sustain the existing social order. Clearly, neither social unrest nor repression is desirable. But at the same time, fairness is a subjective concept, and there can be different views within a polity of what is fair in the employment setting and what is unfair.

Shaping perceptions in the context of a diverse society—particularly one in which history or past repression have produced substantially unequal labor-market outcomes—is a complex task. Efficiency and equity need to be juggled. There is a role for public policy makers at the macro level—as well as managers and unions at the enterprise and organizational level—to deal with that delicate balance. The overriding lesson to be drawn from this book is that such decision-makers are not alone in their quest. There are lessons to be drawn from across the world in achieving fairness in employment and the workplace.

Daniel J.B. Mitchell
Series editor

Preface

The fundamental premise of this book is that equality in employment is compatible with the goals of efficiency and economic growth and prosperity at both *enterprise* and *national and international* levels. We take the view that employment equity/affirmative action (EE/AA) and equality policies for designated groups such as women, racial and ethnic groups, and others need to address real issues of inequality in employment, cultural change, access to skills and promotion, power relations, and structural inequality. Thus, appropriately targeted equality policies can assist the process of efficiency and economic growth. This book is devoted to two groups: women and racial and ethnic groups.

Second, we focus on six countries: South Africa, Malaysia, India, the United States, Canada, and Britain/Northern Ireland. Our rationale for selecting these countries is: (a) to examine EE/AA policies in Malaysia and South Africa that have been designed to assist the majority populations; (b) to examine country experiences with constitutionally sanctioned quota/reservations policies such as those in Malaysia and India as opposed to legislated goals and timetable policies in the United States, Canada, South Africa as well as Northern Ireland and positive action policies in Britain; and (c) to identify the issues and lessons to be drawn, for example, for South Africa and other countries that have recently embarked on EE (such as the Netherlands and the Flemish part of Belgium), based on experiences in the other five countries in the study.

Third, in the light of global competitiveness, increasing trade with Asian countries, and increased international mobility of managers and professional people, we believe that managers in both private and public sectors not only need to understand their home environments, but will also have to master the challenge of working and living in a foreign environment—especially Asian. For this reason, we include historical developments and current analysis of public policies on AA in Malaysia and India, as noted above. It will be instructive to compare the variety of EE/AA policies in the six countries and draw some lessons for managers in both private and public sectors.

Fourth, we offer: (a) conceptual frameworks, (b) comparative perspectives, and (c) operational frameworks for "best practices."

Fifth, we examine systemic discrimination and review the available empirical studies and legal cases pertaining to human resource policies and practices such as recruitment and selection, compensation and equal pay, promotion, training and career development, especially relating to women and racial and ethnic minorities. We hope to show that intellectual capital will become the key to competitive organizations and competitive national economies in this millennium.

The authors would like to acknowledge the important contributions of two guest authors, Professor Simon Taggar and Dr. Nan Weiner. Professor Taggar wrote chapter 3 on the impact on human resources management (such as employer recruitment, selection, compensation, and other staffing policies and practices) of EE/AA legislation; and Dr. Weiner wrote chapter 5 on Fair Pay, providing an examination and an in-depth analysis of policies and practices relating to equal pay for equal work and equal pay for work of equal value and comparable worth.

The senior author wishes to acknowledge partial assistance from the Social Sciences and Humanities Research Council (SSHRC), Human Resources Development Canada and Canadian Heritage, for background research studies; he was a Donald Gordon Visiting Professor at the Graduate School of Business (GSB) at the University of Cape Town (UCT) in early 2002 and wishes to acknowledge the assistance of Professor Frank Horwitz, one of the co-authors, at the UCT, GSB, in providing facilities and consultation to help write a part of the book and especially that of Ms. Elsie Plumb at the GSB. He made field trips to India, Malaysia, the United Kingdom, and the United States and wishes to thank colleagues in these countries for making library and other facilities available. In the UK he wishes to thank one of the co-authors, Professor Peter J. Sloane, for assistance and use of facilities at the University of Aberdeen. He would also like to thank his secretary, Ms. Linda Mirabelli at the Michael G. DeGroote School of Business at McMaster University, for helping him prepare the final manuscript. A part of the book, especially chapter 1, has been presented at the World Conferences of the International Industrial Relations Association (IIRA) in Italy and Japan and at the IIRA African Regional Conference in South Africa.

Employment Equity
and
Affirmative Action

Chapter 1

Introduction

The current millennium has signaled a range of ideas and reflections on whether national policymakers and organizations are capable of meeting the challenge posed by globalization and increasing competition. One such challenge is the extent to which equality of opportunity is afforded to all members of the increasingly diverse labor force in the global economy.

The degree to which comparative convergence in policy and practice may occur is also influenced by the degree of cultural diversity in a country. The concept of diversity includes three types: demographic, cultural, and workforce diversity. The particular mix of these types of diversity varies cross-culturally and internationally. This underlines the importance of skillful management of diversity and change in global and local firms. Learning to manage diversity is one of the greatest challenges in managing human resources in the global economy. Cultural change in firms such as Motorola, Texaco, and Bank of Montreal (BMO) for example, has involved an integrated strategy for recruitment and selection to widen the pool of candidates, identifying talent from minority groups, ensuring fair treatment and practices, holding managers accountable, rewarding attainment of diversity goals, and improving relationships with external stakeholders.

In one sense, globalization may increase the demographic diversity of labor markets, but in another it may in the long run make them more homogeneous. Increasingly, talented people with skills in high demand are becoming internationally mobile. Expatriate professionals and executives are increasing globally as multinational corporations (MNCs) compete for scarce skills and talent. Although MNCs have become more powerful, they cannot assume that identical human resource practices can be applied cross-culturally (Dowling, Welch, and Schuler 1999). This raises the question as to whether specific practices such as employment equity (EE), affirmative action (AA), and diversity are converging or diverging internationally.

Affirmative Action, Employment Equity, and Workforce Diversity

The terms *AA, EE,* and *workforce diversity* are often used interchangeably. However, they are conceptually different. In the North American context, AA originated in the United States as a response to segregation and the disadvantage of blacks in employment, education, and other areas of life. Some have described AA as "hiring by numbers" due to its focus on increasing the representation of designated groups through targeted hiring, and to some extent training and promotion. AA compliance does not emphasize changing organizational policies, practices, and climate so that designated groups could become equal partners with other workers and share with other employees promotion and rewards for their performance (Agocs and Burr 1996). The term *EE* was coined by Judge Rosalie Silberman Abella, appointed chair of a Royal Commission on Equality in Employment in 1984 by the Canadian federal government. Judge Abella set a course different from AA and sought to avoid the controversy and stigma attached to it. EE is designed not only to improve numerical representation of designated groups through hiring, but also to provide supportive organizational culture for the retention, promotion, and training of the designated groups.

Thus, EE is a much more comprehensive strategy that stresses both quantitative and qualitative measures. Accordingly, the emphasis is not only on improving numerical representation but also on providing equality of opportunity through fair staffing procedures and a supportive organizational climate (Jain 1999).

In this book we examine EE/AA with the perspective described above. Both refer to selective policies and programs by government and nongovernmental institutions proactively to redress work-related inequalities that exist within countries along racial, ethnic, gender, caste, disability, and other lines. Diversity management, on the other hand, is a voluntary corporate response and an extension, not substitution, of proactive policies to ensure fair treatment of all employees.

AA/EE programs are legislatively driven, whereas diversity management is strictly voluntary and is a strategic corporate response to the growth of diversity in the workforce and is motivated by business objectives. Diversity management can complement, but not replace, EE/AA (Jain and Verma 1996).

EE/AA is particularly important in assessing the impact of public and organizational policies and human resource practices aimed at addressing unfair discrimination. Globalization implies powerful forces for convergence in respect of diversity and EE, with policies and practices arguably becoming more similar cross-culturally. Yet there is a growing body of evidence supporting the divergence hypothesis, especially regarding enterprise-level policy, practices, and initiatives aimed at differentiating the firm strategically from its competitors.

Convergence may more likely occur at the macro-regulatory and institutional levels, as countries struggle to find the right policies to improve race and ethnic relations and to redress inequalities based on past discrimination in these and other important areas such as gender and disability.

Multinational firms often seek consistency and integration of approach, policy, and practices globally. Theirs is a geocentric approach; which stands in comparison to ethnocentric approaches where little local autonomy is allowed, or a polycentric approach where an MNC subsidiary is treated as a distinct national entity. In the last named, local nationals can exhibit some decision autonomy and management and do not always have to defer to expatriate executives (Heenan and Perlmutter 1979). Regiocentric approaches consider geographic strategies in respect of human resource management and diversity, recognizing the institutional and regulatory context. Some MNCs use a combination of approaches based on a contingency perspective. This view acknowledges that, while basic principles of sound employment practices may apply, unique features of the local context have an impact on the way policies and practices are designed, implemented and monitored. A combination of approaches may be used by the same MNC in different countries (Jain, Lawler, and Morishima 1998).

The propensity for effective management of diversity through EE, AA, and other similar measures is, however, mediated quite strongly by the national and local context. Organizations need to consider an integrated framework that evaluates policy constraints and the appropriate choice or mix of measures and practices used to address unfair discrimination and establish fair labor practices. Factors such as the constitutional and legal framework for employment discrimination and equity, labor market attributes such as supply and demand for particular skills, availability of talent, cultural diversity, and historical relations between ethnic and other groups are key factors that may enhance or limit effective EE/AA policy performance at the firm level. Strategic outcomes are vital in evaluating the effectiveness of both legislation and firm practices in addressing unfair discrimination at work. A key question considered in this book is the extent to which global convergence is occurring in policy and practice, and also how these are best applied given the distinctiveness of certain jurisdictional contexts.

This chapter further examines: (a) the experiences of countries where equal employment and employment equity/affirmative action policies have been designed to assist the majority population such as in South Africa and Malaysia and (b) selected country experiences with quotas/reservations, legislated goals and timetables, and positive action policies and programs. For example, India and Malaysia have affirmative action (AA) programs with constitutionally sanctioned mandatory programs; the United States has Presidential Executive Orders requiring AA for federal contractors and subcontractors with mandated goals and timetables; Canada and South Africa have legislated equal opportunity and employment equity/affirmative action (EE/AA) policies with goals and timetables; Britain relies more on a voluntarist approach; and Northern Ireland in the United Kingdom (UK) has legislated goals and timetables and AA programs for Catholic minorities; and (c) lessons to be drawn from the success/failure of these policies in the six countries; and whether or not such policies can be a source of competitive advantage in the global economy.

The chapter is divided into several sections presenting an examination of: the country experiences for each of the six countries, considering advantages and disadvantages; an outline of the micro-organizational level implications; and conclusions and implications. The plan of the book includes eight chapters. This first chapter deals with equity in selected countries; followed by theories of discrimination in the second chapter; a discussion and empirical analysis of studies dealing with the effect of equal opportunities and EE/AA policies on human resource management policies of recruitment, selection, promotion, and training in the third chapter; an analysis of best practices, including an EE index as well as discussion and analysis of the qualitative and quantitative methods of effective measurement of EE in the fourth chapter; a comparative perspective of pay equity policies in the selected countries in the fifth chapter; labor union equity policies in the sixth chapter; an analysis of public policies in the seventh chapter; and finally, conclusions and implications in the final chapter.

Selected Country Policy Responses to Employment Equity/ Affirmative Action Programs

We have selected several countries to illustrate policy responses to discrimination in employment in the public and private sectors at the macro and micro levels, respectively. These are India, Malaysia, Canada, the United States, South Africa, and Britain, including Northern Ireland. The employment equity/affirmative action (EE/AA) policies of these countries will be examined in some detail.

In Malaysia and South Africa, AA policies deal with the majority communities. As Table 1.1 indicates, in Malaysia, such policies deal with the *Bumiputras* ("sons of the soil") who comprise approximately 66 percent of the estimated 22.3 million population, Chinese 25.3 percent, and Indians 7.4 percent of the population (Treasury, Economic Report 2000). In South Africa, EE policies in the form of constitutional guarantees of equality of opportunity and employment equity legislation and other policies deal with women (both white and black) who make up 52 percent of the total population and with blacks who account for more than 88 percent of the country's population, including men and women such as blacks (76.7 percent), coloureds (8.9 percent), Asians (2.6 percent) (Statistics South Africa 2001), and others. In India, the government's

Table 1.1
Ethnic Distribution of Population in Selected Countries

Ethnic Minorites (%)	USA 2000	Canada 1996	India 1991	Malaysia 2000	South Africa 2001	Britain 2000	Northern Ireland 1995
BLACK	12.3						
HISPANIC	12.5						
VISIBLE MINORITIES		10.3					
ABORGINALS		2.0					
SCs AND STs			21				
MALAY				66			
CHINESE				25			
INDIAN				8			
AFRICANS					77		
EUROPEANS					12		
COLOUREDS					9		
ASIANS					3		
RACIAL MINORITIES						6.5	
PROTESTANTS							58
ROMAN CATHOLICS							42

Source: World Almanac, 1996; Employment Equity, 2001, Pretoria; Census Canada 1996; U.S. Census Bureau, 2002; Treasury, Economic report 2000, Malaysia.

task is one of addressing inequalities for women, who make up 48 percent of the population, and a significant number of minorities such as scheduled castes (SCs) and scheduled tribes (STs).[1] Both groups constitute 21 percent or more than 200 million of the 864 million population as of 1991 (Jain and Ratnam 1994). In Canada and the United States, EE target groups include racial minorities, women, aboriginal people, and persons with disabilities. In both countries, close to 45 percent of the workforce consists of women; racial minorities constitute about 25 percent in the United States and 10.3 percent of the labor force in Canada. In Britain, racial minorities form 6.5 percent of the population, but they have greater visibility because of their concentration in large metropolitan areas (Parekh 2000). Women make up 43 percent of those at work. In Northern Ireland, ethnicity and religion are closely intertwined. For instance, a person's community of origin greatly affects his or her marriage partner, residential area, school to be attended by their children, choice of employers, and the like. (Cormack and Osborne 1991). The Catholic minority is sizable and growing relative to the Protestant majority (58 percent Protestants vs. 42 percent Catholics). AA is the key mechanism, according to the former Fair Employment Commission (FEC) and now the Equality Commission, to affect the working environments inside companies.

Tables 1.3 and 1.4 outline the characteristics of EE/AA programs in the six countries. A brief analysis of the experiences of these countries follows.

The Indian Experience

India is a dominantly patriarchal society. Still, some states like Kerala in southern India and several states in northern India, which are advanced states in the country in terms of United Nations Development Program's (UNDP) Human Development, are matriarchal societies. Mythologically, women enjoyed a special status in India, and constitutionally, there is no discrimination against women. Yet, demographic, social, and economic indicators point out that women continue to be disadvantaged in terms of their access to education and employment. Attitudes about gender roles, social belief systems, customs, and physical infrastructure have perpetuated the relative backwardness and vulnerability of women in society (Jain and Ratnam in press).

The incidence of illiteracy is higher among women than men, in both rural and urban areas. The incidence of illiteracy is higher among the workforce than in the general population, for both men and women. As per the 1991 Census, women account for 28.58 percent of the workforce; 4.21 percent of women workers are employed in the organized sector as against 10.23 percent of male workers. Women's participation rate is less because those who are not in paid jobs (such as household work) are not considered to be working. Labor force participation is low among those who drop out after secondary school and before

Table 1.2
Female and Total Distribution of Population in Selected Countries, 2001 (Millions)

Percentage of Population

USA 51	Canada 50.5	India 48	Malaysia 49.7	South Africa 52	Great Britain 51	*Northern Ireland 50.9
Total population in selected countries						
281.4	31.6	1 billion	22.3	40.5	58	1.7

Source: World Factbook at www.odci.gov/cia/publications/factbook.

*Registrar-General for Northern Ireland, estimated June 30, 2002.

Table 1.3
Characteristics of EE/AA Programs in Six Countries

	USA	Canada	India	Malaysia	South Africa	Britain	Northern Ireland
Legal Provisions	• Presidential Executive Orders Re: AA Requiring Contract Compliance	• EE Act (1995)	• Constitutional Provisions Guarantee AA	• Constitutional Provisions	• Constitution (1996) Bill of Rights (Section 9 Chapter 2) Allows EE	• Race Relations Act, 1976 & Amendments 2001	• Fair Employment and Treatment Order, 1998
	• Court Decisions Under Civil Rights Act & Other Statutes	• Constitution (Charter of Rights & Freedoms) Sec. 15(2) Allows EE	• Seats in Parliament & State Legislatures for SCs & STs	• NEP • OPPI to III • National Vision Plan (NVP)	• EE Act (1998)	• Sex Discrimination Act, 1975	• Race Relations (NI) Order, 1996
		• Human Rights Legislation	• Quotas in Government Jobs & in Public Enterprises		• Promotion of Equality & Prevention of Unfair Discrimination Act (1999)	• Disability Discrimination Act, 1995	• Equal Pay Act, 1970 & Amendments

• Admission into Colleges, Medical & Engineering Schools	• Labour Relation Act (1995)	• Human Rights Act, 1998	• Disability Discrimination Act, 1995
• Tension Exists Between Equality & AA	• Skills Development Act (1998)		• Northern Ireland Act, 1998
• Court Decisions are Ambiguous			• Human Rights Act, 1998

Table 1.4
Characteristics of EE/AA Programs in Six Countries

	USA	Canada	India	Malaysia	South Africa	Britain	Northern Ireland
Target Groups	• Racial & Other Minorities & Women • Vietnam War Veterans • Persons with Disabilities	• Women • Racial Minorities • Aboriginal Persons • Persons with Disabilities	• Scheduled Castes and Scheduled Tribes	• Majority Ethnic Community that is Malay and Indigenous Groups • Persons with Disabilities	• Majority Ethnic Community (Blacks) Women • Persons with Disabilities	• Racial minorities, Women • Persons with Disabilities	• Constitutional Provisions
Scope	Public & Private Sector	Public & Private Sector	Public Sector	Public Sector	Public & Private Sectors	Public & Private Sectors	Public & Private Sectors
Rationale	• Political Necessity for Blacks e.g. Desegregation of Schools etc. • Elimination of Employment Discrimination	• Elimination of Employment Discrimination	• Political Necessity for Elimination of Societal and Job Discrimination	• Political Necessity Due to Racial Riots in 1969 • Broader Economic Development Objectives	• Political Necessity • Elimination of Societal Discrimination	• Elimination of Employment Discrimination	• Elimination of Employment Discrimination

Quotas or Goals & Timetables	Goals and Timetables	Goals and Timetables	Quotas or Reservations	Quotas	Goals and Timetables	• No Affirmative Action Provision • Positive Action in Relation to Training, Outreach Recruitment and Promotion Permissible in Case of Under Representation • However, Codes of Practice Encourage Regular Monitoring and Setting of Targets	• Goals and Timetables • Both Affirmative Action and Contract Compliance

graduation. It is relatively higher among the less educated and among graduates. Overall, women's access to education and employment (as indicated by labor market participation rates) continues to be low (Jain and Ratnam in press).

The 73rd and the 74th constitutional amendments in 1992 granting 33 percent of the seats in local self-government institutions at the village level—*panchayati raj*—to women and the enhanced empowerment of these local bodies have also opened up new possibilities for women's political empowerment and emancipation (Kapur 1999). As of 2001, one of three members and one of three chairpersons in these institutions throughout the country was a woman. Parliament is debating the issue of reserving 33 percent of the positions for legislators at the state (legislative assemblies) and central (members of Parliament) levels for women. The two dominant political parties—the Bharatiya Janata Party (heading the ruling coalition) and the Congress Party (the main opposition party)—are unanimous on this issue. Still, a final decision has been delayed because of questions raised by some other parties on subreservations based on caste. Some state governments announced reservations for women in education and public employment. As in many other fields, here, too, implementation lags behind intent (Jain and Ratnam in press).

At another level, Indian society has traditionally been based on a caste hierarchy that places the priestly caste at the top and those doing manual labor at the bottom. One group of disadvantaged people are the so-called untouchables. They are generally known as the scheduled castes (SCs). The second group are the tribes. They are disadvantaged because they are isolated in remote places. They are known as the scheduled tribes (STs).[2] When India became independent in 1947, the nationalist leadership was committed to removing job and other barriers faced by the two groups. They wrote into the Constitution provisions prohibiting discrimination on grounds of religion, race, caste, sex, descent, place of birth, or residence. The purpose was to eliminate discrimination against the untouchables (SCs) and to facilitate spatial and social mobility for tribal people (STs).

Members of the SCs and STs are predominantly in the unorganized, informal sector, and thus largely unprotected by employment standards and other labor legislation. A substantial majority are dependent on agriculture but do not own land, which leads to very low wages and bonded labor (Kaur 1997).

As a direct result of the constitutional provisions, a reservations or a quota policy came into effect, as noted earlier. The Indian Constitution was ratified in 1950. Both SCs and STs were given seats in the Parliament and in the state legislative assemblies in proportion to their population. Quotas or reservations provisions were also made for employment in government and public sector jobs (i.e., public enterprises) and in the national and state governments, as well as for admissions into schools, colleges, and medical and engineering schools (see the Constitution of India, articles 46, 15, 16, and 35 in Bakshi 2000).

Thus, the Indian experience is one in which AA is defined quite rigidly in terms of reservations and quotas. The rationale for constitutional safeguards and AA programs for women and the socially and economically depressed classes, both men and women, lies in the obnoxious practice of untouchability in respect of SCs and exploitive slavery in respect of both the SCs and STs. Due to repeated criticisms[3] of government policies by the Commission for the SCs and STs (set up in 1978 in the Ministry of Home Affairs), the Constitution was amended in 1992.[4] This provided statutory powers to the commission to investigate and monitor all matters relating to AA measures provided for the SCs and STs. It became mandatory for the federal and state governments to consult the commission on AA measures; the commission was also vested with powers of a civil court examining a suit (Kaur 1997). As a result, several measures were adopted, such as (1) the establishment of the National Scheduled Castes and Scheduled Tribes Finance and Development Corporation—a nonprofit company—to assist in employment generation for SCs and STs; (2) aid to voluntary organizations for SCs such as technical training; (3) national overseas scholarships and transportation grants for higher studies abroad; (4) postsecondary school scholarships for SC and ST students, including payment of all tuition and compulsory fees as well as maintenance allowance; (5) book banks for SC and ST students; and (6) hostels for girls and boys from SCs; as well as (7) coaching schemes offered through pre-examination recruitment training centers to improve SC representation in various services in the federal and state government and in public sector enterprises (Kaur 1997).

In 1990, the Indian government announced that there would be additional quotas or reservations for "other backward classes" (OBCs).[5] The OBCs are socially and educationally backward classes of citizens, consisting of approximately 27 percent of India's population (see Bakshi 2000, 28). The government adopted a quota of 27 percent for the OBCs in addition to the 22 percent provided for the scheduled castes (SCs) and the tribals (STs). Thus, in all, 49 percent of government jobs and admissions into colleges and medical and engineering schools were put aside for approximately three-quarters of the population (Jain and Ratnam 1994). The result was massive demonstrations and violence by the excluded higher castes and others. Several problems contributed to the protests. First, identifying people of designated groups proved very problematic in practice. Allegations of impropriety and corruption in access to reserved seats made it difficult for the government to move rapidly. Moreover, anemic economic growth led to increasing scarcity of opportunities for public employment in the midst of growing unemployment (Jain and Ratnam 1994). Many people felt excluded and saw the government's extension of reservations to the OBCs as a move for political gain rather than in the larger interest of increasing opportunities for all.

Several parties asked the Supreme Court of India to stay the government's order of a quota of 27 percent for the OBCs. In its decision of November 16, 1992, the Supreme Court upheld the government's order (by a majority of 6 to 3) to provide job quotas for the OBCs. The Court decided that reservations for all three groups (SCs, STs, and OBCs) should not ordinarily exceed 50 percent. In addition, candidates selected for reserved positions must meet certain conditions of eligibility to satisfy the requirement of efficiency in administration. The judgment exempted from reservations appointments to certain positions, for example, defense personnel, research scientists, medical scientists, university professors, and others (Sawhney et al. 1992).

Some of the states in India, particularly in South India, have had quotas for OBCs since the 1920s; other states such as West Bengal, which have had no quotas in the past, would be required to introduce job quotas for the OBCs. Some other states such as Karnataka, where job quotas have existed for a long time above the one recommended by the Court, would have to reduce these quotas (Beteille 1993).

The achievements of AA in India are significant, particularly with regard to securing proportionate representation in professional and managerial positions (Jain and Ratnam 1994). There is a small and growing middle class of untouchables and tribals.[6] Although AA programs were originally intended to last ten years from 1950, they have been extended repeatedly over the years. But this is largely because of lack of resources for basic education; only a small proportion of the SC and ST population are qualified for better jobs in government and public enterprises. As per the 1981 Census, only 2 percent of SCs and STs graduated from high school and 0.25 percent were university graduates. Thus, providing access to human resource endowments and entitlements like education, training, and relevant skills, should precede or proceed in parallel with the quota system.[7]

AA in India has survived and strengthened because of popular and political support; more than one out of every five seats in the Parliament are represented and filled by SC and ST candidates as guaranteed by the Constitution. Similar reservations exist with respect to state legislatures, as noted earlier. Continued political pressure from the elected representatives belonging to these communities, who account for 22.5 percent of parliamentarians and legislators, helps keep governments and public enterprise managers on their toes (Jain and Ratnam 1994). Despite these provisions, the progress has been slow on account of a low economic growth rate in the 1950–1990 period. Resources available for the expansion in education and other social services have remained scarce. It has become increasingly apparent that the beneficiaries from the disadvantaged communities are likely to be the better-off and not the worst-off members of the communities to which they belong and in whose name quotas are made. The Supreme Court of India, in its 1992 decision, was concerned about the flow of benefits to what is called "creamy layers" among the disadvantaged and noted that no really effective way has been found to divert the benefits of reservations from the better-off to the worst-off members of backward communities (Beteille 1993).[8] Reservations policies have also exacerbated inefficiency to some extent and the attitude that government employment is a right. There is no incentive for better performance. The entire initiative has been left to the government. The private sector has had no obligations to offer job opportunities to SCs and STs (Beteille 1993).

Experience in Malaysia

Of the estimated population of 22.3 million people in Malaysia in the year 2000, approximately 49 percent were women. As of the year 2000, Malaysia had a labor force of 9.6 million people, of which 6.3 million were male and 3.3 million female. Native Malay had a workforce of 5.7 million, with 3.2 million males and 1.7 million females. The Chinese and Indian proportion of the workforce totaled 2.4 million and 745,000, respectively. There were 1.5 million Chinese males and 871,000 Chinese females in the workforce. Indian males were more than 499,000 and females over 245,000. Others consisted of 1.3 million (Malaysia, Department of Statistics 2001). Male labor force participation rates were 65.5 percent in 2000, while female participation rates were 44.5 percent (Malaysia, Treasury 2000).

The post-independence government in Malaysia was formed by a coalition of three ethnic groups: the Chinese, the Indians, and the Malays. Following independence in 1957, an accord was forged among these three groups: Citizenship was granted to the Chinese and Indians in return for the Malays receiving preferential treatment under the Constitution (Puthucheary 1993; Weiner 1993). However, following the riots after the 1969 elections, it was felt that the ethnic Malay community was economically disadvantaged and that this situation was not conducive to national stability and unity.[9] A new economic policy (NEP) resulted in a fundamental restructuring of the Malaysian economy in order to correct economic imbalances. Several strategies were employed to increase the employment and earned income of *Bumiputras* (native Malay). Quotas were introduced in various areas such as admission to university and equity ownership. Quotas were used extensively in the public sector where *Bumiputras,* especially those with educational qualifications, found ready employment. Appointments in the civil service were made at a ratio of four Malays to one non-Malay.[10] Although there was some resentment on the part of non-Malays, the Chinese leadership within the governing alliance was willing to go along. In fact, a political bargain struck between the Malays and the Chinese elites provided that the Chinese could make money while the Malays could run an administration that pursued pro-growth policies (Emsley 1992).

Substantial changes were made to the Constitution. The special position of

Malays was guaranteed; these provisions could not be removed even by the normal two-thirds majority required for other constitutional amendments. Thus, future governments could not amend this section of the Constitution even if they had a two-thirds majority. In addition, amendments to the sedition laws were passed to make it illegal to question these rights in Parliament or outside.

In the post-NEP period, the government decided to continue the quota program (Mahathir 1991). According to Puthucheary (in Weiner 1993.), the combination of economic growth and special benefits produced a Malay middle class. The NEP came to be increasingly identified with restructuring of society in order to reduce interethnic disparities, especially between ethnic Malay and ethnic Chinese Malaysians (Heibert and Jayasankaran 1999; Jomo 2001).

The NEP has been associated with the economic development policy in three Outline Perspective Plans—OPP-1 for 1971 to 1990; OPP-2 for 1991–2000, and OPP-3 for 2001–2010 and the new National Vision Policy (announced by Prime Minister Mohamad Mahathir in April 2001) is linked to OPP-3. As Jomo (2001) suggests, development policy associated with OPP-2 and then by National Vision Policy (NVP) linked to OPP-3 is still thought to be influenced primarily by the NEP's restructuring of society. The NVP supports the objective of previous plans in 1970s and 1980s to place 30 percent of the country's wealth in the hands of Malays—the *Bumiputras*. In March 2001, following clashes between Indians and Malays, the government for the first time set a 3 percent target of Indian equity ownership; the government is predicting an average economic growth rate of 7.5 percent per annum so that affirmative action policies for the *Bumiputra* and Indian population will not be at the expense of Chinese interests.

Results of the Policies

In 1969, Malays had only 2 percent of equity in firms, and few Malays were in management. Arrangements were made to expand Malay equity capital, so that it reached about 18 percent by 1990 and 20 percent in 2000 (Jomo 2001). Private individual ownership, rather than trust agencies ownership, has risen from less than a third to over 90 percent, though much of this NEP achievement has been subject to dispute. Until the early 1990s, the economy of Malaysia grew at between 6 and 7 percent per year. In private sector employment, the Malays exceeded the 50 percent target set in the first Outline Prospective Plan (OPP-1) reaching 61.8 percent by 1990 in the professional and technical categories. The Malays also improved their representation from 22.4 percent in 1970 to 31.3 percent in 1990 in the administrative and managerial occupational groups, even though their targeted representation level was 49.3 percent. This lower representation attainment level reflects low Malay representation at the managerial and supervisory levels in the manufacturing and service sectors (Hodges-Aeberhard and Raskin 1997).

The most significant change over the years has been the reduction in the incidence of poverty from 74 percent of Malays in 1970 to an overall figure of 6 percent in 1994, and the Malay share of national wealth went up from 1.5 percent in 1969 to 19.4 percent in 1998. The national economy had an economic growth rate of 7 percent a year for most of that period; hence, the Malay's advance did not come at the expense of other races (Heibert and Jayasankaran 1999, 46). Thus, the distribution of income, wealth, and occupations among individuals has achieved a more balanced ethnic mix. In particular, the affirmative action programs have contributed to the establishment of a Malay business community. Through various strategies including the setting up of public enterprises to employ and train Malays and the use of administrative regulations to encourage Malay employment in private sector companies, a more ethnically balanced urban community has come about. Malays now occupy positions that were monopolized by non-Malays in the past. Enrollment in institutions of higher learning increased to such an extent that by 1980, 75 percent of the students in local institutions of higher learning were Malay (Puthucheary 1993).

The high rates of economic growth, as indicated above, resulted in a general increase in the level of income for all ethnic groups, and this has been the most important factor contributing to the success of the affirmative action programs.

Disadvantages of Preference Policies

Although the enrollment of Malay students in educational institutions has increased substantially, talented Chinese high school leavers find it difficult to gain admission to universities because of the preferential system (Lau 2001; Pereira 2001). This results in resentment and causes many to attend universities in other countries such as Singapore. Since Chinese school leavers have better matriculation results than Malays, this situation is perceived as evidence of reverse discrimination. This policy is under review by the Malay government.

Jomo (2001) notes that specific socioeconomic targets of the NEP have largely been achieved; nevertheless, he questions whether this achievement has led to national unity or improved interethnic relations. This is because often interethnic coalitions have been formed over time, with the ethnic Malay partner securing rents for gaining access to government-determined business opportunities and the ethnic Chinese partner with business acumen getting the job done.

This rent seeking and "cronyism" have created what Jomo (2001) describes as growing resentment and interethnic, interclass competition for such government preferential affirmative action policies.

Other negative consequences of AA have been that (a) it has been difficult for the civil service to maintain its image as impartial and politically neutral when it is constantly making political decisions based on ethnic considerations rather than on the objective criteria of need and merit, according to Puthucheary

(1993); (b) AA can result in the perpetuation and even strengthening of ethnic cleavages; (c) AA programs also tend to result in conflicts within the preferential groups themselves since the benefits of AA programs accrue disproportionately to better off than to poorer sections of the groups (this is especially the case between the dominant Malay group and the other indigenous subgroups that together make up the *Bumiputra* category, such as Sarawak and Sabah groups); and (d) some critics have argued that once AA is introduced, it becomes permanently entrenched in the political system, serving the interests of a small minority.

Experience in the United States

The United States had a population of 281.4 million in the year 2000, with 49 percent males and 50.9 percent females. Whites consisted of 75.1 percent of the population, blacks 12.3 percent, Hispanics 12.5 percent, and Mexicans 7.3 percent (www.factfinder.census.gov).

In the United States, initially the country had to address the problem of a disadvantaged minority rather than a majority or large plurality. According to Farley (2000), the United States was essentially a black-white country until 1960. Today, America is becoming a multicultural country with people from numerous nationalities and racial and ethnic backgrounds. This is because of the slowing birthrate of blacks (and whites) and the increasing immigration from Asian and Latin American countries; there were almost 13 million landed immigrants during the 1980s and early 1990s (Farley 2000; Jackson 2000). Farley suggests that the Spanish-origin population will numerically pass the black population within ten years owing to their rapidly-growing population relative to blacks (Farley 2000). In fact, Farley's prediction has already come true. According to the 2000 Census figures, Hispanics have overtaken blacks; there were 35,305,818 Hispanics (or 12.5 percent Hispanics out of the total population of 281,421,906), relative to 34, 658, 190 blacks or 12.3 percent blacks in the same year. This demographic diversity is to be found throughout the United States (Farley 2000), and not just in big cities, and has been confirmed by the 2000 Census (see www.census.usatoday.com; Nasser and Overberg 2001).

According to Farley (2000), 90 percent of blacks lived in poverty at the beginning of World War II, and while relative gains have occurred in the median income of blacks in the 1990s, the black-white earnings gap is likely to continue.

The Civil Rights Act of 1964, title VII, applies specifically to employment; other sections or titles of the Act apply to voting rights, education, accommodations, and the like. Title VII prohibits discrimination on the basis of race, color, religion, sex, or national origin in every aspect of employment. The Equal Opportunity Employment Commission (EEOC) was established to administer the Act; the Act applies to employers, employment agencies, and labor organizations. It was amended in 1972, and its coverage extended to include public and private employers with fifteen or more employees.

The term *affirmative action* first appeared in American law in the Civil Rights Act of 1964, Title VII. All employers of 100 or more employees are required to submit employment statistics reporting employment by race and other protected categories in broad job classifications each year. Although not specifically required under Title VII, affirmative action may be required as part of a conciliated or court settlement among employers and the federal enforcement agencies. According to Leonard (1985), more than 1,700 class action suits were filed under this legislation. These suits have been among the most powerful prods to increasing minority and female employment because they affected the most people, resulted in large awards, and generated the most publicity.

The Civil Rights Act of 1991 covers more prohibited grounds such as age and disability and extends the coverage of the Act to the United States Senate and political appointees of the president and staff members of the elected officials at the state level. The House of Representatives employees are covered by a House Resolution adopted in 1988 (Cascio 1998).

In 1965, the then president Lyndon Johnson issued an executive order requiring affirmative action in employment and promotion of all federal contractors, even if they had never discriminated. Presidential Executive Order 11246 requires affirmative action on the part of all federal contractors with fifty or more employees and a contract of $50,000 or more. A federal contractor's entire organization must abide by the terms of affirmative action; if just one facility in the company has a government contract, all of the facilities of that company are subject to the executive order. The federal contractors are required to submit and implement a written five-year affirmative action plan with goals and timetables, including special measures to achieve the goals. Such goals must be significant, attainable, and specific for planned results. Failure to develop and implement an acceptable AA program within a specified time could result in cancellation or termination of existing contracts, withholding of payments by the government, and disbarment from competing for future contracts (Cascio 1998; Jain 1994). The United States contract compliance program covers more than a quarter of a million companies employing an estimated 27 million workers and providing the federal government with over $100 billion in construction, goods, and services (Cascio 1998, 56).

Leonard (1985) has found that even though the goals may be inflated somewhat by a federal contractor and not usually attained, the contractor that promises to employ more minorities does actually employ more in subsequent years. Finally, affirmative action plans by federal contractors have resulted in employment and occupational advances for minorities in the United States (Leonard 1984b). This trend has continued[11] (Holzer and Neumark 2000a, b; Leonard 1990; Rodgers and Spriggs 1996).

Table 1.5
Percentage of Workforce Representation of Women and Racial Minorities in Canada, 1981–1996

	1981	1986	1991	1996
Females	42.1	44.0	45.9	46.4
Visible minorities	4.9	6.3	9.1	10.3

Source: Census Statistics Canada.

The third annual survey of "America's best fifty companies for minorities" conducted by the nonprofit Council on Economic Priorities on behalf of *Fortune* Magazine found that members of ethnic minorities held about 16 percent of the board seats, made up 22 percent of the officials and managers, and made up 13 percent of the fifty largest paychecks (Mehta 2000, 182). That year's survey was focused on diversity in the upper ranks of each company. According to the magazine, these were key signs that a company had gone beyond political correctness. About 65 percent of the Fortune 1,000 companies had at least one member of the ethnic minority on their board of directors, up from 58 percent in 1998 (Mehta 2000, 183).

Experience in Canada

Canada's population and workforce are becoming increasingly pluralistic. In 1994–1995, 42 percent of Canadians reported origins other than French or British, while 16 percent of Canadians were foreign born (Heritage Canada 1996, 2). Canada had a population of 28.5 million people as per the 1996 Census (31.6 million in 2001)—49.2 percent males and 50.8 percent females. The workforce consisted of 15.5 million, 53.6 percent of whom were males and 46.4 percent females, in 1996. The 1996 Census information regarding racial minorities or visible minorities (VMs), as they are called in official statistics in Canada, indicated that VMs made up 11.2 percent of the Canadian population. They were a growing proportion of the population in Canada's principal cities. For instance, they made up 32 percent of the population of Toronto, 31 percent in Vancouver, as well as 16 percent in Calgary, 14 percent in Edmonton, 12 percent in Ottawa/ Hull, and 11 percent in Winnipeg (Jain et al. 2000, 47). Table 1.5 shows the representation of racial minorities in the Canadian workforce from 1981 to 1996. Their proportion had more than doubled from 4.9 percent to 10.3 percent.

Policy Responses in Canada

In the early 1980s, government in Canada began to investigate the need for policy initiatives in the area of improving the economic status of minorities who faced discrimination in the labor market. The best known of these investigations, commissioned by the federal government known as the Abella Commission Report (Abella 1984), found that significant obstacles confronted the four designated groups, and it therefore recommended early action to head off potential social conflict that might result from inaction. In the same year, the all-party Parliamentary Committee report known as the Daudlin Commission report, *Equality Now!* (Daudlin 1984), reported similar findings on the status of visible minorities. The Edmonds Task Force (Edmonds 1990) examined barriers to advancement of women in the federal public service.

The Canadian responses to improving the status of designated groups such as women and ethnic minorities can be divided into four groups. One category of response is in the form of prohibiting discrimination on enumerated grounds. All the provinces and territories, including the federal government, for instance, have human rights legislation prohibiting discriminatory treatment on several grounds including gender, race, ethnic, origin, religion, and age. The courts have been willing to read in certain grounds of discrimination, even when the legislatures in certain jurisdictions had chosen not to include these grounds into their respective laws. For instance, sexual orientation in the case of the Alberta and the federal human rights statutes was read into the two statutes by the Supreme Court of Canada. The Constitution Act of 1982 contains the Canadian Charter of Rights and Freedoms. Section 15(2) of the Charter guarantees certain rights and freedoms without precluding employment equity programs. This section applies to all government agencies across Canada (e.g., federal, provincial, territorial, and municipal).

The second category of responses has been to enact specific legislation aimed at implementing employment equity programs. This has taken the form of federal Employment Equity Act (EEA) of 1986, revised and amended in October 1995 and strengthened to include federal government agencies for the first time. The 1986 EEA covered employers in mainly three industrial sectors: banking, transportation, and communications. It covered about 343 private sector employers and federal crown corporations with a total of 576,965 employees (Jain 1995).

The third category has been to use administrative policy (as opposed to legislation) to require implementation of employment equity programs. The best example here is the Federal Contractors Program (1986), which requires organizations with 100 or more employees bidding on federal government contracts of $200,000 or more to undertake employment equity programs. This program covers 845 contractors with a workforce of 1.1 million (Longfield 2002). Contractors are required to remove barriers faced by the four designated groups in selection, hiring, promoting, and training; mount proactive positive measures; and come up with specific goals and timetables

The fourth category of response has been the collective agreement provisions under the industrial relations legislation. Approximately half the collective agreements in Canada included antidiscrimination clauses that prohibit discrimination on the basis of the several prohibited grounds or merely incorporate the human rights legislation of the relevant government. These prohibited grounds cover hiring, promotion, job assignment, compensation, and other areas where discrimination may occur (Giles and Starkman 2001, 306). About one-third of collective agreements also contained specific clauses for the protection of older and disabled workers and to prohibit sexual harassment. Some agreements also contain clauses on relatively new grounds such as AIDS, drug use, and electronic surveillance of workers (Giles and Starkman 2001, 307).

Employment Equity

EE is permitted by the Constitution Act of 1982 as well as the Federal Employment Equity Act enacted first in 1986 and revised extensively in 1995.

The Canadian Charter of Rights and Freedoms is a part of the Constitution Act of 1982. The Charter's provisions apply to all government agencies across Canada including federal, provincial and municipal. In addition, the Charter provisions have a direct impact on human rights legislation through the equality provision (McPhillips 2001, 227), section 15, as noted previously.

Section 15 (1) states: Every individual is equal before and under the law and has the right to equal protection and equal benefit of the law without discrimination and, in particular, without discrimination based on race, national or ethnic origin, color, religion, sex, or mental or physical disability.

(2) Subsection (1) does not preclude any law, program, or activity that has as its objective the amelioration of conditions of disadvantaged individuals or groups including those that are disadvantaged because of race, national or ethnic origin, color, religion, sex, age, or mental or physical disability.

In addition, the federal government has had the Contractors Program since 1986, which applies to large and medium-sized provincially regulated employers who supply goods and services to federal government departments and agencies. Both the EE Act and the Contractors Program cover four groups: women, aboriginals, persons with disability, and visible (racial) minorities.

The EE Act applies to employers in the private sector, as noted previously, and to federal government departments with 100 or more employees. The legislation requires these employers to file an annual report with Human Resources Development Canada (HRDC). Employers are required to provide annual information on the representation of the four designated groups by occupational groups and salary range, as well as hires, promotions, and terminations. The public sector employers were required to provide similar information to the Treasury Board of Canada beginning in 1996 (Jain 1997).

Under the 1995 Act, in addition to this statistical information, employers are also required (as of October 1997) to include in their annual reports: (1) a description of the measures taken to implement EE and the results achieved; and (2) the consultations between the employer and its employee representatives concerning EE implementation.

Failure to comply with the filing requirements can result in an administrative penalty for three specific reporting violations (for private sector employers only): (a) failing to file an annual report; (b) failing to include the required information; and (c) knowingly filing a report containing false or misleading information. The amount of monetary penalty is $10,000 for a single violation and $50,000 for repeated and continued violations. All records used in the compilation of the annual reports must be retained by the employer for two years following the submission of the report. The annual reports are made publicly available and also given to the Canadian Human Rights Commission (CHRC) (Jain 1997).

The CHRC was given the authority to conduct on-site compliance reviews (i.e., audits) to verify and ensure employer compliance as of October 24, 1997. The Act also provided for the final enforcement, where necessary by an EE Tribunal. The Tribunal was empowered to hear disputes and issue orders enforceable by courts.

The 1995 Act prescribed four factors to be taken into account in setting goals by an employer (Jain 1997):

1. the degree of underrepresentation of each designated group in each occupational category;
2. the availability of qualified persons in designated groups within the employer's workplace and the Canadian workforce;
3. the anticipated growth or reduction of the employer's workforce during the period of numerical goals; and
4. the anticipated turnover within the employer's workforce in respect of which the numerical goals apply.

Evaluation of the Results

In the private sector firms covered by the EEA since 1986, the overall representation of members of VM groups more than doubled in the thirteen years, 1987 to 1999, from 4.9 percent to almost 10 percent. However, it remained below the 10.3 percent availability rate established by the 1996 Census, (Annual Report 1999, 81). VMs remained concentrated in some occupational groups and underrepresented in others, including senior management (Annual Report 1999, 82).

As indicated by Table 1.6, their representation varied considerably by industrial sector. In banking, their representation was almost 15 percent in 1999 relative to 9.5 percent in 1987. In communications, they made up more than 9.0 percent, more than double their 1987 representation rate of 4 percent. This rate was below availability. Progress was slower in the transportation sector, where the VMs representation rate was almost 9 percent in 1999 relative to 2.6 percent in 1987.

Table 1.6 indicates the progress or lack of it since the Federal Employment Act was enacted. The table also indicates the status of two of the designated groups in 1987, the first year following the enactment of the EEA, 1994, 1996, and 1999 overall and in selected large companies. First we will analyze the overall representation followed by selected company representation. Although the banking industry far exceeds the availability of women, showing the typical ghettoization of women phenomenon, the transportation industry has a long way to go; the communications sector seems to be the only one that comes even close to the external representation of females. Visible minorities show a great deal of improvement in their overall representation from 1987 to 1999; in banking they exceed their external representation, while in transportation and communications their representation has improved but it is still less than their the external availability in the 1996 Census.

Table 1.6 also shows the representation of women and visible minorities in prominent and selected large organizations in each of the three industrial sectors covered by the federal EEA. As can be seen, women are overrepresented in all the six chartered banks relative to their representation in the Canadian labor force in 1996 but not in the other industrial sectors. Females are underrepresented in all of the seven prominent transportation companies, relative to the Census, except for some improvement at the Canadian Airlines (which no longer exists, having been taken over by Air Canada) and to some extent at Air Canada (42.9 and 37.1 percent, respectively); in the six companies in the communications sector, only Bell Canada shows a higher representation of women and CTV comes close relative to the Census as well as the sector.

In the case of visible minorities, except for the National Bank of Canada where their share went down in 1999 to 4.5 percent relative to 9.2 percent in 1996, visible minorities exceed their Census representation in the selected banks both in 1996 and 1999 relative to 1987. However, they are below the Census representation in most of the selected companies in the transportation sector except Canadian Airlines, which no longer exists. In the communications sector, visible minorities exceed their census representation in Purolator and CTV and have improved their share to 9 from 8.6 percent in 1996 in Canada Post.

The CHRC in its 1999 Annual Report found that only a few—four—employers (of the 136 employers audited in the two years) were actually in compliance at the time of the initial audit. However, many have given undertakings to bring themselves into compliance.

The CHRC reported that while there had been progress for some designated groups, "movement towards an equitable federal workplace continues at a snail's

Table 1.6
Representations of Women and Visible Minorities by Sector and Selected Companies, 1987–1999

Designated Groups	Women				Members of Visible Minorities			
Sector and Company	1987 %	1994 %	1996 %	1999 %	1987 %	1994 %	1996 %	1999 %
Sector: Banking	76.1	75.9	74.8	72.8	9.5	13.7	14.1	14.9
Royal Bank of Canada	77.2	77.2	76.3	74.5	7.5	10.8	10.5	13.7
Canadian Imperial Bank of Commerce	78.2	76.5	75.0	72.8	12.2	14.3	13.9	14.6
Bank of Montreal	74.6	75.1	73.2	70.6	9.6	14.1	15.8	17.7
Bank of Nova Scotia	76.9	77.3	76.1	73.0	10.6	16.6	17.0	16.2
Toronto-Dominion Bank	77.4	74.3	72.6	69.1	10.9	17.6	18.4	18.8
National Bank of Canada	77.2	81.5	N/A	77.4	1.3	3.1	9.2	4.5
Sector: Transport	16.9	20.8	21.8	24.6	2.6	4.2	4.8	8.6
Canadian National Railway Company	7.7	7.2	8.4	8.6	2.8	7.0	4.7	4.7
Air Canada	33.5	34.8	36.5	37.1	2.9	4.1	5.8	7.6
CP Rail Division of Canadian Pacific Ltd	6.4	7.6	6.9	8.4	1.8	2.5	2.5	7.6
Canadian Airlines International Ltd	37.1	40.0	40.9	42.9	2.9	6.0	6.6	15.9
Greyhound	16.7	20.9	24.2	22.5	1.6	2.1	1.6	9.1
Via	19.0	19.0	20.6	24.3	4.8	8.0	8.5	7.4
Voyageur	13.2	21.0	26.6	-	1.5	3.1	4.7	-

(continued)

Table 1.6 (continued)

Designated Groups	Women				Members of Visible Minorities			
Sector and Company	1987 %	1994 %	1996 %	1999 %	1987 %	1994 %	1996 %	1999 %
Sector: Communications	39.6	41.5	42.2	41.7	4.1	7.2	8.8	9.0
Canada Post Corporation	36.2	37.5	38.1	39.5	4.0	6.3	8.6	9.2
Bell Canada	50.4	47.2	57.3	54.7	4.1	5.5	8.4	8.0
Canadian Broadcasting Corporation	35.2	40.3	41.3	39.4	2.1	5.1	5.0	4.8
Purolator Courier Ltd	22.6	24.5	23.1	24.4	1.2	4.6	12.6	13.0
CTV	46.2	59.6	45.6	43.7	5.7	14.0	8.3	12.1
CHUM Limited	32.6	33.8	35.9	40.7	1.3	3.8	4.7	5.6

Source: Census Canada 1996 & Annual Employment Equity Reports, Human Resources Development Canada.

pace," (Annual Report 1999, 86) Visible minorities in the public sector "are simply not making acceptable gains."

As noted earlier, the EE Act did not apply to the Public Service (that is, federal government departments and agencies) until 1996. Hence, the data are available since 1997. As of March 31, 1999, the representation of VMs in the federal public service was 5.9 percent relative to 5.1 percent in 1997.

Strengths and Weaknesses of Human Rights Statutes

The strengths of human rights laws across Canada have been that overt discrimination has declined to a great extent. Employees, in general, are more conscious of their human rights in employment, and numerous employers have developed antidiscrimination policies, especially in unionized workplaces.

One of the serious limitations of the human rights legislation across Canada is that it is complaint based, putting the onus of initial proof on an employee or a job applicant. In numerous cases, applicants and employees are reluctant to file a complaint for fear of retaliation and/or losing their jobs. Hence, the complaints filed before human rights commissions represent a tip of the iceberg (Jain and Al-Waqfi 2001). As Deom and Boivin (2001, 511) suggest, in the case of Quebec's Charter of Human Rights and Freedoms, the law of "nothing seen, nothing done" applies. The complaints-based method is rooted in the idea that discrimination in the labor market is an exception rather than the rule. As noted earlier, this is applicable to human rights statutes across Canada (see La Forest, Promoting Equality 2000) since all the statutes are complaint based.[12]

Experience in Britain and Northern Ireland

The population of the United Kingdom was 58 million. In 1999, ethnic minority groups comprised 3.8 million of the population of Britain (Owen, Reza, Green, Maguire, and Pitcher 2000). All minority groups had a younger age profile than the white population (At the Millennium, Women and Men in Britain, EOC website, 3–4). The ethnic minority population has been growing continuously since the late 1940s, reaching 1 million in the late 1960s, 3 million by 1991, and more than 3.8 million of the population of Great Britain in 1999. (Owen, Raza, Green, Maguire, and Pitcher 2000). In the Spring of 2000, 2.4 million people of working age belonged to ethnic minorities in Great Britain.

As in other Western countries, a larger number of men have left the labor force, and this trend is expected to continue. It is projected that only 69 percent of men aged 16 and over will be economically active in 2011. Women's activity rate has been rising steadily since World War II. It is projected that 57 percent of women aged 16 and over will be economically active in 2011, and they will comprise 46 percent of the labor force in that year (EOC website, 4). The proportion of women in the labor market increased from 66 percent in 1984 to 72 percent in 1999, whereas the proportion of men in the same period declined from 88 to 84 percent (EOC website, the labor market, 2).

Women are concentrated in lower skilled and lower paid jobs with less access to vocational training and education. In addition, large numbers of them work part-time, a situation that is closely associated with their family responsibilities (EOC website, 1).

In Britain, equal employment opportunity legislation was initially introduced during the 1970s and has been gradually expanded to include more groups and to cover more aspects of employment.

There is separate legislation covering sex, race, and disability[13] and separate geographical arrangements with separate enforcement agencies in Britain and in Northern Ireland. In Northern Ireland,[14] religion has been the main reason for the Fair Employment legislation.

In Britain, the Equal Opportunities Commission (EOC) and the Commission for Racial Equality (CRE) are the enforcement agencies for the Sex Discrimination Act and the Race Relations Act, respectively. They have the power to request information from employers and other organizations, to undertake "formal investigations," and to issue "non-discrimination notices." Both agencies have the authority to issue Codes of Practice. Although adherence to such codes is voluntary on the part of employers, such noncompliance may be taken into account in legal proceedings. The government, however, plans to merge the EOC and the CRE and have one single all-embracing equality commission, as in Northern Ireland, with a wider range of coverage including religion and age.

Although there is no general provision for affirmative action (AA) in the above-mentioned legislation, AA is permissible in recruitment and training where there have been fewer or no members of one race or sex in particular work in the previous twelve months.

Northern Ireland recently enacted legislation covering racial discrimination (1996), which is to be administered by the Commission for Racial Equality. Religion, not covered by legislation in Britain, has the most extensive legislative coverage in Northern Ireland, with provisions for both AA and contract compliance. Although legislation prohibiting discrimination on the basis of religion has existed in Northern Ireland since the partition of Ireland in 1920, it was not until the enactment of the Fair Employment Act of 1976 that employment discrimination on the basis of religion and political opinion in both public and private employment was outlawed.

Racial and ethnic minorities had no legislative protection until 1996, as noted above, when the (NI) Race Relations Order was enacted. Unlike Britain, it was perfectly lawful to deny someone a job in Northern Ireland because of his or her color and ethnic background.

In Northern Ireland, the Census has never included a question on ethnicity, and therefore no definite figures are available. The best estimate, according to the Multi-Cultural Resource Centre, 2000, in Belfast is that between 1.5 and 2 percent of Northern Ireland's population is made up of blacks and minority ethnic communities (Rogers 2000).

The enactment of the Race Relations (NI) Order (RRO) in 1996 was due mostly to the impetus from the nongovernmental voluntary and community sectors and the criticism of the British government by the United Nations Committee on the Elimination of All Forms of Racial Discrimination (1993) for not providing protection from racial discrimination in Northern Ireland. As Rogers (2000) observes, there were black and minority ethnic communities in Northern Ireland, some second and even third generation. Some of their members undoubtedly suffered racial discrimination and harassment. It took more than twenty years before this legislation was extended from Britain to Northern Ireland.

Racial grounds in the RRO are defined as color, race, nationality, or ethnic or national origins. The legislation covers employment, the provision of goods, facilities and services, housing, and education. It outlaws direct and indirect discrimination and victimization. In relation to employment, it covers recruitment, promotion, training, harassment, and access to benefits.

In April 1998, the Belfast Agreement was signed by the Irish and British governments and ratified by a majority of people in Northern Ireland. Political power was devolved from the British Parliament to Northern Ireland. The equality dimension of this Agreement was translated into legislation in the form of Northern Ireland Act of 1998. The Act provided for the establishment of a new Commission called the Equality Commission. The commission assumed the functions of the existing equality agencies in Northern Ireland: the Commission for Racial Equality, the Equal Opportunities Commission, and the Fair Employment Commission as well as the Northern Ireland Disability Council (Rogers 2000). The new Equality Commission opened its doors to the public in October 1999. As of now, the various agencies are operating independently within the new Commission, and the Equality Commission is faced with the challenge of coming up with a structure to deliver services to a diverse range of constituencies within its mandate.

The RRO empowers the Equality Commission (of Northern Ireland) to assist, financially or otherwise, individual complainants. This is unique since legal aid is not available for cases before the Northern Ireland industrial tribunals relating to employment. No provision is made for class actions (Rogers 2000). The legislation does provide the power to conduct a formal investigation into practices within sectors or specific industries. However, judicial decisions in Britain have limited the effectiveness of this tool thus far. Both the CRE and Equality Commission have recommended that the government must make legislative amendments to ensure that formal investigations are more effective. Apart from enforcement, the Equality Commission has decided to focus on capacity building within the black and minority ethnic sector itself.

In Northern Ireland, the public sector continues to be a major employer, providing work for 34 percent of those in employment. The workforce at present (2000) is around 420,000 (Equality Commission for Northern Ireland 2001). The female participation in the workforce has gone up from 45 to 47 percent in the last decade. As yet, there is no breakdown of workforce on grounds of ethnicity.

Fair Employment and Treatment Order

Because of its ineffectiveness, the first FEA was strengthened in 1989 and 1998 under the Fair Employment and Treatment Order. The 1989 Fair Employment Act was replaced by the Fair Employment and Treatment (Northern Ireland) Order, 1998 (enacted in December 1998). However, the terms of the Order are essentially the same as those of the earlier Act, with minor realigning to transfer the role of the FEC to the Fair Employment Directorate within the new Equality Commission, as noted earlier.

All private sector employers in Northern Ireland with more than ten employees were required to register with the FEC, while public sector employers are automatically registered with the Commission. In 1999, there were almost 3,994 private sector employers and 132 public sector employers registered with the new Equality Commission (Equality Commission for Northern Ireland 2000, 32) representing more than 70 percent of Northern Ireland's total workforce.

Fair employment legislation placed obligations on employers such as the requirement to review employment practices and mandatory monitoring of their workforces. These features have been absent from any other antidiscrimination legislation in Britain. The 1989 FEA provided for: (a) compulsory registration of employers of more than ten workers with the Fair Employment Commission (FEC); (b) annual monitoring of workforces and of applicants for employment; and (c) a review every three years of recruitment, training, and promotion practices to determine whether an affirmative action program needs to be set up to reach the goal of fair participation of both Catholics and Protestants in accordance with FEC's Code of Practice. Penalties under the Act included criminal penalties, economic sanctions, exclusion from tendering for government contracts, and denial of any government grants (Sloane and Mackay 1997).

The FEC and now the Equality Commission (EC) has the power to conduct investigations to determine whether individual employers have complied with the requirements of the legislation. The commission can also obtain a written undertaking from the employer to commit itself to undertaking affirmative actions, including goals and timetables to correct underrepresentation of a religious group. It may apply to a tribunal to enforce the undertakings. According to the latest report of the EC, only 4 of the 4,100 employers required to make a return were prosecuted for failure to submit within the specified time period (Equality Commission for Northern Ireland 2000, 32). According to the EC, the Catholic share of the monitored workforce in 1999 was 39.9 percent compared to a Catholic share of 42 percent of those available to work. The Catholic share of the male monitored workforce, according to EC, increased from 32 percent in 1990 to 36.9 percent in 1999. Among the female workforce, Catholics increased from 38.5 percent in 1990 to 42.5 percent in 1999. After 1990, the Catholic proportion had increased in every occupational group (Equality Commission for Northern Ireland 2000, 28). Even though the monitoring by the EC revealed continued improvement in Catholic participation in the labor market, the gap in employment contributed significantly to the continuing differentials in the experience of unemployment between Catholics and Protestants. Among the long-term unemployed, two-thirds were Catholic (Equality Commission for Northern Ireland 2000, 28).

There is clear evidence, however, that the FEA has had a significant impact on reducing inequalities in the workplace in Northern Ireland (Rogers 2000).

The British RRA, 2000 includes a positive duty on public employers to promote equality of opportunity and monitoring by the CRE, as noted earlier. However, unlike the FEA, there are no such requirements as in the case of the RRO in Northern Ireland. The positive action provisions in both the RRA and RROs are weak, as noted earlier; in addition, there is no contract compliance under these laws.

Some of weaknesses of the Race Relations Order are as follows:

1. Unlike the RRA, there is no requirement for employers to monitor for ethnicity as there is in relation to religious discrimination in the Fair Employment legislation of 1998.
2. The Equality Commission can issue Codes of Practice as in the case of the CRE, but they are not a part of the law. The provisions of these Codes can, however, be persuasive in a tribunal or a court proceeding.
3. The positive action provisions are weak since they do not impose any obligations on employers.
4. There is no provision for contract compliance as there is in the case of the Fair Employment legislation.
5. Unlike the RRA, the RRO provisions do not appear to apply to all public bodies in Northern Ireland (Rogers 2000).

Conclusions and Implications

The Northern Ireland Orders relating to race relations are passive, weak laws since there is no provision of monitoring and there are no goals and timetables as in the case of the FEA in Northern Ireland. The British RRA will include a positive duty on public employers to promote equality of opportunity and monitoring by the CRE. However, unlike the FEA, there are no such requirements in the case of RRO in Northern Ireland. The positive action provisions in both the RRA and the RROs are weak, as noted earlier; in addition, there is no contract compliance under these laws.

Northern Ireland has its own Sex Discrimination Order, 1976, and Equal Opportunities Commission, but legislation covering racial discrimination was enacted recently. Religion, not covered by legislation in Britain, has the most extensive legislative coverage in Northern Ireland with provisions for both AA and contract compliance. Although legislation prohibiting discrimination on the basis of religion has existed in Northern Ireland since the partition of Ireland in 1920, it was not until the enactment of the Fair Employment Act of 1976 that employment discrimination on the basis of religion and political opinion in both public and private employment was outlawed.

The FEC's enforcement powers were substantially greater than those of the EOC and CRE in Britain. However, according to CRE, there was increasing acceptance of ethnic monitoring in the 1990s. Hence, in 1993 the CRE made several proposals to the government, including compulsory monitoring of the ethnic origins of those in employment, contract compliance, powers for local authorities, and class action suits in industrial tribunals.

Britain

As noted previously, Britain has a separate statute to cover race discrimination— the Race Relations Act of 1976. This legislation is administered by the Commission of Racial Equality (CRE).

The commission has issued Codes of Practice for employers, trade unions, employment agencies, and employees in order to provide guidance for eliminating discrimination and enhancing equality of opportunity. The provisions of the Codes are admissible in evidence in proceedings under the two statutes before an industrial tribunal.

The RRA prohibits direct and indirect discrimination on the grounds of race, color, and nationality, including citizenship or ethnic or national origins. Although there is no general provision for affirmative action (AA) in the above-mentioned legislation, AA is permissible in recruitment and training where there have been fewer or no members of one race or sex in particular work in the previous twelve months.

An important development since 1973 has been the role of European Community legislation, which takes precedence over United Kingdom law and has brought about changes in Britain's legislation, especially relating to women (Sloane and Mackay 1997). Britain became a member of the European Economic Community (EEC) in 1973 and is thus subject to the EEC law.

A Race Relations Act (amended) was enacted in November 2000. The amended legislation extends the outlawing of discrimination to all public authorities and the central government, and it also places a statutory duty on these bodies to promote racial equality and eliminate institutional racism (Annual Report 2000, 5–6). Auditing and inspection of public bodies is also mandated under the new Act. CRE expects to make a real, measurable impact on racial equality across Great Britain (CRE Annual Report, 2000, 6). For instance, the duty will apply to the way a public authority carries out its various functions, including employment of staff. The duty on public authorities includes (a) monitoring of staff by ethnicity; (b) assessment of the impact on racial equality of proposed policies and consultation on them; and (c) monitoring of the impact on racial equality of policies and practices.

The CRE has the authority, under the new Act, to issue Codes of Practice containing practical examples of how different types of public authorities can comply with their general and specific duties. Hence, there will be codes for central (federal) government departments, local authorities, educational bodies, police authorities, and the NHS, as well as a general code for all other authorities.

Evidence of Employment Discrimination

According to the *Report on the Future of Multi-Ethnic Britain* (Parekh 2000), seven separate kinds of research evidence demonstrate or imply that inequalities in employment are caused by discrimination. These are census and survey statistics; discrimination testing, that is, special experiments using actors or fictitious applications; interviews with gatekeepers, for example, the staff of employment agencies; interviews and surveys studying the experience of Asian and black people in the labor market or the workplace; the actions of aggrieved employees; investigations conducted by the CRE; and incidents that come to light at employment tribunals.

For instance, statistical analysis of Census data has shown that Asian and black graduates, including those who appear to be doing well, have worse jobs than white graduates. People of Indian, African, and Chinese backgrounds are generally better qualified than whites, but nevertheless have difficulty gaining access to prestigious jobs. This is not because they are new to Britain or have foreign qualifications. The second generation experiences the same pattern and magnitude of penalties as the first generation. Thus, well-qualified people still meet substantial discrimination in the labor market. The top 10 percent of jobs are denied to them by various subtle glass ceilings, (Parekh 2000, 193).

Econometric models are needed to hold constant other nondiscriminatory variables that give rise to differences in employment probabilities across groups.

Strengths and Weaknesses of the Race Relations Act in Britain

The RRA in Britain has had a positive effect, "has helped to curb the worst kinds of discrimination in employment," and "also had invaluable impact on the general climate of opinion" (Parekh 2000, 264).

The weaknesses of the RRA include (a) its failure to deal with institutional racism and organizational culture; (b) its concern with color racism rather than cultural racism; (c) its greater concern with ensuring equality of treatment than with dealing with difference and diversity; (d) its failure to prohibit religious discrimination; and (e) its concern with negative duties, that is, avoidance of discrimination rather than promoting diversity (Parekh 2000, 265). According to the report, *The Future of Multi-Ethnic Britain*, sponsored by the Runnymede Trust, the positive duty in the amendments to the RRA do not extend to private employers (Parekh 2000, 264). A recent survey of the ethnic minorities in the 100 largest corporations in Europe (Foroohar et al. 2002) found that, except in Britain, few minorities reach the top; none of the responding companies had an ethnic minority as a chief executive officer (CEO), and almost all had a dismal representation of racial minorities in the board rooms within European countries. The report cites a survey conducted by the Runnymede Trust in Britain in 2000 and found that ethnic minorities constituted only 1 percent of senior managers (Foroohar et al. 2002).

Experience in South Africa

According to the 1996 Census, the South African population is approximately 40.5 million, with 77 percent Africans, 12 percent white, 9 percent coloured, and 3 percent Indians (Statistics South Africa, 2001). It was estimated that 52 percent of the total population was female. In 1999, 17 million people were in the labor force (World Bank, 2001, 50) while 34 percent of the economically active population (in 1996) were found to be unemployed.

The Employment Equity Act (EEA) was enacted by the Parliament in 1998. It aims to redress the ghettoization of the blacks, including coloureds and Indian women and persons with disabilities (called the designated groups) in the workplace. The objective of the EEA is to achieve equality in the workplace by eliminating unfair discrimination and promoting equal opportunity[15] through the implementation of positive and proactive measures (termed affirmative action measures) to advance the designated groups. The EEA requires employers with either fifty or more employees or certain specified turnover (in monetary terms) to undertake affirmative action measures with a view to ensuring that the designated groups have equitable representation in all occupational categories and levels in an employer's workforce consistent with their availability in the external labor market.

Rationale for Employment Equity Legislation

Historically, the labor market was a distorted one, with inequality in access to education, skills, and managerial and professional work, based on race and ethnicity. Racial discrimination was created in labor legislation, for example, in job reservation clauses that restricted access to skilled jobs (preserving them for white employees), in the Mines and Works Act (1904) and Industrial Conciliation Act (1956). These provisions were abolished in 1980, and significant labor law reforms have occurred in the last five years. However, the apartheid labor market has left most employees inadequately trained and economically disempowered. South Africa's peaceful transition through its 1994 national election and constitutional measures have given hope that the constitutional democracy will provide equal protection and opportunity to all citizens regardless of color, gender, religion, political opinion, or sexual orientation.

The legacy of workplace discrimination against blacks, the majority population, is systematically being eroded, albeit slowly. According to one survey of 161 large firms in South Africa (employing 560, 000 workers), in the year 2000 (Breakwater Monitor Report 2000), 10 percent of managers were black and 5 percent each were coloured and Indian; thus, 80 percent of all managers were white. Of these managers, 79 percent were male and 21 percent female. In 1998, the percentages of blacks, coloureds, and Indian were 6, 4, and 4, respectively, with 86 percent white managers and 84 percent male and 16 percent female (Breakwater Montior Report 2000).

According to the Commission on Gender Equality (CGE), women constituted the major segment of South Africa's population but accounted for only a third of the labor force. They were mainly concentrated in service, retail, and manufacturing sectors. Across all sectors, women were mainly to be found occupying jobs associated with stereotyped domestic roles; thus gender equality[16] within the workplace, according to the CGE, was underpinned by job segregation and perceived roles associated with gender group (CGE 1999).[17]

The Department of Labour (1999) states that whites had a 104 percent wage premium over Africans, and men earned approximately 43 percent higher wages than similarly qualified women in similar industrial sectors and occupations (cited in Thomas 2002).

Another indication is the representation of women and Africans in the senior public sector positions. According to the 1995 Household Survey, men accounted for 78 percent and women for only 22 percent of all legislative, senior officials and management positions in the workforce. Of the 78 percent that were men, 46 percent were white, 23 percent black, 6 percent Asian, and 3 percent coloured. Of the 22 percent that were women, 12 percent were white, 8 percent were black, 1 percent Asian, and 1 percent coloured (Booysen 1999a, 39).

Eighty-seven percent of management in the Public Service (director and above) in 1998 were men, and only 13 percent women (Statistics SA 1998, 41). Over half the men who were public sector managers were white (Booysen 1999a, 39)

Women comprised only 1.3 percent (49) of the 3,773 directors of the 657 companies listed on the Johannesburg Stock Exchange.[18] Only 14 women were listed as either executive directors, chairwomen or managing directors, and less than 1 percent board members were women (Naidoo 1997 in Booysen 1999a).

Employer Obligations under the Employment Equity Act

The EEA requires employers in consultation with unions and employees to:

Conduct a review of employment policies and practices to identify the specific job barriers faced by the designated group members and attempt to remove them;

Conduct a workforce survey and analysis to identify the underrepresentation of members of the designated groups relative to their availability in the external workforce;

Develop an employment equity plan with numerical goals and timetables, monitoring and evaluation procedures; and report on remuneration and benefits in each occupational category and level.[19]

Develop measures an employer will undertake to progressively reduce any disproportional differentials in pay as well as an employment equity plan.

Section 27(2) requires that where disproportionate income differentials are reflected in the statement, a designated employer must take measures to progressively reduce such differentials. Section 27(1) of the Employment Equity Act requires designated employers to submit a statement of remuneration and benefits received in each occupational category and level to the Employment Conditions Commission established by section 59 of the Basic Conditions of Employment Act (1998). Section 27(3) indicates that these measures may include: (a) collective bargaining; (b) compliance with sectoral pay determinations made by the minister of labor in terms of Section 51 of the Basic Conditions of Employment Act; (c) applying norms and benchmarks set by the Employment Conditions Commission; and (d) relevant measures in the Skills Development Act (1998). The Employment Conditions Commission is required to research and investigate norms and benchmarks for proportionate income differentials and advise the minister on appropriate measures for reducing disproportional differentials. The commission is not allowed to disclose information pertaining to individual employees or employers. There is likely to be considerable public and organizational policy debate on what consitutes an acceptable pay curve in respect of differentials within organizations, and indeed whether such pay structuring is possible in a market-driven global economy.

The Employment Equity Act does not set quotas, but rather enables individual employers to develop their own plans. Criteria regarding enhanced representation include national and regional demographic information and special skills availability.

Whenever unfair discrimination is alleged in terms of the Employment Equity Act, a reverse onus of proof is on the employer to establish that the practice is fair. As part of a required employment equity plan, all employers with fifty or more employees are required to review all their employment and human resources practices to remove any provisions or practices that may have a discriminatory effect. This includes recruitment and selection, and remuneration. It is in these two areas, as well as in the provision of substantive benefits and conditions of employment, where discrimination is most likely to be found.

The EEA requires that employers give due consideration to a "suitably qualified person" in their recruitment of designated groups. Such a person may have either formal qualifications, prior learning, relevant experience, or capacity to acquire—within a reasonable time—the ability to do the job.

Capacity to acquire the ability to do the job will require training and support. Currently, few black men and women are qualified to fill semiskilled, skilled, and professional jobs, owing to apartheid practiced by the previous white regime. The EEA along with the Skills Development Act (1998) requires employers to provide training to designated groups.

The EEA encourages employers to provide improved internal grievance procedures against discriminatory behavior and harassment. Labor inspectors have the enforcement powers. Those disputes that cannot be resolved through internal procedures will be referred to the Commission for Conciliation, Meditation and Arbitration (CCMA) and ultimately the Labor court (Hepple 1997).

State of Compliance with the Employment Equity Act by Employers

The Commission for Employment Equity (CEE) recently released its first annual report covering the period 1999–2001 (CEE Report 2001). The commission's report for 2001 is based on 8,250 employers with 3,336,784 employees and shows mixed results.

On the plus side, it indicates that employers, in general, are taking their responsibility seriously for eroding the effects of the apartheid labor market which had left most black workers inadequately trained and disempowered. For instance, the EEC report indicates that black (African, coloured, and Indian) workers improved their labor market position from the 1998 baseline survey (conducted by Jain and Bowmaker-Falconer in 1998 for the South African Department of Labour) to 2001 as Professionals, Technicians and Associate Professionals from 25 to 38 percent, respectively in 1998 to 55 and 48 percent in 2001, respectively (see Table 1.7). The Professionals' position also compares favorably to Statistics South Africa's Household Survey data for 1999.

Blacks lost ground as legislators, senior officials, and managers when their representation declined from 1998 in these occupational categories from 28 per-

Table 1.7
Black Representation per Occupational Category

Occupational category by percent	EE report 2001 Black	OHS '99 Black	Baseline '98 Black
Legislator, senior officials and managers	26.1	45.07	27.88
Professionals	55.1	48.64	24.70
Technicians and associate professionals	47.5	66.89	37.84
Clerks	59.4	64.20	57.71
Service and sales workers	72.0	83.31	62.07
Skilled agricultural and fishery workers	85.6	90.64	90.79
Craft and related trades workers	61.7	84.94	65.88
Plant and machine operators and assemblers	93.7	94.59	92.22
Elementary occupations	97.5	97.67	98.30
Non-permanent works	84.1	N/A	N/A
Total	75.2	80.77	66.11

Source: Employment Equity 2001: Executive Summary of the First Annual Report of the Commission for Employment Equity. South Africa, Department of Labour, Page 10.

cent to 26 percent in 2001; this is even more pronounced than their representation of 45 percent in the Household Survey of 1999. They are primarily concentrated in elementary occupations (98 percent in 2001): plant and machine operators (94 percent in 2001), skilled agricultural and fishery workers (86 percent in 2001), and service and sales workers (72 percent in 2001), as shown in Table 1.7 (Commission for EE Report 2001, 30).

Women (black and white) hold a minority of positions—that is, approximately 22 percent as legislators, senior officials, and managers. In this category, 22 percent, white women hold 15 percent, Indian females 1 percent, African females 3 percent, and coloured females 2 percent (CEE Report 2001, 30).

Table 1.8 indicates that women (both white and black) currently hold only 13 percent of all top management and 21 percent of all senior management positions in SA. However (not shown in the table), African women hold only 1.2 percent of all top management positions (CEE 2001, 19). Women represent 38 percent of total employment and are clearly underrepresented in all management occupational levels (Commission for EE Report 2001, 19 and 24).

Black employees consisted of 31 percent of all levels of management (see

Table 1.8
Summary of Occupational Level Representation by Designated Group in South Africa, 2001

Occupational level	Black%	Female%	Disability
Top management	12.6	12.5	1.2
Senior management	18.4	21.0	1.1
Professionally qualified, experienced specialists and middle-management	44.0	43.1	0.9
Skilled technical, academically qualified and junior management	56.4	40.0	0.8
Semi-skilled and discretionary decision making	82.2	38.6	1.0
Unskilled and defined decision making	98.0	28.6	1.0

Source: Commission for Employment Equity Report, 1999–2001. South Africa, Department of Labour.

Table 1.8). Therefore, an overwhelming majority of managers across all levels of management were white. Employees with disabilities represented only 1 percent of all management levels. The CGE survey (1999) found that employers cited the following problems in integrating women in their workforce: resistance by male employees (across the organizational spectrum); stereotyped perceptions, and poor skills among female employees.

Employers adopted the following criteria for recruitment and promotion (CGE 1999):

a. Psychometric testing, including subjective and culturally biased testing.
b. Emphasis on skills, formal qualifications, and experience.

A paradox thus seems to exist, as noted by the CGE (1999): on the one hand, companies are citing poor skills level among females to be the main barrier. On the other hand, they continue to include it as a criterion for recruitment and promotion. This means that male employees would be the most likely job incumbents, relative to women.

Advantages of Employment Equity (EE)

1. Employment equity (EE) helps employers focus not only on African blacks but all coloureds, Indians, and other designated groups such as women and persons with disabilities.

2. EE encourages more employers to devise new and innovative measures to proactively recruit, promote, and train the designated groups. It goes beyond the poaching of African blacks by one employer from another to plan staffing in a systematic and planned manner. A survey of 23,000 South African employees found that the negative attitudes have increased sharply among black employees. Another recent study (Thomas 2000) suggests that black managers may leave companies ("job hop") for higher salaries and related perks due to not fitting into historically established corporate cultures.

3. EE motivates employers to develop human resources information systems.

4. EE sensitizes employers to the labor market demographics of the designated groups while developing their EE plan.

Disadvantages of Employment Equity

1. According to the South African Department of Labour (SADOL), there was no significant improvement in the representation of designated group members. Similarly, the CGE survey of employers (1999) found that there were significant job barriers in the recruitment and promotion of women. It seems that employers in South Africa have a long way to go as yet. At the same time, one has to realize that the EEA has been in effect only two years and the legacy of apartheid will take some time to overcome.

2. According to Samson (1999), the EEA treats women as a homogeneous category. White and black women currently have extremely different levels of education and training, job opportunities, and wages. Even among black women, there are significant differences. Legislation at present does not require companies to disaggregate their information on race and disability by gender. This presents the possibility that targets for women will be met by advancing the already privileged, thereby denying black women access to training and traditionally male jobs. In addition, companies below the threshold limit of fifty employees are not covered by the EEA. Since the vast majority of African women work in the informal sector or as domestic workers, most of them will remain uncovered by EEA in their workplaces (Samson 1999).

An evaluation of the compliance with the EEA must take into consideration (a) the economic and financial factors relevant to the sector in which the employer operates; (b) present and anticipated economic and financial circumstances of the employer; (c) progress in implementing EE by other employers;

and (d) reasonable efforts made by the employer to implement EE (Samson 1999). In fact, some of these factors regarding the employer's economic and financial circumstances and plans are outlined in the Canadian (federal) EEA.

Conclusion

Although progress has been made in enhancing racial and gender representation in the workplace, this is an incremental process that has to be supported by coherent human resource development priorities through the implementation of the Skills Development legislation and changes in the organizational culture. This is vital at both public policy and organizational levels. An increasing earnings gap has an adverse impact on mainly black people, in spite of the increasing diversity and multiracial character of a growing middle class. The biggest priority must be human resource development and education in skills and competencies needed in a society in transition.

Both the government and the Black Economic Empowerment Commission recognize this reality. The commission has made important recommendations to the government to "kick-start" the economy and enhance economic growth through state-driven measures to ensure black participation in the mainstream economy. Proposed measures include a national integrated human resource development strategy, legislated deracialization of business ownership in the private sector, national targets—which include land distribution and ownership, and equity participation in economic sectors. The commission further recommends targets for senior and executive management in private sector firms of more than fifty employees to be black. The commission's proposals, which have been accepted by the government in principle, are a significant policy basis for improving access to capital and skills and economic empowerment for the majority of South Africans. These overall measures, along with the progress in implementing employment equity, will greatly improve the chances of majority blacks to have their just share in the South African economy.

Micro-Organizational Level Implications

At a micro-organizational level, much of the success or failure of EE/AA programs can be attributed to whether employees believe that staffing processes for designated groups were procedurally fair, that is, perceived equity of the recruitment, selection, promotion processes used to make managerial decisions relating to the target groups. If the process appears unfair, designated groups suffer negative self-perceptions of competence. Several studies support the notion that employees have higher perceptions of fairness when EE/AA is achieved through certain competitive advantage arguments (Greenberg 1990; Heilman, McCullough, and Gilbert 1996). Studies have also shown the relationship between procedural fairness and organizational outcomes such as trust in a decisionmaker.

Similarly, micro-organizational determinants such as the status of the EE/AA officer can have an impact on the success or failure of such programs. Pfeffer, Davis-Blake, and Julius (1995) found that salary paid to the head of EE/AA affected the amount of change in the racial and gender composition of senior positions. An officer with higher status and higher pay relative to other administrators in the same organization was more likely to mobilize resources and have a higher proportion of women and other designated groups.

In addition, research on diversity in general and racial diversity in particular shows support for improved group performance (O'Reilly et al. 1997); that diverse groups do better than homogeneous groups on both process and performance effectiveness (Watson et al. 1993); and that racial diversity interacts with business strategy in determining firm performance measured in terms of productivity, return on equity, and market performance (Richard 2000).

Conclusions and Implications

Tables 1.9 and 1.10 list the pros and cons of EE/AA policies in the selected countries. It is obvious that countries with mandatory AA programs such as India, Malaysia, and the Northern Ireland part of UK, as well as those with Contract Compliance programs such as the United States, have made significant progress in improving the employment and earnings of the designated groups, although they still have a long way to go.

EE/AA policy measures stimulate positive changes in the workforces of affected employers. In particular, such public policy measures:

1. help broaden the focus of the affected employers to designated groups in the selected countries;
2. require employers to collect both stock and flow data on the designated groups in several countries such as Canada, the United States, and South Africa;
3. encourage many employers to devise new and innovative measures to attract, retain, and motivate designated group workers by adopting proactive hiring, training, promotion, and compensation policies;
4. persuade many employers to relate their human resource management plans to corporate plans by revamping the human resource function, and in many cases, developing human resource information systems to benefit both designated and other workers; and
5. sensitize employers to the changing demographics in their respective societies, thereby helping managers develop policies to cope with these developments.

Table 1.9
Characteristics of EE/AA Programs in Six Countries: Advantages

Evaluation	USA	Canada	India	Malaysia	South Africa	Britain	Northern Ireland
Advantages	• AA Effective in Contract Compliance Programs (Leonard Study of 68,000 Establishments) Found Employment Gains and Occupational Upgrading for Minorities. • Employers Who Established	• Helped Employers Broaden the Focus to Four Groups. • Encouraged Employers to Devise New and Innovative Measures to Proactively Recruit, Promote and Train Women and Minorities.	• Secured Proportional Representation of SCs and STs in Professional and Managerial Jobs. • Small and Growing Middle Class of SCs and STs. • One of Five Seats in Parliament Held by SCs and	• In 1969, Malays had 2% equity in firms. In 2000, Malays owned 22% of their National Economic Assets • AA produced a Malay middle class • Almost all PS jobs are held by Malay	• 2001 Report of the Commission for Employment Equity showed some improvements. • Some of the pros listed under Canada may apply.	• Not known except for Case Studies of formal investigations and industrial tribunal awards.	• *According to the 10th (1999) Annual Report of The Equality Commission (NI)—Established in October 1998—in 1990 Catholics comprised of 40% of those available for work and yet they were in ex-

(continued)

Table 1.9 *(continued)*

Evaluation	USA	Canada	India	Malaysia	South Africa	Britain	Northern Ireland
Advantages *(continued)*	Goals did Actually Employ More Minorities Relative to Others (Leonard). • Holzer & Neumark Study (2000) Found that AA programs have successfully redistributed economic resources to minorities & women	• Helped Employers to Develop HR Information Systems. • Sensitised Employers to the Changing Demographics. • Overall, EE is Relatively Successful Primarily for Women and to Some Extent Visible Minorities.	STs; 22.5% of all Parliament and State Assembly Members are from SC and ST Classes.				cess in only 3 of the 9 occupational classifications. However, in 1999 their labour availability was 42% and they had representation in excess of 40% in 6 of the 9 occupational classification. • As well, the Report notes that

in both the public and private sectors the share of applicants has increased; Male and Female appointees in the two sectors were in excess of 45%.

Source: Equality Commission for Northern Ireland (Belfast), May, 2000.

Table 1.10
Characteristics of EE/AA Programs in Six Countries: Disadvantages

Evaluation	USA	Canada	India	Malaysia	South Africa	Britain	Northern Ireland
Disadvantages	• Recent Supreme Court decisions may nullify gains. • Changing political climate	• The previous (1986) Federal EE Act was relatively ineffective: Coverage was limited and goals and timetables were not mandatory. • Threshold limit and monitoring and enforcement not clearly defined. • Glass ceiling for upper level management is still in place for Women and VMs.	• AA fell short of proportional representation. • Demonstrations and violence condemned AA extension for other backward classes (OBCs). • Government political gain agenda. • Lack of pool of qualified SCs and STs due to poor educational funding.	• May create problems if economic growth discontinues.	• 2001 Report of the Commission for Employment Equity shows employers have a long way to go to reflect Black, Female, Disabled Persons Labour Market Representation.	• No provisions for goals and timetables as yet. • Progress is mixed. • Substantial differences remain in employability. • Occupational segregation across groups.	• Employment discrimination a continuing problem.

There are powerful forces at work to reduce disparities in the labor market opportunities of ethnic minorities and women. We have deliberately chosen six countries which are diverse both in terms of culture and economic development to show that responses to this challenge vary according to the circumstances of each country but usually involve a degree of legal intervention. Although there may be widespread agreement on the need for reform, the precise mechanisms for achieving this reform are the subject of much debate and controversy. Nowhere is this more clearly seen than in the case of affirmative action and to some extent employment equity programs, which may be perceived to have detrimental effects on individual members of nondiscriminated against groups.

Malaysia and South Africa are distinctive insofar as protection is offered to the ethnic and racial majority as opposed to minority groups. In India the problem arises from the caste system. In the UK a distinction is made between Northern Ireland and Britain. In Northern Ireland, religion, which is aligned with political leanings, is a major issue, while this is largely absent in the rest of the UK. In England, the problem of racial discrimination is influenced by the fact that racial minorities are largely concentrated in large urban areas. In each of the developing countries, there may be problems of illiteracy, and in the UK and elsewhere problems of language, which reduce the productivity potential in employment of certain members of these groups and make it more difficult to detect whether differences in employability and pay are caused by discrimination. In the United States racial minorities include a diverse array of groups including blacks, Hispanics, and Mexicans, with nonwhites making up 25 percent of the population. What is clear from the U.S., Canadian, and UK experience is that the outcomes differ not only between the minorities and majority groups, but also across minority groups, with some achieving better labor market performance than others. In the United States and Canada there are a wide range of measures, including affirmative action and employment equity plans, respectively, for federal contractors and protection against age and other prohibited grounds of discrimination. Much of this legislation has been influential elsewhere as in the case of affirmative action in Northern Ireland.

Notes

1. SCs comprise 135 million persons and STs consist of 66 million persons, as of 1991. STs are made up of some 400 communities varying greatly in size, physical characteristics, linguistic and religious usages, as well as traditional modes of livelihood. They do not however, have a distinctive racial, religious, or even linguistic identity that marks them off from the nontribal communities. They remain relatively backward and live in isolation in remote communities. Unlike the tribals (STs), SCs are found in every part of the country and have been closely involved in the life of their respective communities. They speak the language of the region they inhabit. In the past, they occupied the lowest position in the economic hierarchy and have been

engaged in manual and menial occupations. The Constitution of India has abolished the practice of untouchability, but they continue to suffer from many disadvantages (Beteille 1993).

2. According to Sowell (1990), "India is not only the world's largest multi-ethnic society but also one of the most socially fragmented, with powerful religious, caste, regional and ethnic differences cross-cutting the society. There are an estimated 180 languages in India and more than 500 dialects." In India, preferential policies for majorities are state or local, while preferential policies for less fortunate minorities such as untouchables and tribal groups are national, supplemented by local programs.

3. The representation for SCs and STs was well below the quotas; 5 percent in Class 1 jobs against a quota of 15 percent for SCs and 1.04 percent versus a quota of 7.5 percent for STs.

4. A National Human Rights Commission was established through the Protection of Human Rights Act in 1993. It institutionalized the concept of human rights. All proceedings before the commission are deemed to be judicial proceedings, and the commission is deemed to be a civil court. The chairperson and other members of the commission are appointed by the president of India on recommendation by the prime minister, speaker of the House, leader of the opposition in the House, and others. The chairperson of the commission has to be a former chief justice of the Supreme Court.

5. Mandatory constitutional provisions of reservation of seats in the Parliament and the state legislatures apply only to the SCs and STs, and not to the OBCs.

6. Currently, of the 365 districts in India, 60 to 70 are headed up by district officers who are members of SCs and STs; some of them are also vice-chancellors at universities, doctors, airline pilots, and lawyers. In addition, there are SC teachers in a fairly large number of village schools, and they play an important role in changing attitudes toward SCs (Beteille 1993). AA has been successful in large part in altering the image that other people have of SCs and STs.

7. In the past, it has often been pointed out that jobs reserved for the STs and SCs could not be filled for want of qualified candidates. This is partly a direct result of governments not giving effect to the constitutional directive for universal elementary education. Hence, job reservation, according to Beteille (1993), has been an easy way out for governments; it is a cheap mechanism, implemented at low cost. All that it requires is that places are set aside in the public service (Beteille 1993). Beteille goes on to point out that an effective job reservations program would have required much more active intervention by both the government and other agencies in society.

8. In India, a vast majority of the population is concentrated in villages. Job reservations divert attention from the masses who are too poor even to be seeking jobs in their names. Hence, job reservations can only attend to the problems of middle-class SCs and STs.

9. According to Sowell (1990), "an escalation of preferential policies of Malays occurred after the race riots of May 1969, in which Malays unleashed mob violence against the Chinese. The Malay government promulgated its 'New Economic Policy,' designed to achieve what it called 'racial balance.'"

10. According to Puthucheary (1993), the NEP aimed at assisting Malays and other *Bumiputras* to move from agricultural occupations to the more lucrative urban occupations where opportunities for socioeconomic advancement were much greater. Affirmative action programs were introduced to education, employment, and in the corporate sector where wealth was measured in terms of equity ownership. In edu-

cation, ethnic quotas were introduced for admission to local universities. In the private sector, statistical targets were set for "economic restructuring." It was envisaged that within a twenty-year period, the proportion of Malay ownership of share capital would increase from less than 2 percent in 1969 to about 30 percent by 1990. In addition, laws were passed making it compulsory for firms over a certain size to employ a certain number of Malays at all levels of the hierarchy. Companies wishing to expand their operations were also required to set aside a proportion of their new capital for Malay ownership. The price of shares offered to Malays was lower than the market value, thus giving opportunity to those who were allocated these shares to make quick returns. The emphasis of the NEP was on equality of results, that is, on ensuring that the distribution of income, wealth, and occupations is in proportion to the population of each group. Emphasis was placed on getting the right ethnic "mix" in employment at all levels and in both public and private sectors.

11. Holzer and Neumark in their article entitled "Assessing Affirmative Action" in the September 2000 issue of the *Journal of Economic Literature,* provide an extensive review of more than 200 studies of affirmative action in the United States. The authors' conclusions are, in part, based on the results of longitudinal studies, national surveys, statistics, and so on. Their overall conclusion is that AA programs that resulted in the successful redistribution of income to women and minorities have not seriously affected efficiency. Their review shows that discrimination is the most logical empirical explanation for historical wage and achievement gaps and that discrimination is a continuing problem. They also indicate that any efforts to bolster the status of women and minorities in the public and private sectors do not affect economic efficiency to any significant extent. The authors also conclude that AA programs increase the participation of women and minorities anywhere from 10 to 15 percent. Their review of 200 studies, as mentioned above, show no evidence of weaker job performance or educational qualifications. Even where women and minorities do have weaker credentials, they still perform about as well as nonminorities (CAUT Bulletin 2001).

12. Moreover, complaints are subject to lengthy delays owing in part to the inadequate funding of the human rights commissions, and almost all human rights laws focus on dealing with individual rather than systemic complaints.

13. The Race Relations Act of 1976 makes it unlawful to discriminate on grounds of color, race, nationality including citizenship or ethnic or national origin in employment, training, and related matters. The Sex Discrimination Act of 1975, as amended, makes it unlawful to discriminate on grounds of sex and marriage when recruiting, training, promoting, dismissing, or retiring staff (Jain and Bowmaker-Falconer 1998).

14. In Northern Ireland, legislation bans discrimination in employment on grounds of religious belief or political opinion. All public authorities and private sector employers with more than ten employees are required to register with the Fair Employment Commission—now the Equality Commission—and submit annual reports to the commission on the religious composition of their workforces. Failure to do so is a criminal offense that is punishable by a fine and in some cases by economic sanctions, such as loss of government grants and contracts (*Northern Ireland* 1995). The commission has power to direct an employer to take affirmative action, such as the encouragement of job applicants from an underrepresented group. It can also set goals and timetables in cases where fair participation by both Protestant and Catholic communities in employment is not being secured. The Fair Employment Tribunal adjudicates on individual complaints of discrimination. It can award unlimited compensation to victims of discrimination and may order remedial action by an employer.

It also has powers to fine an employer and provide details of the commission's directions to the employer to high court in order for an employer to obey its orders. The high court has unlimited powers of fine (*Northern Ireland* 1995).

15. The legislative armory against unfair discrimination is now quite formidable. For example, Chapter 2 of the Employment Equity Act (1998) in South Africa prohibits unfair discrimination against designated employees. These include black people, women, and employees with disabilities. Legislative prohibitions against unfair discrimination are also intrinsic to South Africa's Constitution (1996). Chapter 2 (the Bill of Rights) contains an equality clause, and like the Employment Equity Act specifies a number of grounds that constitute unfair discrimination. In addition, Schedule 7 of the Labour Relations Act (1995) considers unfair discrimination either directly or indirectly as a residual unfair labor practice. Grounds include race, gender, ethnic origin, sexual orientation, religion, disability, conscience, belief, language, and culture. Labor laws have been at the forefront of the post-apartheid government's determination to remove unfair discrimination. A new act, The Promotion of Equality and Prevention of Unfair Discrimination Act (1999) seeks to prohibit discrimination in both civil society and in employment practices.

The draft Constitution adopted by the Constitutional Assembly on May 8, 1996, was approved by the Constitutional Court in November 1996 (Corder 1996). Section 9(2) of the Bill of Rights in the Constitution states in part: To promote the achievement of equality, legislative and other measures designed to protect or advance persons, or categories of persons, disadvantaged by unfair discrimination may be taken.

Similarly, section 2(2) of Schedule 7 of the Labour Relations Act of 1995 stipulates that "an employer is not prevented from adopting or implementing employment policies and practices that are designated to achieve the adequate protection and advancement of persons or groups or categories of persons disadvantaged by unfair discrimination, in order to enable their full and equal enjoyment of all rights and freedoms."

EEA sets out the purpose of the Act to achieve equity in the workplace.

a. promoting equal opportunity and fair treatment in employment through the elimination of unfair discrimination; and

b. implementing affirmative action measures to redress the disadvantages in employment experienced by designated groups, in order to ensure their equitable representation in all occupational categories and levels of the workforce.

16. Sex vs. Gender: A person's sex refers to the biological characteristics that make the person male or female. Biological differences between men and women are as follows: (1) only women can get pregnant and (2) women menstruate and men do not.

Gender refers to the characteristics that society expects a person to have, based on their sex. It refers to economic, social, and cultural roles, behaviors, attributes, and opportunities that are associated with being female or male such as women are meant to do certain types of work and men other types of work.

17. More than a quarter of African males and 60 percent of African females in the formal sector were in the elementary occupations such as cleaning, garbage collection, and agricultural labor. Similarly, 41 percent of coloured women were in these elementary occupations, while 40 percent of Indian women were in clerical occupations.

About 18 percent of African women and 19 percent of coloured women were in managerial or professional jobs, while 11 percent of African men, 14 percent of coloured men, and 37 percent of Indian men were in managerial or professional jobs (Erasmus and Sadler 1999).

18. There is also a concentration of managerial control through a system of interlocking directories where the same person(s) serve on the boards of several corporations. This social closure has limited the upward mobility of black managers and women. However, South Africa's reentry into the international business community has forced an awareness about its relative competitiveness in the manufacturing and service sectors.

Recently, statutory and governmental tender requirements have been directed toward employment equity and diversity at all levels. Several black directors have been appointed to boards of directors. Although less than 15 percent of South Africa's company directors are black or women, this is likely to change significantly by the year 2005.

19. The Employment Equity Act does not set quotas, but rather enables individual employers to develop their own plans. Criteria regarding enhanced representation include national and regional demographic information and special skills supply/availability. Section 27(1) of the Employment Equity Act requires designated employers to submit a statement of remuneration and benefits received in each occupational category and level to the Employment Conditions Commission established by Section 59 of the Basic Conditions of Employment Act (1998). Section 27(2) requires that where disproportionate income differentials are reflected in the statement, a designated employer must take measures to progressively reduce such differentials. Section 27(3) indicates that these measures may include: (a) collective bargaining; (b) compliance with sectoral pay determinations made by the minister of labor in terms of Section 51 of the Basic Conditions of Employment Act; (c) application of norms and benchmarks set by the Employment Conditions Commission; and (d) relevant measures in the Skills Development Act (1998). The Employment Conditions Commission is required to research and investigate norms and benchmarks for proportionate income differentials and advise the minister on appropriate measures for reducing disproportional differentials. The commission is not allowed to disclose information pertaining to individual employees or employers.

References

Abella, R.S. 1984. Equality in Employment. A Royal Commission Report. Ottawa: Supply & Services.

Agocs, Carol, and Burr, Catherine. 1996. "Employment Equity, Affirmative Action and Managing Diversity: Assessing the Differences." Jain, Harish C. and Verma, Anil, eds., "Workforce Diversity and Competitive Strategies: Human Resource Policies and Practices in the 1990s." *International Journal of Manpower* 17: 30–45.

Annual Report. 2000. London: Commission for Racial Equality.

Annual Report, 1999. 2000. Ottawa: Canadian Human Rights Commission.

Bakshi, P.M. 2000. *The Constitution of India.* Delhi: Universal Books.

Beteille, A. 1993. "India: Equal Opportunities for All and Special Opportunities for Some." In *Development and Democracy.* M. Weiner, ed. Johannesburg: The Urban Foundation, 3–20.

Booysen, Lize. 1999a, Autumn. "Towards More Feminine Business Leadership for the 21st Century: A Literature Review and a Study of the Potential Implication for South Africa." *South African Journal of Labour Relations* 23: 31–54.

Booysen, Lize. 1999b, Winter/Spring. "Male and Female Managers: Gender Influences in South African Managers in Retail Banking." *South African Journal of Labour Relations* 23: 25–54.

Breakwater Monitor Report. 2000. Pretoria: Department of Labour website. www.labourgov.za.

Britain 1996. *An Official Handbook.* London: HMSO.

Cascio, Wayne F. 1998. *Managing Human Resources: Productivity, Quality of Work Life, Profits.* Boston: Irwin McGraw-Hill.

CAUT Bulletin. 2001, March. "Report Assesses Affirmative Action Programs in the United States." (Taken from Campus Clips, American Federation of Teachers).

Commission for Employment Equity Report, 1999–2001. www.labour.gov./za/docs/legislation/eea/commission.html.

Commission for Employment Equity Report, 1999–2001. 2001. Pretoria, South Africa: Department of Labour.

Commission for Gender Equality Report. 1999. *Survey of Employers Regarding AA Policies and Practices. Gender in the Private Sector.* Pretoria, South Africa: Commission for Gender Equality.

Corder, H. 1996, Summer. "South Africa's Transitional Constitution: Its Design and Implementation." *Public Law*.

Cormack R.J., and Osborne, R.D., eds. 1991. *Discrimination and Public Policy in Northern Ireland.* Oxford: Clarendon Press.

Daudlin, R. 1984, March. *Equality Now! Report of the Special Committee on Visible Minorities in Canada Society.* Ottawa: House of Commons.

Deom, Esther, and Boivin, Jean. 2001. "Union-Management Relations in Quebec." In *Union-Management Relations in Canada,* eds. Morley Gunderson, Allen Ponak, and Daphne Taras. Toronto: Addison-Wesley Longman, 486–520.

Dowling, P.J., Welch, D.E., and Schuler, R. 1999. *International Human Resource Management.* 3d ed. Cincinnati: Thomson.

Economic Report. 2000. Government of Malaysia: Ministry of Treasury.

Edmonds, J. 1990. *Beneath the Veneer.* Volumes 1–4. Ottawa: Supply and Services Canada.

Emsley, I. 1992, November. "Malaysia, Affirmative Action: The Malaysian Experience." *OPTIMA*.

Equal Opportunities Commission. Undated. *Women and Men in Britain.* www.eoc.org.uk.

Erasmus, B.J., and Sadler, E. 1999, Winter/Spring. "Issues Affecting Women in the South African Workplace: A Comparative Analysis of Findings." *South African Journal of Labour Relations* 23: 4–19.

Farley, Reynolds. 2000. "Demographic, Economic and Social Trends in a Multicultural America." In *New Directions: African Americans in a Diversifying Nation,* ed. James S. Jackson. Washington, DC: National Policy Association.

"Focus on South East Asia." 2002. Allens Arthur Robinson, www.aar.com.au/publications/forseaju101.htm.

Foroohar, Rana, Theil, Stefan, Marais, Samia, Pepper, Tara, Weidekind, Heike, Nadeau, Barbie, and Daly, Emma. 2002, February 18. "Race in the Boardroom: A Newsweek Survey of Corporate Europe Finds Plenty of Confusion about the Continent's Changing Identity Just As New Laws are about to Require More Clarity." *Newsweek,* 28–32.

Ganguly, S. 1997. "Ethnic Policies and Political Quiescence in Malaysia and Singapore." In *Government Policies and Ethnic Relations in Asia and the Pacific,* eds. Michael Brown and Sumit Ganguly. Cambridge, MA: MIT Press.

Giles, Anthony, and Starkman, Akivah. 2001. "The Collective Agreement." In *Union-*

Management Relations in Canada, eds. Morley Gunderson, Allen Ponak, and Daphne Taras. Toronto: Addison-Wesley Longman, 272–313.

Greenberg, J. 1990. "Organizational Justice: Yesterday, Today and Tomorrow." *Journal of Management* 16: 392–432.

Heenan, D.A., and Perlmutter, H.V. 1979. *Multinational Organizational Development.* Reading, MA: Addison-Wesley.

Heibert, Murray, and Jayasankaran, S. 1999, May 20. "Affirmative Action Policies Enacted after Riots 30 Years Ago Still Play a Vital Role in Forecasting Racial Harmony." *Far Eastern Economic Review,* 45–47, 162.

Heilman, M.E., McCullough, W.F., and Gilbert, D. 1996. "The Other Side of Affirmative Action: Reactions of Nonbeneficiaries to Sex-Based Preferential Selection." *Journal of Applied Psychology* 81: 346–357.

Hepple, Bob. 1997. "Equality Laws and Economic Efficiency." *Industrial Law Journal* 18.

Heritage Canada. 1996, January. *Annual Report 1994–1995 on the Operation of the Canadian Multi-Culturalism Act.* Ottawa: Heritage Canada.

Hodges-Aeberhard, J., and Raskin, C., eds. 1997. *Affirmative Action in the Employment of Ethnic Minorities and Persons with Disabilities.* Geneva: International Labour Office.

Holzer, Harry J., and Neumark, David. 2000a, January. "What Does Affirmative Action Do?" *Industrial & Labor Relations Review* 53(2): 240–271.

Holzer, Harry J., and Neumark, David. 2000b, September. "Assessing Affirmative Action." *Journal of Economic Literature,* 483–568.

Jackson, James S., ed. 2000. "Introduction and Overview." *New Directions: African Americans in a Diversifying Nation.* Washington, D.: National Policy Association.

Jackson, Richard. 2001. "Collective Bargaining Legislation in Canada" In *Union-Management Relations in Canada,* eds. Morley Gunderson, Allen Ponak, and Daphne Taras. Toronto: Addison-Wesley Longman, 175–210.

Jain, H.C. 1994. "Canadian Federal Employment Equity Policies." In *New Approaches to Employee Management,* ed. David Saunders. Greenwich, CT: JAI Press.

Jain, H.C. 1995, September. "Employment Equity in Canada." *Human Resource Management in Canada,* 50, 045–50, 060.

Jain, Harish C. 1997, November. "Employment Equity in Canada." *Human Resources Management in Canada,* 50, 043–50, 058.

Jain, Harish C. 1999. "Foreword" in *Achieving Employment Equity: A Guide to Effective Strategies, Developing the Fabric of Organizations,* Adele Thomas and David Robertshaw. Randburg, South Africa: Knowledge Resources (pty) Ltd.

Jain, Harish C. 2000, July 7. "A New Approach to Rights: Our Human Rights Commission Needs a New Mandate to Combat Systemic Discrimination." *Hamilton Spectator,* A-13.

Jain, H.C., and Bowmaker-Falconer, A. 1998. *Employment Equity/Affirmative Action Codes of Practice and Best Practices in USA, Britain, Canada and Other Selected Countries.* Pretoria, South Africa: Departmentof Labour.

Jain, H.C., and Hackett, R. 1989. "Measuring Effectiveness of Employment Equity Programs in Canada: Public Policy and a Survey." *Canadian Public Policy* 15: 189–204.

Jain, H.C., Lawler, J., and Morishima, M. 1998. "Multinational Corporations, Human Resource Management and Host-Country Nationals." *International Journal of Human Resource Management* 9: 553–566.

Jain, H.C., and Ratnam, C.S.V. 1994. "Affirmative Action in Employment for the Scheduled Castes and the Scheduled Tribes in India." *International Journal of Manpower* 15(7): 6–25.

Jain, Harish C., and Ratnam, C.S.V. In press. "Gender Equality in India." In *Workplace Equality*, ed. Carol Agocs.

Jain, Harish C., Singh, Parbudyal, and Agocs, Carol. 2000, Spring. "Recruitment, Selection and Promotion of Visible Minority and Aboriginal Officers in Selected Canadian Police Services." *Canadian Public Administration* 43(1): 46–74.

Jain, Harish C., and Verma, Anil. 1996. "Introduction: Workforce Diversity and Competitive Strategies: Human Resource Policies and Practices in the 1990s." *International Journal of Manpower* 17: 5–13.

Jain, Harish C., and Al-Waqfi, Mohammad. 2001. "Racial Discrimination in Employment in Canada." In *Industrial Relations in a New Millenium: Selected Papers from the XXXVIIth Annual CIRA Conference,* eds.Y. Reshef, C. Bernier, D.Harrisson, and T. Wagar, 47–63.

Jomo, K. Sundaram. 2001, September. Malaysia's New Economic Policy and "National Unity." Paper prepared for the United Nations Research Institute for Social Development Conference on Racism and Public Policy, Durban, South Africa.

Jones, R.E., Chair. 1997, December. *Task Force Report on Best Equal Employment Opportunity Policies, Programs, and Practices in the Private Sector.* Washington, DC: Equal Employment Opportunity Commission.

Kapur, Aanchal ed. 1999. *Women Workers Rights in India: Issues and Strategies—A Reference Guide.* New-Delhi: International Labor Organization.

Kaur, A. 1997. "India." In *Affirmative Action in the Employment of Ethnic Minorities and Persons with Disabilities,* eds. Jane Hodges-Aeberhard, and Carl Raskin. Geneva: International Labour Office.

La Forest, Gerard V. Chair. 2000. "Promoting Equality: A New Vision." Report of the Canadian Human Rights Act Review Panel. Ottawa: Ministry of Justice.

Lau, Leslie. 2001, May 1. "KL Treads Minefield on Bright Students: The Government Knows Not Giving Top Non-Bumi Students in Universities is a Political Hot Potato and It Has to Find a Solution." *Strait Times,* 15.

Leonard, J. 1984a. "The Impact of Affirmative Action on Employment," *Journal of Labour Economics* 2: 439–463.

Leonard, J. 1984b. "Employment and Occupational Advance under Affirmative Action." *Review of Economics and Statistics* 66: 377–385.

Leonard, J. 1985. "What Promises Are Worth: the Impact of Affirmative Action Goals." *Journal of Human Resources* 20: 3–20.

Leonard, Jonathan. 1990. "The Impact of Affirmative Action Regulation and Equl Employment Law on Black Employment." *Journal of Economic Perspectives* 4: 47–63.

Longfield, Judi, Chair. 2002, June. *Promoting Equality in the Federal Jurisdiction: Review of the Employment Equity Act.* Report of the Standing Committee on Human Resources Development and the Status of Persons with Disabilities, House of Commons, Canada.

McPhillips, David. 2001."Employment Legislation in Canada." In *Union-Management Relations in Canada,* eds. Morley Gunderson, Allen Ponak, and Dephanie Taras. Toronto: Addison-Wesley Longman, 211–233.

Mahathir, M. 1991, June 18. "Speech at Parliament." *New Straits Times.*

Malaysia, Department of Statistics. Labour Force. 2001.

Malaysia, Treasury. Economic Statistics. 2000.

Mehta, Stephanie N. 2000, July 10. "Best Companies for Minorities: What Minority Employees Really Want. It's Simple: Inclusion, Encouragement, and Opportunity. But How Do You Know You Are Really Providing It?" *Fortune.*

Naidoo, G. 1997, May."Empowerment of Women in the Corporate World." *People Dynamics* 15: 30–35.

Nasser, Haya El, and Overberg, Paul. 2001, March 15. "Index Charts Growth in Diversity:

Despite 23% Jump Segregation Is still Going on, Researchers Say." *USA Today*, 3A and 10A.

Northern Ireland. 1995 London: HMSO.

O'Reilly, C., Williams, K., and Barsade, S. 1997. Demography and Group Performance: Does Diversity Help. Paper presented at the annual meeting of the Academy of Management, Boston.

Owen, D., Reza, B., Green, A., Maguire, M., and Pitcher, J. 2000, November. "Patterns of Labour Market Participation in Ethnic Minority Groups." *Labour Market Trends*, 505–510.

Parekh, B., Chair. 2000. *Report on the Future of Multi-ethnic Britain*. London: Profile Books.

Pereira, Brenda. 2001, May 7. "Non-Malay Brain Drain Fears Worry Mahathir: If Malays Can't Meet Criteria to Enter University, Their Places Should Go to Chinese and Indian Students, Says PM." *Strait Times*, 1.

Pfeffer, J., Davis-Blake, A., and Julius, D.J. 1995. "AAA Officer Salaries and Managerial Diversity: Efficiency Wages or Status." *Industrial Relations*, 34.

Puthucheary, M. 1993. "Malaysia: Safeguarding the Malays and the Interests of Other Communities." *Development and Democracy*. Johannesburg: The Urban Foundation, 23–40.

Ramaposa, C., Chair. 2000. *Report of the Black Economic Empowerment Commission*. www.beecom.org.za/html/home.htm.

Richard, Orlando C. 2000. "Racial Diversity, Business Strategy, and Firm Performance: A Resource-Based View." *Academy of Management Journal* 43: 164–177.

Rodgers, William, and Spriggs, William E. 1996. "The Effect of Federal Contractor Status on Racial Differences in Establishment Level Employment Shares: 1979–1992." *American Economic Review* 86: 290–293.

Rogers, S. 2000, November. Employment Equity: The View from Northern Ireland. Paper presented at the Fifth International Metropolis Conference, Vancouver.

Samson, M. 1999. "Training for Transformation." *Agenda* 41: 6–17.

Sawhney, Indra, et al. 1992, November 16. *Petitioners v. Union of India and Others*, Respondents.

Sloane, P.J., and Mackay, D. 1997. "Employment Equity and Minority Legislation in the UK after Two Decades: A Review." *International Journal of Manpower*, 18.

Sowell, T. 1990. *Preferential Policies: An International Perspective*. New York: W. Morrow.

Statistics South Africa. 2001. Government of South Africa.

Thomas, Adele. 2000. A Piano of Discord: Reasons for Job Mobility among Black-Managers. Unpublished paper, University of Witwatersrand Johannesburg.

Thomas, Adele. 2002. "Employment Equity in South Africa: Lessons from the Globals School." *International Journal of Manpower* 23: 237–255.

Twomey. B. 2000, January. "Labour Market Participation of Ethnic Groups." *Labour Market Trends*, 29–42.

United States Census Website: http://www.factfinder.census.gov.

Watson, W.E., Kumar, K., and Michaelsen, L.K. 1993. " Cultural Diversity's Impact on Interaction Process and Performance: Comparing Homogeneous and Diverse Task Groups."*Academy of Management Journal* 36: 590–602.

Weiner, M. 1993. *Development and Democracy*. Johannesburg, South Africa: The Urban Foundation.

World Bank. 2001. Washington, D.C.

Wright, P., Ferris, S.P., Hiller, J.S., and Kroll, M. 1995. "Competitiveness through Management of Diversity: Effects on Stock Price Valuation." *Academy of Management Journal* 38: 272–287.

Chapter 2
Theories of Discrimination

Introduction

The basis of discrimination against particular groups in the labor market has been a matter of considerable debate among social scientists. In general, it appears that an attempt has been made to apply a common framework to different groups, whether it be race, gender, religion, or age. An example is Gary Becker's approach in the *Economics of Discrimination* (1957), which is based on the premise that certain groups have a taste for discrimination based on an aversion to other groups, for which they are prepared to pay a price as for any other commodity. But distinguishing, for instance, between race and gender, we can see that there are important differences between the two cases. Although races tend to remain separate entities, men and women most frequently marry. Therefore, the potential gains to racial discrimination to the extent that they exist seem larger than to gender discrimination in the context of a gains from trade model. Does the aversion have to do with physical distance at work or social distance? That is, is simple contact at work the issue or who gives and who takes orders? Marriage causes intermittent labor force participation for most women, and this may influence job choice. Genetic differences are more significant across gender than across race, and the same is possibly true in relation to tastes for particular types of work. This raises the question as to whether in the context of this book separate theories are needed to explain the phenomenon of discrimination in the three advanced industrialized countries represented here and the three developing economies with very different social and political structures.

In this chapter, we will attempt to define what constitutes discrimination, recognizing that equality of opportunity does not necessarily imply equality of outcomes. Consideration then turns to identifying the major discriminators—employers, trade unions, co-workers, consumers, or governments. This raises the important question of who benefits and who loses in financial terms from such discriminatory practices—the key groups being blacks, whites, males, females, capitalists, and workers. Attention then turns to the thorny question of estimating the extent of discrimination. Can we in fact put a precise figure on it or even a general order of magnitude? Finally, we attempt to estimate what effect, if any, the various pieces of legislation have had on labor market outcomes.

Who Is Discriminated Against?

Before a group can be subjected to discrimination, it must be clearly identifiable (Sloane 1985). Gender, color, age, and language clearly fall into that category; marital status and religion less so, though such information can be acquired through appropriate questions on a job application form. The group that most easily falls into this category is immigrants. They are not only clearly identifiable, but also lack knowledge of the indigenous labor market and its cultural norms. From an empirical point of view, it can be difficult to establish whether the inferior position of an immigrant is a consequence of discriminatory treatment or of inferior attributes related to productivity. Two contrasting features dominate the immigration literature (Sloane and Gazioglu 1996): the assimilation hypothesis and the enclave hypothesis. The assimilation hypothesis suggests that over time the earnings of immigrants will tend to converge with those of comparably qualified indigenous workers as they acquire skills appropriate to the host country. Also, as they become more efficient in information gathering, they will tend to move into jobs where they have a productivity advantage. The assimilation effect should also incorporate host country language proficiency. If the host country language is learned after arrival, assimilation is one means by which upward mobility may be achieved. Language ability may also influence occupational choice, given that jobs are heterogeneous in their language requirements and likewise earnings because of the requirement to accept lower productivity jobs than are implied by the possession of other skills. For this and other reasons we may expect that the first- and second-generation offsprings of immigrants will be better assimilated than their parents.

It has been widely noted that immigrants tend to locate in areas where immigrants of their own country of origin have settled, and this concentration may extend into the workplace. Thus, for example, De Freitas (1991) found that over half of the Mexican immigrants into the United States worked principally with members of their own ethnic group and frequently in small establishments. The presence of such enclaves gives rise to the possibility in particular of self-employment catering for customers who are predominantly from one's own ethnic group and who are likely to demand products of which the immigrant has particular knowledge. For immigrants who are not fluent in the host country language, self-employment in such an enclave minimizes language disadvantages. This might explain Kossoudji's (1988) finding that lack of English language ability does not necessarily lead to loss of productivity. The assimilation and enclave hypotheses together suggest the possibility of multiple equilibria, with those immigrants who have skills complementary to those of indigenous workers gaining the most benefit from assimilation and those lacking such skills gaining the most from employment in enclaves where they have a comparative advantage.

A further inference from the above is that it is inappropriate to treat minority groups as homogeneous. When, for example, Gwartney and Long (1978) examined the relative earnings position of eight minority groups in the United States, they found a wide disparity in outcomes, with the Japanese and Chinese faring better in the labor market and Mexicans worse than other minority groups. Similarly for the UK, Leslie et al. (1998) found that the Chinese did relatively well, whereas the Pakistanis and Bangladeshis did very poorly in terms of both earnings and employment prospects. They note that certain groups such as the Black-Caribbeans have been in the UK for a long period, whereas others such as the Bangladeshis are of relatively recent arrival. Thus, only by looking at separate ethnic groups can we gain an accurate picture of the extent of racial minority disadvantage.

Who Discriminates?

Discrimination can derive from several sources—employers, co-workers, and trade unions, consumers, or the government, and some of these may act against discrimination rather than perpetuate it. Most analyses have focused on employer discrimination, though it is by no means certain that this dominates other forms. The Becker taste-based model assumes that an individual employer forfeits profits by refusing to hire members of minority groups, even under competitive conditions and even when the marginal value product of such workers exceeds the marginal cost of hiring them. Thus, where the wage required to hire such workers is *w,* the employer behaves as though this wage is $w(1+d)$ where d represents the employer's discrimination coefficient. This is tantamount to a leftward shift in the demand curve for that category of labor, resulting in lower wages for members of minority groups and lower employment, assuming a conventional upward-sloping supply curve of labor. However, employer discrimination suffers from a certain degree of ambiguity in a world characterized by large-scale multiproduct oligopolistic industries, with a divorce between ownership and control. Why should a manager in a head office be concerned about the racial composition of the workforce in a branch that he rarely visits? There is also the prediction that such behavior would be eliminated in the longrun through competitive forces, since discrimination must mean foregone profits, and hence discriminators would be unable to survive unless monopoly rents were available.

A number of economists have suggested that employee discrimination is more plausible than employer discrimination. Indeed Becker himself came to precisely this conclusion in his Nobel lecture. It is employees who have direct contact with members of minority groups and who may attempt to deny access to jobs altogether or oppose being subject to orders from members of minority groups in supervisory positions. Alternatively, members of minority groups and particularly immigrants insofar as they are represented in substantial numbers may be seen as a threat to both job and income security. Under such circumstances, majority group employees may be prepared to trade off short-run wages against the benefit of excluding minority workers, either to avoid contact with the minority at work or to maximize long-run wage levels. If majority and minority groups are perfect substitutes and wage rates are initially identical, employers will face increased wage bills if they attempt to integrate their workforces. Thus, a rational, nondiscriminatory employer will hire a completely segregated workforce, and competition will ensure that any wage differences between the two groups are eliminated. This would follow because, if minority wage rates were to fall below those of the majority, competition by nondiscriminatory employers would force up the price of such labor until equality was achieved. Thus, long-run equilibrium implies completely segregated firms, or perhaps completely segregated occupations when the two groups are complements rather than substitutes.

In parallel with the above, consumer discrimination occurs when prejudiced consumers refuse to purchase goods from members of minority groups unless goods are cheaper than when purchased from majority employees. It has been suggested that consumer-based discrimination is unlikely to play a major role because most goods are not produced with customer contact (see Cain 1988). However, we should remember that the majority of workers are now employed in services rather than manufacturing. Other economists have suggested that customer discrimination is a more plausible source of the racial wage gap than either employer or employee discrimination, for it will not be eliminated through competitive forces, since it results in lower productivity for the group discriminated against (see Nardinelli and Simon 1990). In such circumstances, we would expect that racial minority workers would specialize in the production of goods where customer contact is minimal and thus avoid being paid a wage lower than that received by the white majority. If crowding in such jobs led to pressure toward lower wages, whites would move into jobs with consumer contact until wages became equalized in the two sectors. Segregation by race, as with employee discrimination, is the predicted outcome. Kahn (1991b) has noted that the impact of antidiscrimination legislation is different under consumer discrimination than under the other two cases above. If a government imposes both equal pay and employment equity for minorities, the resulting allocation of resources will, under particular assumptions, be identical to the nonconsumer discrimination case and discrimination would be eliminated. Governments can influence the degree of discrimination either positively or negatively. First, by providing education, government determines the amount of human capital with which the various groups enter the labor market. Second, the government is itself a major employer of labor and also regulates activities in a number of other industries. Third, governments can introduce equal opportunities legislation to limit the extent to which minority groups are discriminated against. Becker (1957) noted that in a political democracy we would expect governments to act on the basis of the median taste for discrimination among the electorate. As the size of the minority population relative to the total population will reflect the number of votes at stake, we would expect discrimination to decline as the size of the minority group increased. Yet, when this happens the minority group becomes more of a perceived threat to the majority in terms of job competition and an influence on wage rates in particular occupations, so that a priori the outcome is indeterminate. If, however, the issue of minority rights is critical to minority voters but marginal for majority voters, more votes are to be gained from implementing equal rights than are to be lost from frustrating them. Borjas (1982) has formalized this into a vote-maximization hypothesis, which predicts that the economic status of minorities in federal agencies will depend on how important such minorities are in gaining political support for those agencies. Knight and McGrath (1977) noted that the most overt cases of wage discrimination in South Africa were to be found in the public sector where a three-tier salary structure operated for whites, Asians and coloureds, and Africans. In the 1970s, however, the government moved towards acceptance of the principle of equal pay for equal work.

Alternative Approaches

Differences in pay and occupational distribution may arise from reasons that have nothing to do with a taste for discrimination, from wherever it originates. Many economists measure discrimination as a situation in which minority workers receive lower pay than majority workers for a given level of productivity, but this can arise under conditions of monopsony, which may play a central role in explanations of male-female earnings differences. Monopsonistic exploitation—the payment of a wage below the marginal revenue product of labor—may arise where employers are faced with upward-sloping labor supply schedules and given the existence of different wage elasticities for various labor market groups are able to split labor into different categories. If, for example, men and women are perfect substitutes in production, equilibrium requires that the male and female marginal revenue products be equated. Thus, the profit-maximization condition can be expressed as

$$W_M(1 + 1/E_M) = W_F(1 + 1/E_F) \hspace{4cm} [1]$$

where

W_M and W_F represent male and female wage rates and E_M and E_F their elasticities of supply.

Sex discrimination will occur if $E_M \neq E_F$ even under conditions of profit maximization, since the marginal wage costs rather than the wage rates of the two groups of workers are equated.

Monopsony is a function of a lack of perfect mobility of labor and in this case is related to the crowding hypothesis first put forward by Edgeworth in 1922. Edgeworth's hypothesis in turn has much in common with the concept of labor market segmentation and its subsidiary dual labor market hypothesis which became fashionable in the 1970s. The essence of the crowding hypothesis is that minority workers are excluded from higher paying occupations or industries and are, therefore, crowded into other areas of employment, where the enforced abundance of supply lowers marginal productivity and hence wages.

In their work on the dual labor market, Doeringer and Piore (1971) highlighted the extent to which large firms in the United States had largely insulated themselves from the external labor market by recruiting only through limited ports of entry and relying on internal promotion for more senior jobs. If current employees are given preference over outside applicants, members of minority groups may be excluded simply because race or gender is used as a screening device. Dual labor market theory suggests that the labor market is divided into a primary and a secondary sector. "Good" jobs are limited to the former, but minority workers become trapped in the secondary sector, where education and training do not lead to improved wages, but rather job instability leads to a higher probability of unemployment.

Statistical discrimination may arise in well-developed internal labor markets. Suppose that an employer knows the distribution of the productivity of minority and majority groups, but not the productivity of any single individual with accuracy prior to employment. Mean productivity is known to be higher for majority than minority group workers. Hiring decisions are based on a performance test that measures the true performance level, q, imperfectly. Then

$$y = q + u \hspace{4cm} [2]$$

where

q is normally distributed with constant variance and u is a normally distributed error term.

In such circumstances statistical discrimination could arise from differences in the means of abilities between the groups, differences in the variance of

Figure 2.1 **Labor Market Segmentation and Equilibrium**

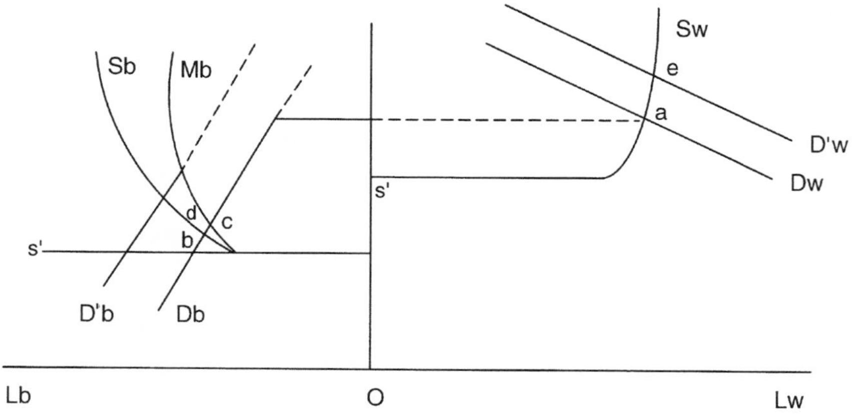

abilities between the groups, or differences in the variance of u (that is, the ability to predict accurately true performance from test scores). In such cases, there will be no group discrimination, since the probability of being hired is related to average rates of productivity for the groups. Within-group discrimination is, however, inevitable when the performance can only be revealed through observation after the worker has been hired.

Yet another explanation for differences in pay and employment between majority and minority workforces is Lang's language theory of discrimination (1996). Lang defines language not only in a verbal sense but also in a nonverbal one, including such elements as posture, gesture, and eye-contact. Blacks and whites or men and women can be said to "speak" different languages in this sense. Overcoming such barriers will involve transaction costs, which will lead to segregation based on speech communities.

To what extent are these theories relevant to developing as well as developed economies? Knight and McGrath (1977), for example, reject the relevance of taste-based models to the explanation of wage discrimination in South Africa, though recognizing that internal labor markets, segmentation theories, and job crowding may all have a role to play. Their arguments are summarized in Figure 2.1.

The labor market is segmented into a black labor force (*Lb*), which is unskilled, and a white labor force (L_w), which is educated, with separate demand curves D_b and D_w. Market forces produce equilibrium at *a* for whites, and assuming that whites can be substituted for blacks, this provides an upper limit to the black wage. Blacks have a lower supply price than whites as indicated by *S'b*, with *b* representing equilibrium. Alternatively, labor supply may be limited as represented by *Sb*. Then M_b represents the marginal cost curve facing the employer, with *c* representing the equilibrium point in the monopsony case and *d* in the competitive labor market case. In all of these cases, black wages are lower than those for whites.

If demand for white labor increases, the degree of upward shift in the demand curve will depend on the extent to which employers negotiate the transfer of black workers into jobs previously reserved for whites (*e* representing such a modified position); whether the black wage will respond depends on whether *S'b* or *Sb* is the relevant supply schedule. This illustrates the importance to blacks of removing the educational and occupational color bars that existed in South Africa until comparatively recently.

How Much Discrimination Is There?

The estimation of discrimination is problematical for a number of reasons, not least because the most common approach—the residual approach—does not attempt to measure the phenomenon directly. Thus, in a very detailed survey, Sloane (1985) concluded that

> the labour market experiences of minority and majority group employees are influenced by a large number of factors which make it difficult to detect the extent to which discrimination plays a role in determining outcomes. Indeed, there can be few areas in economics where so many conflicting findings have been produced in empirical work based on various methodologies and data sets. On the most plausible assumptions the removal of discrimination might raise the earnings of women by as much as 10 per cent and those of racial minority workers by rather more, but some differences in earnings and occupational distributions would remain because of differing human capital endowments among the various groups.

Since many studies have been undertaken since the mid-1980s, the question arises as to how far the above conclusions remain true today. In the United States the unadjusted ratio of earnings of full-year black employees relative to whites was 0.70 in 1990 for males and 0.90 for females. Even adjusting for human capital, the first of these does not rise above 0.85. Hamermesh and Rees (1993) report that the median discrimination coefficient for black males was 15 percent and for black females less than 10 percent in 1988. However, this does not adjust for quality of schooling or on-the-job training among other things. The position of racial minorities in the United States appears to have improved in the 1970s but thereafter not to have changed appreciably. It has been suggested that part of the improvement may have reflected the withdrawal of a high proportion of low-wage black employees from the labor market in search of government transfer payments. However, Vroman (1990) finds that of the 13.2-

percentage point improvement between 1964 and 1985, only 1.8 percentage points (or 14 percent) can be attributed to sample selection. He attributes most of the improvement to the unusually tight labor markets that operated in part of this period and the active pursuit of equal employment opportunities (EEO) policies, especially in the southern states. The latter is supported by Hamermesh and Rees, who note the correlation between Equal Employment Opportunities Commission (EEOC) expenditures and increased earnings ratios and further that those firms induced to set higher goals in affirmative action programs achieved the greatest gains in black employment in the late 1970s.

Particularly revealing have been studies of the racial composition of jobs. Both Ragan and Tremblay (1978) and Sorensen (1989) found that the wages of white employees diminish as the percentage of the immediate workforce that is nonwhite increases. In a further study, Hirsch and Schumacher (1992) found that the wages for both races decreased significantly as the percentage of black workers in a labor market increased. Their regression results suggest that wages among white male workers decrease by 52 percent as we move from an entirely white to an entirely black male workforce, while the figure for blacks is 39 percent. This result is inconsistent with taste-based models of employer or employee discrimination, which suggest that white wages and the wage gap should increase as minority employment increases. These results are also inconsistent with consumer and statistical discrimination theories, but they are consistent with theories of quality sorting and partially consistent with theories of racial crowding and language discrimination.

The recent literature has also focused much more on consumer discrimination than earlier work. Thus, Yinger (1998) notes that several studies show that under certain circumstances housing agents and car dealers may discriminate in order to boost their profits. Thus, three audit studies of car dealers in Chicago in the 1990s found that profits on the dealers' initial and final offers were highest for black males, followed by black females and white females relative to white males. Moreover, these differences were quite large. Further, a study of 356 fast-food restaurants in Pennsylvania and New Jersey in 1992 found that meal prices rose about 5 percent for a 50 percent rise in the black population. Even more telling are studies of consumer discrimination in professional team sports where it is possible to differentiate consumer discrimination from variations in ability on the pitch. For example, Kahn and Sherer (1988) found that a 20 percent wage gap between black and white basketball players in the NBA remained after controlling for measures of performance. Furthermore, basketball attendance is strongly and positively related to the proportion of a team who are white. Positional segregation on the basis of race or ethnicity has also been detected in baseball, football, and ice-hockey (Kahn 1991a). Further evidence of consumer discrimination is found in the market for sportsmen trading cards. Thus, Nardinelli and Simon (1990) found that baseball cards of nonwhite players sell for about 10 percent less than those of whites of comparable ability in the case of hitters, while the differential is 13 percent in the case of pitchers. Not dissimilar results were found by Anderson and La Croix (1991). In the case of basketball trading cards, Stone and Warren (1999) were unable to detect overall customer discrimination. However, the effect of career length on trading card prices was lower for white than for black players, and the card price premium for players who subsequently coached in the NBA is lower for blacks than for whites.

Other forms of direct evidence of discrimination can be found in court cases and audit studies. Thus, Darity and Mason (1998) argue that a sample of job discrimination lawsuits over recent years demonstrates that discriminatory practices have occurred in some highly visible U.S. multinational companies, including General Motors, Texaco, and USAir, relating to employment, training, promotion, tenure, layoff policies, and the working environment. Another source of direct evidence is to be found in the audit studies conducted in the early 1990s involving matched pairs of job applicants. In such a study conducted by the Urban Institute, it was found that black and Hispanic males were three times as likely to be rejected for a job opening as members of the white male majority. However, Heckman (1998) challenges the validity of such approaches, which are likely influenced by unobserved variables. He also notes that Neal and Johnson (1996) found substantial differences in the mean scores of young blacks and whites in the Armed Forces Qualifying Test, which on their own can explain virtually the whole of the racial difference in earnings. Likewise, Loury (1998) concludes that the substantial skills gap between blacks and whites is a key factor in explaining racial labor market inequality.

In Britain there are also substantial differences in labor market outcomes for the various ethnic groups. In 1996, the unemployment for nonwhite males was 19 percent compared to 9.1 percent for white males, and for nonwhite females, 15 percent compared to 5.9 percent for white females; the unemployment gap has widened since the 1970s. According to the Labour Force Survey (1992–1995), the average gross hourly earnings for white males was £5.48 compared to £4.89 for nonwhite males and £3.93 for white females compared to £3.89 for nonwhite females (Leslie et al. 1998). There are, however, substantial differences across the various ethnic minorities. The likelihood of unemployment is significantly higher for Pakistanis and Bangladeshis than for Indians or Chinese. Sloane and Mackay (1997) show that improvements in education and training would not by themselves be sufficient to eliminate the unemployment differential. In the case of earnings, Leslie et al. found that Pakistanis, Bangladeshis, and Black-Africans suffer the largest wage penalty (about 20 percent); as these also have the highest unemployment rates, they are doubly penalized. However, a recent study by Borooah (1999), which compared the occupational attainment of Black-Caribbeans and Indians relative to whites, suggests some cause for optimism when the sample is split according to age-group. The younger cohort of blacks suffered much less from occupational disadvantage; this narrowing was largely due to younger blacks acquiring post-18 education, particularly degrees.

As far as gender issues are concerned, the United States was one of the earliest countries to pass equal pay legislation in 1963, but its impact was curtailed by the relatively decentralized nature of collective bargaining. Unlike the European countries, both the United States and Canada have experimented with comparable worth policies that allow comparisons across organizations as well as within them, but these have not been pursued at the federal level. In the 1980s and 1990s, gender wage differentials narrowed in the United States. According to Blau, Ferber, and Winkler (1998), in 1981 the annual earnings of women who were employed both fulltime and year round were only 59 percent of men's annual earnings. By 1995, this figure had risen to 71 percent. Darity and Mason (1998) suggest three explanations for this narrowing of the gender differential. First, the wage distribution has altered in favor of women. For example, a study by Gottschalk reveals that over the period 1973 to 1994 men below the 78th percentile actually experienced absolute real wage decreases, while the real earnings of women rose throughout the female distribution. Second, the gap in endowments of human capital between men and women narrowed. Third, legal pressures widened the range of job opportunities available to women.

Yet a considerable degree of gender segregation remains. Killingsworth (1990) notes that there are two stylized facts regarding female intensity of employment. First, both women and men earn less as the female percentage of employment rises. Second, the negative relationship between earnings and female intensity is stronger among men than among women. This phenomenon was subsequently examined in some detail by MacPherson and Hirsch (1995) using various U.S. data sets over the period 1983–1993. Their results indicate that the gender composition effect is substantial and broadly similar for men and women. That is, earnings are 7 percent lower in a typical female occupation than in a typical male occupation. This does not necessarily imply discrimination, however. They suggest that female intensity may be a proxy for a relative absence of (unmeasured) skills, preferences, and job attributes.

In Britain, women's earnings as a percentage of men's earnings for full-time employees aged 18 and over rose from 63.1 percent in 1970 to 83.3 percent in 1996 for hourly earnings (excluding overtime) and from 54.5 percent in 1970 to 74.4 percent in 1996 for weekly earnings (including overtime). As equal pay legislation was phased in from 1970 and a substantial upward movement in female relative pay occurred in the 1970s, it is tempting to attribute the major part, if not the whole, of this improvement to the legislation. However, Sloane and Theodossiou (1994), using disaggregated New Earnings Survey data, show that this improvement applied not only to integrated occupations with male comparators but also to totally segregated occupations where no valid comparisons could be made under the legislation. They attributed this finding to a general increase in the demand for female labor relative to males. In fact, males have a higher probability of unemployment in Britain than do females. Sloane and Mackay (1997) also show that only 20 percent of the unemployment gap is due to the fact that men are employed in industries or occupations that are particularly prone to unemployment.

Joshi and Paci (1998) find that on average 33-year-old women would be paid 6 percent more if employed in a predominantly male job, mirroring the U.S. findings. They also find that over the period 1978 to 1991 the measured discrimination coefficient for full-time women fell by 7 percentage points. This contrasts with the position of part-time women whose relative position has worsened, despite the fact that protection has been extended to them through European legislation. It remains to be determined how far the newly introduced national minimum wage will assist low-paid women and particularly part-time women, but three-quarters of those directly affected by this legislation are female.

Finally, another factor to emphasize is the importance of breaks in employment in depressing the pay of women. Using British Household Panel study data, Manning and Robinson (1997) show that there is no significant difference in earnings growth between men and women who are in continuous employment, although there is a small gap in absolute pay. They suggest that labor market interruptions are the main cause of women's disadvantage, particularly among part-time female employees.

Conclusions

Despite the substantial amount of research on the relative position of labor market minority groups and women in North America and Britain, there is still some disagreement about the extent to which the disadvantaged position of these groups is attributable to discrimination, from which sources this is largely derived, and to what extent legislation has influenced outcomes. Overall, the relative position of these groups does seem, however, to have improved over time, though not necessarily evenly. To some extent, the focus has shifted from employer discrimination toward employee and customer discrimination; these latter categories can explain why discrimination can persist over time.

References

Anderson, T., and La Croix, S.J. 1991, October. "Customer Racial Discrimination in Major League Baseball." *Economic Inquiry* 24: 665–677.

Becker, G.S. 1957. *The Economics of Discrimination.* Chicago: University of Chicago Press.

Becker, G.S. 1993. "Nobel Lecture: The Economic Way of Looking at Behavior." *Journal of Political Economy* 101(3): 385.

Blau, F., Ferber, N., and Winkler, A. 1998. *The Economics of Women, Men and Work.* 3d ed. Englewood Cliffs, NJ: Prentice-Hall.

Borjas, G.J. 1982. "The Politics of Employment Discrimination in the Federal Bureaucracy." *Journal of Law and Economics* 25: 271–300.

Borooah, V.K. 1999, March. How Do Employers of Ethnic Origin Fare on the Occupational Ladder in Britain? Paper Presented at the Royal Economic Society Annual Conference, University of Nottingham..

Cain, G.G. 1988. "The Economic Analysis of Labor Market Discrimination: A Survey." In *Handbook of Labor Economics,* eds. O. Ashenfelter and P.R.G. Layard, Amsterdam: Elsevier.

Darity, W.A., Jr., and Mason, P.L. 1998, Spring. "Evidence on Discrimination in Employment: Codes of Color, Codes of Gender." *Journal of Economic Perspectives* 12(2): 23–40.

De Freitas, G. 1991. *Inequality at Work: Hispanics in the U.S. Labor Force.* New York: Oxford University Press.

Doeringer, P., and Piore, M. 1971. *Internal Labor Markets and Manpower Analysis,* Lexington, MA: Lexington Books.

Gwartney, J.D., and Long, J.E. 1978. "The Relative Earnings of Blacks and Other Minorities." *Industrial and Labor Relations Review* 31: 336–346.

Hamermesh, D.S., and Rees, A. 1993. *The Economics of Work and Pay.* New York: HarperCollins.

Heckman, J.J. 1998, Spring. "Detecting Discrimination." *Journal of Economic Perspectives* 12(2): 101–116.

Hirsch, B.T., and Schumacher, E.J. 1992, Fall. "Labor Earnings, Discrimination and the Racial Composition of Jobs." *Journal of Human Resources* 27(4): 602–628.

Joshi, H., and Paci, P. 1998. *Unequal Pay for Women and Men.* Cambridge, MA: MIT Press.

Kahn, L.M. 1991a, April. "Discrimination in Professional Sports: A Survey of the Literature" *Industrial and Labor Relations Review* 44(3): 395–418.

Kahn, L.M. 1991b, July. "Customer Discrimination and Affirmative Action." *Economic Inquiry* 29(3): 555–571.

Kahn, L.M., and Sherer, P.D. 1988, January. "Racial Differences in Professional Basketball Players' Compensation." *Journal of Labor Economics.* 6(1): 40–61.

Killingsworth, M.R. 1990. *The Economics of Comparable Worth.* Kalamazoo: Upjohn Institute for Employment Research.

Knight, J.B., and McGrath, M.D. 1977. "An Analysis of Racial Wage Discrimination in South Africa." *Oxford Bulletin of Economics and Statistics* 39: 245–272.

Kossoudji, S. 1988. "English Language Ability and the Labor Market Opportunities of Hispanic and East Asian Men." *Journal of Labor Economics* 6: 203–228.

Lang, K. 1996, May. "A Language Theory of Discrimination." *Quarterly Journal of Economics* CXI, 363–381.

Leslie, D., et al. 1998. *An Investigation of Racial Disadvantage.* Manchester: Manchester University Press.

Loury, G.C. 1998, Spring. "Discrimination in the Post-Civil Rights Era: Beyond Market Interactions." *Journal of Economic Perspectives.* 12(2): 117–126.

Manning, A., and Robinson, H. 1997, September. "Something in the Way She Moves: A Fresh Look at an Old Gap." Centre for Economic Performance, London School of Economics.

MacPherson, D.A., and Hirsch, B.T. 1995. "Wages and Gender Composition: Why Do Women's Jobs Pay Less?" *Journal of Labor Economics* 13(3): 426–471.

Nardinelli, C., and Simon, C. 1990, August. "Customer Racial Discrimination in the Market for Memorabilia: The Case of Baseball." *Quarterly Journal of Economics* 105(3): 575–595.

Neal, D.A., and Johnson, W.R. 1996, October. "The Role of Pro-Market Factors in Black-White Wage Differences."*Journal of Political Economy* 104(5): 869–895.

Ragan, J.F., Jr., and Tremblay, C.H. 1978. "Testing for Employee Discrimination by Race and Sex." *Journal of Human Resources* 13(4): 524–544.

Sloane, P.J. 1985. "Discrimination in the Labour Market." In *Labour Economics,* eds. D. Carline et al. Essex: Longman, 78–158.

Sloane, P.J., and Gazioglu, S. 1996, December. "Immigration and Occupational Status: A Study of Bangladeshi and Turkish Fathers and Sons in the London Labour Market." *Labour Economics* 3(4):399–424.

Sloane, P.J., and Mackay, D. 1997. "Employment Equity and Minority Legislation in the UK after Two Decades: A Review." *International Journal of Manpower,* 18(7): 597–626.

Sloane, P.J., and Theodossiou, I. 1994. "A Generalised Lorenz Curve Approach to Explaining the Upward Movement in Women's Relative Earnings in Britain." *Scottish Journal of Political Economy* 41: 464–476.

Sorensen, E. 1989. "Measuring the Effects of Occupational Sex and Race Composition in Earnings." In *Pay Equity: Empirical Enquiries*, eds. R.T. Michael, H.I. Hartman, and B. O'Farrell. Washington, DC: National Academy Press.

Stone, E.W., and Warren, R.S., Jr. 1999, June. "Customer Discrimination in Professional Basketball: Evidence from the Trading Card Market." *Applied Economic,* 31(6): 679–686.

Vroman, W. 1990, October. "Black Men's Relative Earnings: Are the Gains Illusory?" *Industrial and Labor Relations Review.* 44(1): 83–98.

Yinger, J. 1998, Spring. "Evidence on Discrimination in Consumer Markets." *Journal of Economic Perspectives* 12(2): 23–40.

Chapter 3

A Comparative Look at the Impact on Human Resources Management of Employment Equity Legislation

Simon Taggar

This chapter takes a comparative look at the efforts made by six countries to improve equity in the workplace through structured human resources management (HRM) systems concerned with fairness and bias. It focuses on the UK, United States of America, Canada, South Africa, India, and Malaysia.

HRM practices (e.g., job analysis, recruitment and selection, training and development, performance appraisals, and compensation) are the mechanisms through which equity initiatives impact organizations. These mechanisms are designed and implemented by practitioners who are governed to varying degrees by professional standards of conduct. How employment equity/affirmative action legislation impacts HRM, or the practitioners responsible for HRM, is a topic that has largely been neglected. Previous research generally treats employment equity programs as a "black box" and generates only estimates of employment outcomes. The present chapter differs from previous work on employment-related equity initiatives by providing a fuller answer to the question, "How do equity initiatives impact HRM and HRM practitioners?" Moreover, previous research has generally lacked theory. This chapter also suggests a theoretical framework that yields testable hypotheses.

Conceptual Model

Equity policies may be conceptualized as falling along a continuum of required legislated compliance. For the six countries of interest in this chapter, this is illustrated in Figure 3.1. At one end lay the Indian private sector and the UK, where there is little reliance on legislation to achieve the goal of employment equity. At the opposite end, in Malaysia and the Indian public sector, equity

Figure 3.1 **Legislative Continuum of Structured HR Systems and Professional Standards Concerned with Fairness**

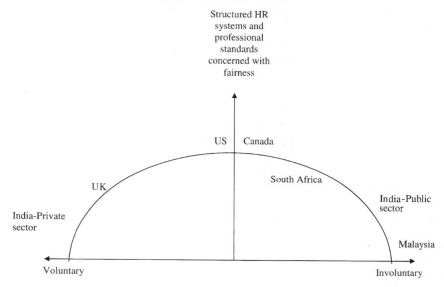

Legislative continuum

initiatives are implemented in a top-down fashion in the form of strict requirements; the most notorious of which is the use of quotas.

American, Canadian, and South African employment equity legislation falls at about the midpoint of the spectrum in Figure 3.1. In general, countries close to the midpoint of the continuum believe that equity legislation and regulatory bodies are necessary, but they shy away from the use of quotas.

The vertical axis in Figure 3.1 indicates the degree to which structured human resource (HR) systems exist in organizations and the extent to which professional standards govern the actions of HR practitioners. When equity initiatives fall close to the midpoint on the continuum of legislated compliance, Figure 3.1 suggests that there is likely to be a sufficient legislative framework to encourage HRM practitioners to be proactive in compliance with employment equity legislation. For organizations captured under these legislative systems, the cost and consequences of litigation can be substantial; therefore, it behooves them to maintain HRM systems that assure they live up to their promise of fair employment practices. Given their concern for fairness, organizations close to the middle of the continuum are likely to have relatively structured HR systems characterized by formal job evaluation, testing for job applicants, training needs analyses, training evaluation, performance-related pay, and formal career paths.

Although structured HR systems are likely to be most prevalent when organizations are close to the midpoint of the continuum, at the two poles HRM systems are likely to be relatively unstructured. Organizations operating under limited equity legislation, or legislation that is not enforced, may be asked to voluntarily implement fair employment practices. They have considerable discretion in the types of HR practices they can use. Due to the reduced risks of litigation on the grounds of the fairness of employment practices, there may be less impetus for these organizations to consider structured HR practices.

At the other extreme, when outcome decisions for HR practices are legislated, there is little need for structured HR practices aimed at generating fair decisions. For instance, there is little impetus for formal testing of job applicants when an organization knows that it must hire from a designated group to fulfill a quota. Once quota requirements are met, there is little or no additional legislated incentive to implement equity initiatives for other groups of employees.

Placement of Countries in Figure 3.1

United Kingdom

The keystones of the UK's civil rights law are the Race Relations, Sex Discrimination, and Fair Employment Acts (the latter covering religious discrimination in Northern Ireland). While a complete review of the UK's equity legislation is provided in previous chapters of this book, a brief summary of the Race Relations Act (RRA) is provided to illustrate the UK's approach and to justify its placement at the voluntary end of the legislative continuum in Figure 3.1.

The core of the RRA is its definition of racial discrimination, particularly its focus on being race-neutral: "A person discriminates against another . . . if on racial grounds he treats that other less favourably than he treats or would treat other persons" (RRA, Part I, Section 1). Using differential standards to benefit minority groups is called "positive discrimination" and is forbidden by the RRA. An exception exists for genuine occupational qualifications (RRA, Part II, Section 5). There are no specific equity requirements for government contractors, no requirements for government to do business with minority-owned businesses, and no required recordkeeping of a firm's employment of minorities, as exist in Canada, South Africa, and the United States. Hence, according to Teles (1998), the consequence of both the law and its interpretation by the courts and administrative bodies is that there is little, if any, hard employment equity or affirmative action in the UK.

United States of America

The Civil Rights Act covers private employers with fifteen or more employees, federal, state, and local governments, educational institutes, employment agencies, and labor unions. It prohibits discrimination on the basis of race, color, religion, national origin, and sex in pay, promotion, hiring, training, and termination. The legislation dictates that the management practices that the plaintiff initially alleges to have caused adverse impact are unlawful unless the employer can successfully rebut the charges. The law permits exemption based on bona fide occupational requirements only for sex, religion, and national origin and not for race and color. Executive Order 112246 covers federal contractors with contracts in excess of $50,000, or fifty or more employees, and requires the development and implementation of a written Affirmative Action Plan.

Separate Acts cover people with disabilities. In addition to the above federal laws, there are also state and local level laws. These laws are often patterned after federal laws; however, their basic provisions vary substantially from state to state.

In essence, affirmative action in the United States is somewhat voluntary (see *United Steelworkers v. Weber* in 1979), and, other than in the case of the Federal Contractors Compliance Program, the limits of affirmative action are left to the courts. Since the late 1980s, the Supreme Court has been distancing itself from its past position of pushing for social equity (Tummala 1991).

Canada

In contrast to the U.S. system where the limits of affirmative action are left to the courts, in Canada there is detailed legislation that specifies the scope of affirmative action. Equity legislation in Canada consists of a family of federal and provincial acts. The acts outlaw discrimination based on race, color, religion, national origin, marital status, sex, age, and often disabilities. They encourage HRM decisions based on merit, but they also allow for the development of special programs to reduce the disadvantages experienced by women, aboriginal people, visible minorities, and persons with disabilities.

The Canadian Human Rights Act applies to all federal government departments and agencies, crown corporations, and businesses and industries under federal jurisdiction. Besides prohibiting intentional direct discrimination, the Human Rights Act covers systemic or indirect discrimination. The employer must not only show that there was a genuine business reason for adopting a policy or practice, but also that the company took reasonable steps to accommodate the complainant, short of undue hardship.

The Canadian Federal Contractors Compliance Program requires that companies with 100 or more employees that wish to bid on federal contracts for goods or services worth $200,000 or more, implement an employment equity program. Under this program, contractors are required to sign a certificate of commitment to design and carry out an employment equity plan. The contractors are not required to file an employment equity plan with the government, only a commitment to develop and implement such a plan subject to on-site compliance reviews by employment equity officers from Human Resources Development Canada. Those contractors that do not meet their commitments may ultimately face exclusion from future government contracts.

South Africa

The Labour Relations Amendment Act (1988) made discrimination on the grounds of race or gender an unfair labor practice. Under the new Constitution (May 1996), previously disadvantaged groups are entitled to preferential treatment in hiring, promotion, university admissions, and the award of government contracts. Chapter 10 of the Constitution states that public administration "must be broadly representative of the South African people, with objectivity [and] fairness," and it needs "to redress the imbalances of the past to achieve broad representation."

The Employment Equity Act obliges firms with more than fifty employees to submit annual progress reports to the government on their efforts to make their workforce "demographically representative." In the event that a complaint is lodged, it is up to the employer to prove his or her innocence. Designated groups are defined as black people (including Africans, coloureds, and Indians), women, and people with disabilities.

A job applicant is defined as an "employee" in the Act, making unfair discrimination in recruitment and selection procedures impermissible. This includes the wording of job advertisements, application forms, psychometric testing and types of questions asked in an interview.

Following the notion of "inherent requirements of the job," the Employment Equity Act further refers to the notion of a "suitably qualified person" (Sections 15 (2) and Section 20 (3). As in the Canadian jurisdiction, it also requires "reasonable accommodation" measures, for example, for people with physical disabilities who meet the inherent job requirements.

Affirmative action measures for people from designated groups are designed to ensure that suitably qualified people from these groups have equal employment opportunities and are represented in all occupational categories and organizational levels. An area that could be the subject of disputes is the interpretation of what a "suitable qualification" is for a particular job, job category, or competency level. In this regard, an applicant's lack of the necessary qualifications is not a sufficient reason for hiring a nondesignated group member applicant instead. The employer must prove that the designated group member applicant could not have acquired the relevant skills in a reasonable time. Chapter II of the Act notes that measures taken in pursuit of affirmative action do not constitute "unfair discrimination." The Act does not require hiring or promotion quotas, only targets. The Labour Court has also found that the use of derogatory terms and language, names, or labels constitutes an unfair labor practice and is a form of unfair discrimination. Passive acceptance is not considered a valid defense.

The EEA, which takes precedence over all laws except the constitution, obliges firms that have more than fifty employees or that have turnover above a certain threshold to obtain demographic proportionality.

India

The Indian Constitution of 1950 officially abolished untouchability and casteism, and the government instituted a policy of reserved jobs and educational opportunities for those of the traditionally oppressed lowest castes for public service positions. Reservations denote a set of quotas for recognized minorities. Reservations in public employment are now open for three groups: Scheduled Castes, Scheduled Tribes, and other Backward Classes. Despite the fact that females are in a minority in public service, there is no preference based on sex, even though Article 15 (3) of the Constitution permits the state to make special provisions for women and children. For the federal government in India, a quota of 15 percent for Scheduled Castes and 7.5 percent for Scheduled Tribes (roughly in proportion to their population strength) is set for direct recruitment on an open competitive examination given throughout India (Tummala 1999). State governments have similar reserved positions, though with slight variations in the ratios.

The private sector is not covered under this policy of reservations. The Indian government has done very little to protect employees in the private sector from discrimination. What legislation exists for private sector workers is generally not strictly enforced (Kuruvilla 1996). In addition, multinational corporation subsidiaries operating in India may tend to adopt local private sector HR practices rather than implement HR practices used in countries other than India (Lawler, Jain, Ratnam, and Atmiyanandana 1995). Hence, in Figure 3.1, India is split into public and private sector firms due to the relatively large disparity in the enforcement of legislation between the two sectors.

Malaysia

Affirmative action was launched in 1971 as the New Economic Policy (NEP). The NEP's aim was to redistribute wealth from Malaysia's non-Malays to the indigenous Malay population (*Bumiputras*) through grants, licenses, entitlements, and quotas. At the heart of Malaysia's affirmative action initiatives is the goal that Malays should own at least 30 percent of the country's business capital. Through the use of quotas, Malays are granted special protection under the Constitution (querying Malay constitutional rights is treasonable) in the areas of employment, education, and business.

In August 2000, the government tabled a new scheme to create *Bumiputra* storeowners. The scheme, entitled Prosper, offers interest-free loans, bank guarantees, low-rent premises to be purpose-built by a government-controlled bank, and training for management. Later that same month, the government announced another effort to create *Bumiputra* entrepreneurs. In the months following the 1997 Asian economic crisis, the government bought up large numbers of shares of non-Malay owned companies to prop up the currency and the stock market. The government is now selling off these shares but only to *Bumiputras*.

Degree of Structure in HR Practices: Voluntary Legislation

For organizations close to the voluntary end of the legislative continuum, we would expect relatively few structured HRM practices and professional standards for HR practitioners that are driven by a concern for fairness and reduced bias. In the UK, a study by the Employment Department Group of Capita Management Consultancy found that despite the fact that such action is permissible under the RRA, 51 percent of employers did not specifically state that "applications from people belonging to ethnic minorities were particularly welcome" (Edwards 1995). This is in contrast to Canada, South Africa, and the United States, where a best defense against charges of systemic discrimination is to show that every attempt has been made to attract members from designated groups. As a result, many recruitment advertisements encourage members of designated groups to apply in order to obtain a representative applicant pool. For instance, almost any job application from any major U.S. organization would now indicate that the organization is an equal employment opportunity employer.

In the UK, there was no evidence that employers had embarked on the systematic selection or promotion of ethnic minority individuals on racial grounds (Welsh, Knox, and Brett 1994, Section 4.7). In terms of selection, controversies over the fairness and bias associated with the use of ability tests have been frequent in Canada and the United States but in comparison, have not occurred in the UK. Perhaps in recognition of the voluntary nature of British equity legislation, the British Psychological Society is attempting to provide some professional guidelines to HRM practitioners. It refers to the International Test Commission's *Guidelines on Test Use (Psychological Testing: A User's Guide)* recommendations that (a) the tests are unbiased and appropriate for the various groups that will be tested, (b) the constructs being assessed are meaningful in each of the groups represented, (c) evidence is available on possible group differences in performance on the test, (d) evidence relating to differential item functioning is available, where relevant, (e) there is validity evidence to support the intended use of the test in the various groups, and (f) effects of group differences not relevant to the main purpose (e.g., differences in motivation to answer or reading ability) are minimized. When tests are to be used with people with disabilities, it is recommended that (a) adequate arrangements are made when test takers include people with hearing, visual, or motor impairments, or other disabilities (e.g., learning impairments, dyslexia), (b) use of alternative assessment procedures, rather than modifications to tests, is considered (e.g., other more suitable tests, or alternative structured forms of assessment), and (c) modifications, when necessary, are tailored to the nature of the disability and are designed to minimize impact on score validity.

Teles (1998) examined the compensation situation of African Caribbeans and Indians in the UK because they are the two largest minority groups. Although hourly pay for black males was far below that of white males (£7.01 per hour versus £8.34 per hour), black female earnings were slightly higher than white female earnings (£6.71 per hour versus £6.59 per hour). Unemployment levels for blacks were very high: In the spring of 1995, 24 percent of blacks versus 8 percent of whites were unemployed, as well as 39 percent of young black workers versus 14 percent of young whites (Office of National Statistics 1996). Indians have high labor force participation levels approaching the level of whites, and their unemployment rates are much lower than those of blacks, Pakistanis, and Bangladeshis (Jones 1996; see Table 5.1). Their male hourly earnings, at £8.01/hour, are comparable to those of whites at £8.34/hour (Jones 1996, Table 4.17). Of even greater significance is the very impressive educational qualification of Indians: 61 percent of 21- to 23-year-olds have two General Certificate of Education (GCE) A levels or equivalents, compared to 43 percent of whites (Office of National Statistics 1996).

In India, the government has done very little to protect employees in the private sector from discrimination, and what legislation exists for private sector workers is generally not strictly enforced (Kuruvilla 1996). In a recent survey, Budhwar and Khatri (2001) reported that private sector organizations in India are likely to recruit their management employees from their current employee stock. They use a word-of-mouth strategy when recruiting externally rather than search firms or consultants (Budhwar and Khatri 2001). Employers in the private sector may choose whomever they want; hence, recruitment and selection in these firms is primarily governed by familial, communal, and political considerations (Sharma 1992). Widespread bribery and nepotism is practiced in the selection process.

Given the orientation toward personalized relationships in India rather than toward performance (Kanungo and Mendona 1994), it is not surprising that formal performance appraisals are rare in the private sector. When the applicant's performance is a concern, Indian organizations prefer to use reference checks, work samples, and unstructured interviews rather than psychological tests and inventories (Tripathi 2001). Moreover, rules regarding practices such as recruitment, training, promotions, and layoffs are ad hoc in nature and subject to easy manipulation by employers (Ratnam 1995).

Although there is little current data on the state of HR practices in India in the extant literature. In a 1965 study by Negandhi and Estafen, only a few business units used a formal and systematic performance appraisal program. Feedback and rewards were almost entirely based on the impressions of superiors and top management. In a survey of 82 Indian organizations in 1968 with follow-up of forty-nine Indian organizations in 1976, Tripathi (2001) reports that when performance appraisals were conducted, they gave very little performance feedback, and even less developmental feedback. The appraisals generally increased employee anxiety, lowered morale, and reduced commitment.

In a review of four surveys conducted on Indian training practices, Tripathi (2001) concluded that (a) only in a few big industrial organizations is training based on a needs assessment, (b) supervisory recommendations, poor job performance, and employee suggestions determine who gets training and the type of training they get, (c) small organizations generally do not provide training, and (d) in the majority of Indian organizations training is a "neglected and secondary function" (p. 152). None of the organizations studied spent over 1 percent of sales on training.

Similarly, Sparrow and Budhwar (1997) reported on a 1995 survey that led them to conclude that in the Indian private sector relatively little importance is attached to the early identification of high-potential employees, establishment of multiple and parallel career paths, reward of employees for enhancing skills and knowledge (rather than performance or customer service), use of customer and peer assessment of such skills and knowledge, and provision of continuous training and development and basic education. Moreover, one would expect little communication of the business direction, problems, plans, and facilitation of employee involvement. In addition, Sparrow and Budhwar (1997) found that 48 percent of the Indian HRM professionals saw little or no value in adopting 360-degree performance appraisal systems, 48 percent saw no role for using new technology to promote communication, and 45 percent saw no role for providing employees with more direct access to information systems. Only 14 percent of the sample believe that sharing the benefits, risks, and costs with employees is of high importance (compared to 43 percent in the United States), while 49 percent saw no value in doing this. A full 50 percent of the sample saw no value in implementing pay systems that promote sharing in business success or failure.

Degree of Structure in HR Practices: Mid-continuum Organizations

In Canada, South Africa, and the United States, employment equity requires HRM to identify and remove barriers that adversely affect designated group members, implement actions to further diversity, make reasonable accommodations to ensure equal opportunity, and make efforts to train, develop, and retain minorities. HR managers in organizations that fall close to the center of the legislative continuum need to be proactive in order to be compliant with employment equity legislation. In these organizations, employment-related litigation covers a relatively large number of employers. Thus, many HR managers study employment law, and employers require that HR managers be able to handle legal processes and procedures. Moreover, many employers seek professionally accredited HRM practitioners who must abide by certain ethical and professional standards.

Mid-continuum organizations use relatively sophisticated HR practices because HR procedures such as recruitment and selection, performance appraisal, and pay determination have to use objective rather than subjective criteria in order to adhere to employment law. These practices require that the organization conduct a job or work analysis as a basis for HR decisions (Cronshaw 1998). The job analysis is used to determine job specifications (list of skills and experiences that a person should possess in order to perform the job adequately) and job descriptions (list of tasks, duties, and responsibilities). Job specifications form the basis of the recruitment and selection process. They help determine the appropriate recruitment methods and selection tools. Pre-employment selection tools should (a) identify the applicants who will become the most effective employees and (b) offer equal employment opportunities to applicants of all designated groups.

Bias and Fairness in HRM Decisions

In the United States, there has been much debate over what constitutes fairness, bias, and hence, when a selection procedure should be subject to review by the courts. *Bias* refers to systematic errors in measurement, or inferences made from measurements, that are related to designated group membership (AERA et al. 1999). *Fairness* refers to value judgments people make about the decisions or outcomes based on a selection measurement. Decisions may be empirically correct, yet may be perceived as unfair by a group of people. In Canada a "relatively large body of jurisprudence on the need for 'fair and equitable' criteria in the recruitment, selection and promotion of visible minorities, aboriginal people, and women has developed, which puts the onus on the employer to maintain a workplace free from all forms of illegal discrimination" (Jain, Singh, and Agocs 2000, 54).

Some clarification as to what is fairness and bias can be found in the Uniform Guidelines on Employee Selection Procedures (Equal Employment Opportunity Commission 1978), a document intended to establish a uniform basis of selection procedure criteria in the U.S. Federal sector. In both Canada and the United States, litigants, courts, and HRM practitioners rely on the Uniform Guidelines heavily.

In the United States, The Standards for Educational and Psychological Testing (AERA et al. 1999), Principles for the Validation and Use of Personnel Selection Procedures (1987), and The Ethical Practice of Psychology in Organizations (Society for Industrial and Organizational Psychology 1987) are additional professional documents regarding validity and ethical use of occupational tests. In Canada, the Canadian Psychological Association has published Guidelines for Educational and Psychological Testing. All these professional documents are congruent with, and elaborations of, the Uniform Guidelines. Although the U.S.-based Uniform Guidelines, Standards for Educational and Psychological Testing, and Principles for the Validation and Use of Personnel Selection Procedures (1987) are not Canadian, they are often cited in Canada as representing professional standards and are often used by enforcement agencies in assessing professional programs. The Industrial/Organizational Psychology section of the Canadian Psychological Association adopted the principles outlined in the Uniform Guidelines for developing equitable selection systems for use in Canada (Latham and Sue-Chan 1999).

Adverse impact. Adverse impact is any substantial disparity in hiring, promotion, layoff, or other HRM action between a designated group and a comparison group. The comparison group is the most favored group. For instance, blacks are compared to whites and women are compared to men. In terms of adverse impact, the Uniform Guidelines on Employee Selection Procedures state that a selection rate for any race, sex, or ethnic group which is less than four-fifths (4/5) (or 80 percent) of the rate for the group with the highest rate will generally be regarded by the federal enforcement agencies as evidence of adverse impact, while a greater than four-fifths rate will generally not be regarded by federal enforcement agencies as evidence of adverse impact. While intended as a rule of thumb, the four-fifths or 80 percent rule has become a commonly used standard for determining whether or not there is adverse impact in both the United States and Canada (Vining, McPhillips, and Boardman 1986). Even if an entire selection process composed of a battery of selection tools does not show adverse impact, it may be necessary to justify any portion of the selection procedure that has an adverse impact (*Connecticut v. Teal* 1982).

Since validated tests can be used in discriminatory ways, Section 11 of the Uniform Guidelines states:

> A selection procedure, though validated against job performance following the Guidelines, cannot be imposed upon members of a race, sex, or ethnic group where other employees, applicants, or members have not been subjected to that standard. Disparate treatment occurs where members of a race, sex, or ethnic group have been denied the same employment, promotion, or other employment opportunities as have been available to other employees or applicants.

Validity. In all mid-continuum organizations, validity and reliability concerns permeate the recruitment, selection, and performance appraisal situation. For instance, Section 8 of the South African Employment Equity Act (1998) prohibits the use of psychometric testing unless the test or assessment being used (a) has scientifically been shown to be valid and reliable, (b) can be applied fairly to all employees, and (c) is not biased against any employee or group. In the Canadian case of *Andrews v. Treasury Board and Department of Transportation* (1994), a Canadian Human Rights Tribunal heard expert witnesses criticize a hearing test that cost over $100,000 to develop. The test consisted of fourteen different subsets administered to the applicant on the bridge of an operating Coast Guard ship. The applicant's responses to the subset scenarios were recorded and then compared to predetermined standards. The practical hearing test was criticized because of (a) a lack or reliability and validity, (b) incomplete technical development, (c) insufficiently standardized conditions when administered, and (d) an absence of norm data on which to compare and interpret the applicant's scores.

In North America, a major document that HRM practitioners refer to is the Principles for Validation and Use of Personnel Selection Procedures (Society for Industrial and Organizational Psychology 1987). This document describes content, construct, and criterion-related validity. Although reliability, construct validity, and content validity are important considerations, relating scores on a procedure to measures of performance on some relevant criterion is paramount in the employment situation in Canada, South Africa, and the United States. Some researchers argue that users of selection measures should investigate differences in criterion-related validity for designated groups. Various investigations can be conducted; Appendix 1 at the end of this chapter, provides a brief overview of some of these. The guidelines relating to validation of selection procedures are intended to be consistent with generally accepted professional standards for evaluating standardized tests and other selection procedures (any measure, combination of measures, or procedures used as a basis for an employment decision), such as those described in the Standards for Educational and Psychological Tests (American Psychological Association 1974).

Cascio (1992) suggests evaluating predictive systems for differential and single-group validity. He does, however, acknowledge that the occurrence of these systems is rare. Differential validity occurs when there is a significant difference between the validity coefficients obtained for two groups and when the correlations with the criteria in one or both groups are found to differ significantly from zero (see Appendix 1 for a more detailed discussion). When the two groups show no significant difference between their validity coefficients, but a given predictor exhibits validity significantly different from zero for one group, then there is single-group validity. Of concern is when differential validity and single-group validity result in unfair discrimination. Unfair discrimination

Figure 3.2 **Relationship between a Predictor and Criterion when a Cut Score is Used**

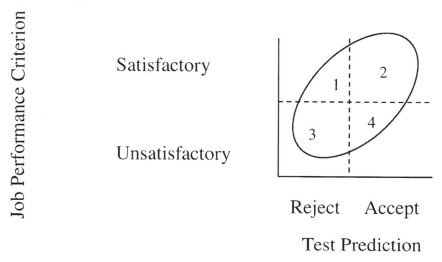

exists when persons with equal probabilities of success have unequal probabilities of being hired.

Cascio (1992) describes five models of selection fairness. Figure 3.2 is an aid to understanding each model's definition of fairness.

The "regression model" compares the regression slopes and intercepts of subgroups. For a test to be fair, there should not be a higher proportion of individuals from any one subgroup in regions 1 and 4 of Figure 3.2. The same applies to the "subjective regression model" where a constant is added to or subtracted from the predictor score. This is equivalent to using different cutting scores for subgroups. In the "equal risk model," separate predictor cutoff points are set for each subgroup. Above cutoff points, applicants have equal probabilities of job success. In this model, if 1 (1 + 4) is equivalent over subgroups, then the selection tool is fair. Using a "constant ratio model," a selection measure should select the same proportion of minority applicants that would be selected by a perfectly valid selection measure. This is a form of quota setting. If 2/4 is constant over groups, then the selection tool is fair. Lastly, the "conditional probability model" suggests that fairness exists when both minority and nonminority group members achieve a satisfactory criterion score, so that there is the same probability of selection despite group membership. According to this model, for a test to be fair, each subgroup should have the same number of cases in 1 (1 + 2).

The regression model is the most widely advocated method of determining selection fairness (Guion and Gibson 1988). This method is adopted by the Uniform Guidelines on Employee Selection Procedures. According to Cleary

(1968), a test is biased if the criterion score predicted from the common regression line is consistently too high or too low for members of the subgroup. With two subgroups—"designated group and comparison group"—one regression line may be used to represent both groups, or two regression lines are used—one for each group. Figure 3.3 in Appendix 1 represents the first situation, and Figure 3.4 the second situation.

Maxwell and Arvey (1993) show that the objectives of achieving high validity and minimizing adverse impact are identical within the class of fair tests (where fairness is defined according to Cleary's [1968] model). They show that "maximizing validity also minimizes adverse impact" (p. 433; see also Schmidt and Hunter 1974).

Validity generalization. In 1986, an appeal board of the Canadian Public Service Commission heard a complaint from job applicants who alleged that the use of a paper-and-pencil cognitive ability test lacked appropriate validation (*Maloley et al. v. Department of National Revenue (Taxation)*; Juriansz 1987). The appeal board ruled that the test was validated through validity generalization determined by meta-analytical studies.

Some scholars now believe that there is rarely a need for any organization to develop its own employment test, unless the job or context is very unique. Rather, a procedure called meta-analysis is used to combine validity coefficients for similar predictor and criterion measures reported by different validation studies. This challenges the conventional argument that a validity coefficient was specific to the context or environment in which it was measured. In combining the data, meta-analysis weights the results from each separate validity study according to its sample size. Generally, the results from studies with few subjects get smaller weights than those with more subjects. Inconsistencies in validity coefficients across studies can be attributed to statistical artifacts such as the range of scores in each study, the reliability of the criterion measures, and sample size. Once the effects associated with study size and other artifacts are removed, the validity between a predictor and criterion remains relatively stable between occupations (Schmidt and Hunter 1977). If a meta-analysis database is large and the results are relatively consistent, adequately representing the type of job to which it will be generalized in the local situation, there is a strong case for using the validity generalization data (AERA et al. 1999). Validity generalization studies for tests validated using U.S. samples have shown that validities from U.S. workers generalize to Canadian workers (Getkake, Hausdorf, and Cronshaw 1992).

Job Analysis

Job analysis refers to the process of collecting information about jobs. It is the cornerstone of the development and continued validity of HR systems. In the validation process, a job analysis ensures that criteria measures represent important work behaviors or outcomes. In the United States, the Principles for the Validation and Use of Personnel Selection Procedures (1987) emphasize the management practices of job analysis, criterion-related, content-oriented, and construct-oriented validation strategies, and validity generalization. In 1975, the U.S. Supreme Court made a precedent-setting decision when it criticized the Albermarle Paper Company for its failure to use a job analysis to demonstrate the job relatedness of its selection procedures (*Albermarle Paper Co. v. Moody*). Canadian Human Rights commissions and courts recognize U.S. legal precedents, guidelines, and professional standards. Hence, in Canada, job analysis is an essential step in protecting the organization should its selection and performance appraisal procedures be challenged in court (Ash 1988). For example, in *British Columbia (Public Service Employee Relations Commission) v. BCGSEU*, 1999, with respect to the use of criterion measures in selecting forest fire fighters, the Supreme Court of Canada ruled that a criterion must be reasonably related to the accomplishment of work-related purposes. The absence of a job analysis as part of criterion development will likely cast suspicion on any performance measurement system (Landy 1989). In *B.L. Mears v. Ontario Hydro* (1984), a tribunal under the Ontario Human Rights Commission decided that black employees were unfairly ranked for layoffs, compared with white employees, through use of a vague and undefined criterion.

Recruitment

Holzer and Neumark (2000) used survey data from employers to investigate how affirmative action in recruiting and hiring influences hiring practices, personnel policies, and, ultimately, employment outcomes in the United States. They found that affirmative action increases the number of recruitment and screening objectives used by employers, raises employers' willingness to hire stigmatized applicants, increases the number of minority or female applicants as well as employees, and increases employers' tendencies to provide training and to formally evaluate employees. In Canada, Jain et al. (2000) found that in order to obtain a representative sample of applicants, Canadian police services used numerous innovative and traditional recruitment strategies, including visits to community and minority organizations being used by 69 percent of police services. Specifically, with respect to the recruitment of visible minority and aboriginal officers, their data revealed that the use of qualified and trained recruiters, aboriginal and visible minority community presentations, consultation with aboriginal and visible minority organizations, and advertisements within the minority group's media were prevalent.

Holzer and Neumark's (2000) results suggest that U.S. employers who undertake affirmative action in recruiting cast a wider net than they otherwise would, thus generating more minority and female job candidates. By using more screening methods (particularly more formal ones), they obtain more information about each candidate and pay less attention to more obvious but potentially noisier signals of quality (such as education or previous employment and criminal histories). Although employers no doubt bear some cost in obtaining the extra information, doing so probably enables them to avoid hiring candidates whose productivity would be considerably weaker as a result of affirmative action. The extra training that these establishments appear to provide their employees might also be a way to compensate for any initially weaker credentials or performance among their "protected group" hires and thus to offset potential productivity losses (cf. Caplan 1997; Davidson and Lewis 1997; Penn, Percy, and Harold 1986). Holzer and Neumark's (2000) study shows that, although there is some evidence of lower educational qualifications among blacks and Hispanics hired in the United States under affirmative action, there is little evidence of substantially different job performance among most groups of minority and female affirmative action hires. Parker, Baltes, and Christiansen (1997) studied the work attitudes of four groups of federal employees. White men did not associate support for affirmative action and equal opportunity with loss of career development opportunities, organizational injustice, or negative work attitudes. Women expressed positive attitudes regarding organizational justice and increased career opportunities. In short, Holzer and Neumark (2000) found that when affirmative action was used in recruiting, it generally did not lead to lower credentials or performance of those women and minorities who were hired.

The focus of mid-continuum organizations on recruitment practices has spurred a good amount of research. A brief review of this research is offered below. Designated group members will not apply for a job or accept a job offer if they have a negative perception of the organization (Elkins and Phillips 2000). One way this perception is formed may be through the initial contact that recruiters make with the applicant. However, Rynes (1991) concludes that recruiter characteristics, such as sex and ethnicity, probably do not have a large impact on applicants' job choices—when effect sizes are found, they are generally small.

Taylor and Bergmann (1987) studied applicants over a five-stage recruitment process, from the campus interview stage to the job offer decision. Although samples at the later stages were small ($N = 24$ being the smallest), it was found that only at the early stages of the recruitment process, when actual job attribution information is low, do recruiter characteristics, interview characteristics, and applicants' perceptions of recruiter empathy relate to organizational attractiveness and the probability of job offer acceptance. Job attribute information showed strong significant relationships with applicants' reactions throughout the later stages of the recruitment process.

In research on the effects of sources of recruits, significant support exists for lower turnover when employee referrals are used (Rynes 1991). The greatest concern with using employees as a source of recruits is the possibility that it may produce charges of discriminatory hiring practices, specifically adverse effect discrimination. Adverse effect discrimination occurs when an employer in good faith adopts a policy or practice that has an unintended, negative impact on members of a designated group. In referring friends and relatives, employees are likely to refer individuals from their own ethnic, racial, or gender groups; this can work against meeting employment equity goals.

Practically all employers in North America use application forms to collect information that will allow them to assess whether the candidate is minimally qualified. Where there is adverse impact against members of a designated group, whether intentional or otherwise, the standards used to screen applicants must be demonstrably job related. Employers cannot ask for information prohibited on discriminatory grounds unless it can be established that the information being asked for is a bona fide occupational requirement. In addition to risking lawsuits, employers who include questions that are likely to discriminate against members of designated groups are likely to create a negative impression on applicants, applicants are less likely to pursue employment with the organization, less likely to accept an offer of employment, and less likely to recommend the organization to a friend (cf. Saks, Leck, and Saunders 1995).

Selection

Jain et al. (2000) found that Canadian police services use a "variety of selection instruments and criteria" in selecting candidates, including the use of structured and semistructured interview formats. In Canada, as in the United States, it is necessary that any selection tool "accurately assess the individual's performance or capacity to perform the essential components of the job in question safely, efficiently, and reliably" (Canadian Human Rights Commission 1988, 11).

Commonly used predictors in HR selection are reviewed subsequently. In mid-continuum organizations, selection measures must meet prevailing psychometric and professional standards, among the most important of which is validity. Table 3.1 provides validity coefficients reported by Schmidt and Hunter (1998) across job criteria and perceptions of fairness reported by Steiner and Gilliland (1996) and Stinglhamber, Vandenberghe, and Brancart (1999). Perceptions of a lack of fairness from applicants can lead to a legal challenge. Such challenges are less likely when the selection method incorporates: (a) job relatedness, (b) an opportunity for the candidate to demonstrate ability, (c) sympathetic interpersonal treatment, and (d) questions that are not considered improper (Gilliland 1993).

Assessment centers. Assessment centers are a series of standardized assessment procedures taken over two to three days to evaluate candidates for selection, classification, and promotion. Usually ability tests, personality inventories,

Table 3.1
Validity Coefficients from Meta-Analytical Studies

Selection tool	Mean validity	Fairness perceptions in U.S.
Assessment center	0.37	Not available
Conscientiousness	0.31	Below average
Integrity tests	0.41	Below average
Cognitive ability	0.51	Average
Unstructured interview	0.38	Above average
Structured interview	0.51	Above average

situational exercises, and interviews are used. Gaugler, Rosenthal, Thornton, and Bentson (1987) conducted a meta-analysis of assessment center validity. In their study, assessment center purpose (promotion, early identification of management potential, selection, and research) resulted in a variation in average corrected validity coefficients ranging from .30 to .48; this reflects the lack of standardization and the variance in the tools used in different assessment centers. Study of different criteria (ratings of job performance, management potential, managers' job performance on the dimensions used in the assessment center, performance of managers in a training program, and career advancement) results in variation in average corrected validity coefficients ranging from .33 for dimensional ratings to .53 for management potential. Assessment center scores correlate well with general cognitive ability tests and show less adverse impact (McDaniel and Nguyen 2001; Thornton and Morris 2001).

Overall, Gaugler et al. (1987) provide strong support for the predictive validity, validity generalization, and situational specificity of assessment centers. Situation specificity occurs when validity is specific to situations—as when the assessment center has high validity in one location or organization and is invalid in another. If in a meta-analysis one can show that all observed validity variance is due to artifacts, then one has also shown that no moderators are likely operating. This allows the conclusion that the mean corrected correlation is equivalent to the population correlation and that all contributing studies are from a single population. Under this condition, there is validity generalization.

Gaugler et al. (1987) reported that in the total sample and in five of the studied subgroups of validities, more than 40 percent of the variance in correlations could be explained by artifacts. All of the variance for career progress, early identification, and research validities appears to be artifactual. Nevertheless, based on the 75 percent decision rule (Hunter and Schmidt 1990), the authors could not reject the situational hypothesis in the total sample as artifacts explain 54 percent of the variance and the remaining variance (situational variance) indicates that moderators may exist. Situational variance could account for as much as 46 percent of the observed variation in validity coefficients. Although a fairly large proportion of the observed variance may be accounted for by situational variance, the residual standard deviation is fairly small and validity generalization is still possible (Schmidt, Hunter, and Pearlman 1981). When an average corrected validity coefficient for the total sample was calculated, it was above the 90 percent credibility value (.21), and the authors concluded that the validity of assessment centers does generalize.

Personality measures. Personality traits are stable characteristics that help to explain an individual's behavior. In North American organizations, self-report inventories are the most frequently used measurement tool for assessing personality. The Society for Human Resources Management reports that over 20 percent of its members use personality inventories for new as well as existing hires. Hogan (1991) maintains that the criticisms against using personality psychology in HRM have been rejected on empirical grounds. He reports that validity coefficients of personality measures can be greater than .30.

The five broad dimensions of personality (Big Five) recommended by Hogan (1991) are extroversion, agreeableness, conscientiousness, neuroticism, and openness to experience. These dimensions, he counsels, are the minimums required to appraise "person-job fit." Off-the-shelf convenience measures of traits, such as "type A" personality, fail to measure the prerequisite dimension and are therefore insufficient (Hogan 1991). He notes that personality inventories are especially useful because they are race and gender blind in many cases.

Hogan notes that validity may be a function of applicant defensiveness, self-knowledge, presentation skills, and situational strength. Nonetheless, in Hogan's view, the implications for a practitioner are clear: "Structured personality measures, when competently developed, are reasonably valid predictors of occupational performance" (p. 898). When used in selection, the dimensions of personality that are most important vary with the job in question. Thus, it is important to conduct a job analysis to determine which dimensions are bone fide occupational requirements. Otherwise, a mid-continuum organization will most certainly lose any litigation involving the use of personality measures (Hogan, Hogan, and Roberts 1996).

Barrick and Mount (1991) used the Big Five personality dimensions to investigate the relationship of personality to three job performance criteria—job proficiency, emotional stability, and HR data. Their meta-analysis found that only some personality dimensions are valid predictors of some occupations and some criterion. This further illustrates the need for job analysis to determine the appropriate personality dimensions for a given job.

Barrick and Mount's four main findings have implications for the practitioner and researcher. First, it was found that only conscientiousness is a valid predictor for all occupational groupings. For the remaining personality dimensions, validities varied by occupational group and criterion type. Second, the meta-analysis found that extroversion is predictive for occupations requiring frequent interactions. Thus, for jobs requiring a large amount of social interaction, consideration of extroversion is warranted. Third, openness to experience was found to predict training proficiency and may identify readiness for training. Measuring the "openness to experience" trait can help to identify the best candidates for training. This dimension had the highest correlation to cognitive ability (Barrick and Mount 1991). Lastly, agreeableness was not found to predict performance; however, this latter finding is not conclusive due to range restriction problems.

Whereas Barrick and Mount found conscientiousness to be the best predictor across all job types, Tett, Jackson, and Rothstein (1991) found in their meta-analysis that the validity of conscientiousness was surpassed by that of agreeableness, openness to experience, and emotional stability. The weighted mean of Tett et al.'s uncorrected validities for the Big Five was .14 compared to .06 as reported by Barrick and Mount. An even higher mean validity (.38) was obtained based on studies using job analysis for the selection of personality traits. With respect to moderator variables: (a) differences in mean validities for subjective vs. objective, professional vs. nonprofessional, and managerial vs. nonmanagerial were found, (b) fakablility was not an issue, and (c) tenure strengthened the relationship between personality measures and peer ratings. From the Tett et al. study, one may glean that the usefulness of personality tests for selection is more promising than Barrick and Mount's meta-analysis leads one to believe.

Mount, Barrick, and Strauss (1994) examined the validity of observer ratings (supervisor, co-worker, and customer) and self-ratings of personality measures. Observer ratings provided significant incremental validity beyond self-ratings for the job-relevant personality constructs. The three ramifications of this study are as follows. First, supervisor, co-worker, and customer ratings of conscientiousness and extroversion are valid predictors of sales performance. Practitioners may wish to include measures of personality with reference checks. Second, having several observers rate an applicant improves the validity of the personality measure. Lastly, customer ratings may be heavily weighted because they have higher validities. Findings also suggest "that organizations should provide feedback to sales representatives about customer perceptions" (p. 278).

Although faking is possible, according to Hogan it does not appear to be a problem in an applied setting. Ones and Viswesvaran (1998), using meta-analytic data, argue that socially desirable responses do not affect the validity of personality inventories that are used in work settings. Alliger and Dwight (2000) disagree with the conclusion drawn by Ones and Viswesvaran (1998). Therefore, the results from self-report inventories should not be used in isolation but rather in conjunction with a candidate's complete file for evidence of distortion (Rosse, Stecher, Miller, and Levin 1998).

Bias does not appear to be a concern with respect to personality inventories.

There is no evidence that psychometrically sound personality inventories have any adverse impact on any protected group (Hogan et al. 1996). In fact, it appears that adding a personality or personality-based integrity inventory to a selection battery that includes a measure of cognitive ability may reduce bias in selection (Ones, Visewesvaran, and Schmidt 1993). Personality measures may help people with disabilities demonstrate their qualifications as they do not differ significantly on personality from the comparison group (Hogan et al. 1996).

Applicants may perceive an invasion of privacy when personality inventories are used for selection (Steiner and Gilliland 1996). With respect to perceptions of fairness, Rosse, Miller, and Stecher (1994) found that including a cognitive ability test within a selection battery could offset adverse reactions with job applicants to personality assessments, which candidates tend to view negatively.

Cognitive ability tests. Cognitive abilities are related to intellectual abilities, such as numerical, verbal, reasoning, and problem solving. General cognitive ability has been related to successful job performance in many different types of occupations (Ree and Carretta 1998). It has been related to how easily people can be trained to perform job tasks, how well they can adjust and solve problems on the job, and how satisfied they are likely to be with the demands of the job (Gottfredson 1986). Lubinski and Dawis (1991) report that cognitive abilities generally have at least some validity for all jobs—predictive validities can be as high as .50, and they note that explaining "25% of the variance in any socially important area with one class of attributes is impressive" (p. 40).

Cognitive ability tests have withstood court challenges both in Canada and the United States and provide predictions of subsequent work performance that are more or less equally accurate across different ethnic groups—there is no differentially "unfair" (Cleary 1968) predictions for members of different ethnic minority groups. Nonetheless, because minority groups do obtain lower scores on these tests, even though there is no differential validity, it is not always wise to use cognitive ability tests.

Lubinski and Dawis (1991) consider the debate about whether "g" general cognitive ability, the "underlying factor common to all forms of cognitive func- tioning" (p. 6) should be used instead of multiple measures of ability. They posit that multiple cognitive ability tests may appear to index different constructs but do not, in fact, have unique nomological mappings and often do not show in- cremental validity over general ability measures. The predictive validity of mul- tiple cognitive ability tests is often due to their common variance with "g."

There may be two ways in which cognitive abilities and measures of cognitive abilities covary by content or complexity (Lubinski and Dawis 1991). It is through content and complexity evaluations that the correct cognitive test can be selected for occupations. After a review of the literature, Lubinski and Dawis (1991) conclude that "although the scientific significance of general intelligence and its central role in Industrial/Organizational Psychology are quite robust, multiple ability dimensions are worthy of both applied and theoretical attention" (p. 20). For lower level occupations, the authors recommend "g"-based tests. For more complex occupations, they recommend multiple ability tests that measure the specific content-focused abilities necessary for a given cognitively demanding occupation.

From a study by Rosse et al. (1994), a number of practical suggestions regarding use of personality and cognitive ability tests can be gleaned. They found that personality tests have the potential to offend some applicants. However, when a job-relevant and inoffensively worded personality test is used in conjunction with a face valid ability test, applicant reactions can be as positive as those in interview-only conditions. It is also important to note that most litigators and potential job incumbents judge the fairness of a personality test by its wording.

Integrity tests. Ones et al. (1993) conducted a meta-analysis to investigate integrity tests and found that integrity tests predict job performance with moderate and generalizable validity. Overt integrity tests assess attitudes regarding dishonest behaviors by specifically asking about past illegal and dishonest activities. Personality-based integrity inventories predict a broad range of counterproductive behaviors based on measures of personality traits. Ones et al. (1993) found that overt and personality-based integrity measures correlated significantly with both externally measured and self-reported counterproductive behaviors. They report the estimated mean true validity of integrity measures for predicting supervisory ratings of job performance was .41. Validities were positive across situations. Faking was not controlled for and, to the extent that it occurred, the estimated mean validity was encouraging. Since there is no doubt about the purpose of an overt integrity test, applicants may be more susceptible to faking (Alliger, Lilienfeld, and Mitchell 1996). A more recent meta-analysis by Sackett and Wanek (1996) supports the conclusions reached by Ones et al. (1993) that integrity tests provide valid information about an applicant's potential to engage in dysfunctional behaviors.

Assuming correlations between ability measures and integrity measures are close to zero (an assumption sufficiently supported by research), the expected incremental validity of integrity tests over ability tests should be substantial (up to 59 percent). Therefore, Ones et al. recommend the use of a weighted composite of the scores of ability tests and integrity tests. This reduces the mean difference between the scores of blacks and whites by 22 percent as compared to ability tests alone (Ones et al. 1993).

Dalton, Metzger, and Wimbush (1994) reviewed integrity test literature, noting that some studies rely too heavily on technical reports that may overinflate validities. Dalton et al. conclude that the validity of integrity tests is not altogether confirmed, nor is the role of moderators. In support of this conclusion, they cite a meta-analysis that found much smaller validities than did Ones et al. (1993). Consequently, the validity of integrity tests remains somewhat questionable. In addition, there is no conclusive evidence as to whether integrity tests are measuring a "conscientiousness" or "honesty" construct.

Dalton et al. (1994) discuss the base-rate validity interaction problem in depth. Their main concern is the high level of false negatives when an integrity test is used. Although this issue may be one for practitioners in tight labor markets, generally practitioners are most concerned with false positives. Nevertheless, in a tight labor market, the use of integrity tests may result in turning away potentially good candidates. Therefore, an integrity test may be best used as an initial screening device or as a "red flag" initiating the gathering of further information related to applicant integrity.

Vocational interest, value, and preference tests. Sex and race may significantly predict vocational aspirations and interests (see Mau and Bikos 2000). Dawis (1991) assessed vocational interest, value, and preference tests. A person's interests and values determine whether he or she applies for a specific job. He notes that there is little agreement on the precise definitions (neither operational nor conceptual) of interests, values, and preferences. One way to distinguish the three is to view interests as the attraction or repulsion of a person towards objects, situations, or events, while values may be viewed as the criterion by which people judge these objects, situations, or events. Interests and values are manifested in preferences. Research has shown that interests, values, and preferences are stable dispositions in most individuals when measured by self-report inventories (Dawis 1991).

Using established self-report instruments, Dawis (1991) reported a number of significant, if modest, conclusions. First, interests and values can predict occupational membership, tenure, and job satisfaction, with values predicting better than interests. Second, interest and value measures can be useful in predicting worker-satisfactoriness; however, ability is a much better predictor. Third, interests, values, and preferences are distinct from conventional personality traits, and finally, interests, values, and preferences are associated with life-history variables.

Due to validity problems associated with many established questionnaires, Dawis makes the following observations, "multiple measurement, if not multimethod measurement, is not just desirable, at the current level of measurement technology, we cannot afford not to require it" (p. 862). Empirical methods may produce the most useful scales for professional practice, but two problems exist. First, such scales function more as indicators of the target criterion group than as measures of the predictor. Second, selection decisions are not based on the probability of group membership given a score, but on the probability of a score given group membership. These are equal only when the base rate and the selection rate are the same, which is improbable.

There are numerous dimensions on which to classify interest, value, and preference tests. The choice of tests is large, and comparing tests is difficult. Furthermore, differing tests can lead to conflicting psychometric information (Dawis 1991). Definitions should distinguish clearly between interests, values, and preferences. One cannot assume that interest, value, and preference tests do not reflect abilities or measure personality constructs. Furthermore, one cannot yet assume a strong link between interests, values, and job satisfaction. Nor is there sufficient evidence to recommend use of these measures to predict job tenure and change. Some tests have been sufficiently assessed (such as the Strong Vocational Interest Blanks [SVIB]) however, in general, more research and theory development is required before interest, value, and preference tests can be wholeheartedly recommended to predict tenure, job satisfaction, and worker-satisfactoriness. These tests, if used during selection, should be combined with personality and ability tests and should incorporate expressed preference measures (Dawis 1991).

The Employment Equity Career Development Office (EECDO) of the Public Service Commission of Canada, which has a mandate to facilitate the effective career development of designated group members with the federal Public Service, commissioned a report that evaluated vocation interest and preference tests. The report made three recommendations (Gruber 2000). The first is that research into the reliability and validity of interest and preference inventories for designated groups be encouraged. The second is that, given that test norms for designated groups are unlikely to be made available by test publishers in the short to medium time period, it is recommended that the Federal Public Service take steps to develop "local" norms. And the third recommendation is that the Federal Public Service look for collaborative opportunities with commercial inventory publishers to foster research and inventory development work into vocational interest inventory usage for diversity groups. With respect to interest, value, and preference tests, the report concludes that there is a lack of validity research specific to the use of these inventories with designated group members in a career assessment context.

Employment interviews. Schmidt and Hunter (1998) and Schmidt and Rader (1999) believe that interviews measure a mixture of experience, cognitive ability, specific abilities, and aspects of personality such as conscientiousness. McDaniel, Whetzel, Schmidt, and Maurer (1994) conclude that the interview is an acceptable means of selection and even the unstructured interview has respectable and generalizable validity. The structured interview (mean validity of .44) outperformed the unstructured interview (mean validity of .33) in predicting job performance. Characteristics of a structured interview include (a) interviewer questions are job-relevant and standardized across applicants, (b) answers to questions are scored immediately, (c) scoring guides are used (i.e., behavioral anchors and/or benchmarks), and (d) scores for answers to individual questions are summed or averaged. More recently, Salgado (1999) reported corrected validity coefficients of .56 for highly structured interviews and .20 for interviews with very little predetermined structure.

Huffcutt and Roth (1998) conducted a meta-analysis on racial group differences in employment interview evaluations and found that differences in employment interview scores were quite small for structured interviews and much less than for unstructured interviews. Moscoso (2000) found that interviews show only a small adverse impact, but this impact decreases if behavioral structured interviews are used. However, behavioral interviews may be associated with negative applicant reactions. Structured interviews should be designed so that applicants do not perceive them to be boring or fakable. Also, applicants perceive that they are being treated fairly when they have a chance to present their credentials and qualifications. Standardization of the interview allows applicants to be compared on the basis of the same criterion and the interviewer to obtain a better picture of the merits of each applicant relative to other applicants. Moreover, the standardized treatment of each applicant is perceived to be fairer than the nonstandardized treatment, thereby reducing the chances of discrimination-related litigation. In addition, the use of job-related interview questions and a standardized scoring system should improve the organization's ability to defend itself against litigation (Hackett, Rose, and Pyper 2000). Board interviews were found to be no more valid than interviews by individual interviewers. Lin, Dobbins, and Farh (1992) found that boards consisting of all black interviewers gave slightly higher scores to black applicants than did boards made up of all white interviewers. They found less evidence of race bias when structured board interviews were used than when unstructured board interviews were used.

A content analysis of 158 U.S. federal court cases involving hiring discrimination was conducted by Terpstra, Mohamed, and Kethley (1999). They assessed the relative frequency of litigation associated with nine selection devices: unstructured interviews; structured interviews; biographical information blanks; cognitive ability tests; personality tests; honesty tests; physical ability tests; work sample tests; and assessment centers. The outcomes of the cases (whether the devices were ruled to be discriminatory) for each of the nine types of selection devices were also examined. Findings include the following: (1) the unstructured interview was the most frequently challenged selection device; (2) cognitive and physical ability tests were also significantly overrepresented; (3) regarding outcomes of the legal challenges, the structured interview survived 100 percent of the legal challenges mounted against it, while the unstructured interview survived only 59 percent of its legal challenges.

Dipboye (1994) notes that, contrary to evidence of superior structured interview validity, unstructured interviews still appear to dominate HRM practices. Continuous monitoring and interviewer training can counter a tendency for structured interviews to become less structured over time. Dipboye suggests that structure declines due to interviewer boredom, relinquishing of power, decrease in satisfaction, decrease in autonomy, and perceptions of low-growth potential. Unstructured interviews may have a place in collecting "applicant fit" information that may help the organization make better hiring decisions. Dipboye (1994) suggests that unstructured interviews allow for richer communication, resolution of conflict between alternative job applicants, organizational justice, ascertainment of applicant fit, and increased interviewer commitment to his or her decision.

A solution to the structured versus unstructured interview dilemma is to use both types of interviews. Structure may aid in the assessment of knowledge, skills, and abilities (KSAs) and intuitive unstructured processes, used in the last stages of the selection process, may aid in estimating applicant-organization fit. Although unstructured interviews are generally less reliable and valid than structured interviews, research on semistructured interviews has found no evidence of age or gender bias in their semistructured interviews (Arvey, Miller, Gould, and Burch 1987).

Drug and alcohol tests. Random and mandatory drug testing by Canadian companies is not as common as it is in the United States. Only 2 percent of Canadian companies had a drug-testing program in place compared to 75 percent of U.S. companies (Jain, Piczak, and Zeytinoglu 1998; "Storm over Drug Testing" 1992). The image of the typical drug abuser as a minority inner-city teenager may no longer fit—according to the American Council for Drug Education, 68 percent of drug users are currently employed, and 76 percent are white (Zetlin 1991). Nevertheless, when Normand and Salyards (1989) examined the relationship between drug-test results (DTRs) and two job performance indicators— turnover and absenteeism—they found that males and blacks had higher DTRs than females and whites, respectively. DTRs were significantly associated with involuntary separation (turnover) and absenteeism.

The Federal Court of Canada stated that if a company cannot link the drug testing to job performance, then it contravenes the Canadian Human Rights Act (Ayed 1998; Gibb-Clark 1996). Similarly, Section 7(1) of South Africa's Employment Equity Act (1998) prohibits medical testing of an employee unless legislation permits it, or it is justifiable in the light of medical facts, employment conditions, social policy, the fair distribution of employee benefits, or the inherent requirements of the job. The latter is a key test, and the onus of proof is on the employer in this regard. Section 7 (2) prohibits HIV testing unless such testing is determined as justifiable by the Labour Court.

Some U.S. states have enacted statutes that are specifically designed to regulate drug and alcohol testing in the workplace. Most restrict employee testing to instances where probable cause exists that an employee is a user and job performance is being affected. In *Hennessey v. Coastal Eagle Point Oil Com-*

pany, a discharged employee challenged the validity of the company's drug testing program. He argued that the constitutional safeguard against unreasonable search and seizure, as well as the constitutional right of privacy, established a clear mandate of "public policy." He charged that his employer violated his rights by conducting random urinalysis testing of employees when there was no suspicion of individual drug use. The lower court agreed with the plaintiff's argument, but it was reversed on appeal. The New Jersey Supreme Court's decision turned on the result of a balancing test in which the company's interest in a safe workplace weighed more heavily than the plaintiff's privacy rights. Harris and Trusty (1997) provide empirical evidence to suggest that the relationship between substance abuse and job performance may be insignificant.

Performance appraisals. Performance appraisal ratings help determine pay levels, promotions, training needs, and who is retained or let go. According to Latham, Skarlicki, Irvine, and Siegel (1993), in 1988 94 percent of U.S. organizations were using performance appraisals. Analyses of court cases indicate that courts are scrutinizing appraisal systems as sources of unfair discrimination (Cascio and Bernardin 1981). One meta-analysis with a cumulative sample size of 13,706 found a small and consistent tendency for white employees to receive higher ratings than do black employees (Kraiger and Ford 1983). Brugnoli, Campion, and Basen (1979), found that blacks were rated lower than whites on global performance scales but the same as whites on specific behavioral dimensions.

Latham et al. (1993) suggest that the legal defensibility of North American performance appraisal tools are enhanced when they are based on a job analysis, focus on specific performance-relevant behavior rather than on traits or outcomes only, the rater is trained in how to avoid rating biases, there is consistent application of job-related performance and promotion requirements, the appraisal and performance are documented, employees are provided the opportunity to improve, and the ratee has recourse if (s)he does not agree with his or her rating.

According to the Canadian Psychological Association's Guidelines for Educational and Psychological Testing (1987):

> Promotion decisions are sometimes distinguished from selection decisions when the individual being considered for promotion has an established job performance record in the organization. Thus, the employer may know considerably more about the individual than is known about new applicants. In many situations, however, the distinction between promotion and selection is blurred and of no practical consequence.

Latham and Wexley (1994) review three types of performance appraisal instruments. Of the instruments that focus on behaviors, including BARS (behaviorally anchored rating scales), BES (behavioral expectancy scales), and BOS (behavioral observation scales), BOS seems to have the highest reliability and validity.

This is because it focuses on observed frequencies (rather than value or quality) of behavior and because it concentrates on one behavior at a time that aids in rater recall. BOS also incorporates more critical incidents per dimension and is developed by statistical analysis, while other instruments are developed by more subjective means. However, for BOS to be content valid for legal purposes, many items are necessary. Furthermore, because BOS is not a true ratio scale, all behaviors on the scale have equal importance. The authors note that no measurement scale is free of rating error. Nevertheless, the more behavioral the times to be rated, and the less subjectivity allowed in the form of value or trait judgments, the less the incidence of bias.

According to Latham and Wexley (1994), there are several nontraditional sources of appraisal. Peer evaluations have higher reliability and validity than other sources of evaluation. Subordinate evaluations are congruent with participation and commitment values. Self-appraisals are a good source of information, increase employee dignity, and allow the appraiser to be viewed as a counselor. Different methods may be effective in different circumstances, and a combination of methods is appropriate.

To enhance perceptions of fairness, employees should participate in the selection of the individuals that allocate rewards. The rules for making decisions should be standard, public, and applied fairly. This includes methods of ensuring that decision-making bodies do not abuse their power. The perception of justice is particularly important when firing an employee, when discussing poor work habits, and when taking disciplinary action (Latham and Wexley 1994).

Making Selection Decisions

Sackett and Roth (1991) evaluated eight different selection methods using the Monte Carlo technique. The "strict top-down" method offered the best quality workforce, but also the greatest adverse impact against low-scoring designated groups. Top-down selection within groups (also called race norming) had been used in the past when reporting test scores. According to this procedure, the scores for members of different designated groups were based on a comparison with the scores of other members of the same group. Using a strict top-down procedure under these circumstances results in a quota in which the proportion of minority applicants hired equals that of the nonminority applicants. Race norming was forbidden by the Civil Rights Act of 1991. Since the obvious strategy for reducing adverse impact by adjusting test scores in a way that reduces or removes group differences (e.g., within-group norming) is expressly forbidden in the United States by the Civil Rights Act of 1991, an alternative approach of test score banding is receiving increasing attention (Cascio, Outtz, Zedeck, and Goldstein 1991).

Some banding procedures could substantially reduce the adverse impact of selection tests, with relatively small decreases in overall selection utility (Cascio et al., 1991; Sackett and Roth 1991). Furthermore, some banding procedures have survived strict legal scrutiny, up to the level of the Supreme Court (Murphy 1994). Banding involves grouping applicants based on ranges of scores, taking into account the standard error of measurement. Applicants whose scores fall within the band are considered tied. The procedure that could potentially most benefit minorities is the sliding band with minority preference within that band when the top scorers are selected. In the sliding-band procedure, the band from which the applicants are selected shifts downward when a person within that band is selected. However, Sackett and Roth (1991) conclude:

> [W]e found small differences between different banding approaches in mean test scores of selected individuals. Although strict top-down selection produced the highest mean test performance of any of the selection rules examined, none of the banding procedures produced mean test scores as much as .1 SD lower than top-down selection."
>
> (p. 239)

Sackett and Roth note that selecting randomly from the band also does little to increase minority or female participation. On the other hand, giving minority group members preference may raise public policy issues and protests from male and nonminority applicants who are passed over. Those who are passed over argue that any deviation from strict rank order is unfair. The counterargument often forwarded is that precise ranking is a fiction and that there is no noticeable difference in the potential performance of applicants whose scores are virtually the same.

A problem arises when management does not promote one of the higher scoring applicants. In this case, the high scorer acts as a limit on how much the band can slide, since eventually the upper boundary of the band would slide past the high scorer. If there is some compelling reason not to hire or promote the high scorer, the decision maker may justify the decision to eliminate him or her from consideration.

Degree of Structure in HR Practices: Involuntary Legislation

In the Indian public sector, the scope of reservations over time has been widened from recruitment to include promotions. There is little formal performance appraisal in the public sector (Kanungo and Mendona 1994), and rules regarding HR practices are ad hoc in nature (Ratnam 1995). Lifetime employment is still prevalent (Ratnam 1995), and the compensation of public sector employees is based on seniority and experience because this is a legal requirement (Budhwar and Khatri 2001).

Malaysia follows the Indian public sector policy of reservations and quotas. These policies require that key positions be filled by *Bumiputras*. HR managers must ensure that training and education programs are undertaken so that the *Bumiputras* are prepared to hold a job and get ready for promotion to higher-level positions. As in India, Malaysian HR managers have to create a huge recording system that allows them to show that they are in compliance with government legislation.

Conclusions

More research is needed to better determine the effects of affirmative action initiatives on HRM practices and HRM practitioners. One goal of this chapter was to provide a framework that allows testable hypotheses on which to base future research. If some equity legislation increases the use of structured and sophisticated HRM systems concerned with fairness and legal compliance, and these same practices improve firm performance (see Becker and Gerhart 1996), then there may be previously unarticulated benefits to policies that place an organization at the mid-level of the legislative continuum. For instance, Huselid (1995) in a United States study, found that a one standard deviation increase in the use of sophisticated HR practices decreased turnover by 7 percent and increased sales by $27,000 per employee per year. More research needs to be conducted in order to evaluate the differential effects of programs that are perceived as being government imposed, such as affirmative action and/or quotas versus those that are perceived as being management imposed, such as diversity management and combinations thereof.

Although mid-continuum countries generally contain more structured HR practices than organizations at the two poles of the continuum, research suggests that there is considerable variance in the structure of HR practices used within mid-continuum organizations (e.g., Jain et al. 2000). For instance, in most countries the theory of representative bureaucracy is adhered to—which suggests that if public service personnel become more diverse and representative of all segments of the community, the service itself will become more responsive to the needs of all. Antecedents of the variance in HRM practices both within and between countries requires further study.

References

Books and Articles

Alliger, G.M., and Dwight, S.A. 2000. "A Meta-analytic Investigation of the Susceptibility of Integrity Tests to Faking and Coaching." *Educational and Psychological Measurement* 60: 59–73.

Alliger, G.M., Lilienfeld, S.O., and Mitchell, K.E. 1996. " The Susceptibility of Overt and Covert Integrity Tests to Coaching and Caking." *Psychological Science* 7: 32–39.

American Educational Research Association, American Psychological Association, and National Council on Measurement in Education (AERA). 1999. *Standards in Educational and Psychological Testing.* Washington, DC: American Educational Research Association.

American Psychological Association. 1974. Standards for Educational and Psychological Tests. Washington, DC: Author.

Arvey, R.D., Miller, H.E., Gould, R., and Burch, P. 1987. "Interview Validity for Selecting Sales Clerks." *Personnel Psychology* 40: 1–12.

Ash, R.A. 1988. "Job Analysis in the World of Work." In *Job Analysis Handbook for Business, Industry, and Government,* Vol. 1, ed. S. Gael. New York: Wiley, 3–13.

Ayed, N. 1998, July 24. "TD Drug testing Policy Discriminatory." *Canadian Press Newswire.*

Barrick, M.R., and Mount, M.K. 1991. "The Big Five Personality Dimensions and Job Performance: A Meta-analysis." *Personnel Psychology* 44: 1–26.

Becker, B., and Gerhart, B. 1996. "The Impact of Human Resource Management on Organizational Performance: Progress and Prospects." *Academy of Management Journal* 39: 779–801.

Brugnoli, G.A., Campion, J.E., and Basen, J.A. 1979. "Racial Bias in the Use of Work Samples for Personnel Selection." *Journal of Applied Psychology* 64: 119–123.

Budhwar, P.S., and Khatri, N. 2001. "A Comparative Study of HR Practices in U.K. and India." *International Journal of Human Resource Management* 12: 800–826.

Canadian Human Rights Commission. 1988. *Bonafide Requirement Policy"* Ottawa: Minister of Supply and Services Canada.

Caplan, L. 1997. *Up Against the Law: Affirmative Action and the Supreme Court.* Washington, DC: Brookings Institution.

Cascio, W.F. 1992. *Applied Psychology in Personnel Management.* 2d ed. Reston, VA: Reston Publishing Co.

Cascio, W.F., and Bernardin, H.J. 1981. "Implications of Performance Appraisal Litigation for Personnel Decisions." *Personnel Psychology* 34: 211–226.

Cascio, W.F., Outtz, J., Zedeck, S., and Goldstein I.L. 1991. "Statistical Implications of Six Methods of Test Score Use in Personnel Selection." *Human Performance* 4: 233–264

Cleary, T.A. 1968. "Test Bias: Prediction of Grades of Negro and White Students in Integrated Colleges." *Journal of Educational Measurement* 5: 115–124.

Cronshaw, S.F. 1998. "Job Analysis: Changing Nature of Work." *Canadian Psychology* 39: 5–13.

Dalton, D.R., Metzger, M.B., and Wimbush, J.C. 1994. "Integrity Testing for Personnel Selection: A Review and Research Agenda." *Research in Personnel and Human Resource Management* 12: 125–160.

Davidson, R., and Lewis, E. 1997. "Affirmative Action and Other Special Consideration Admissions at the University of California, Davis, School of Medicine." *Journal of the American Medical Association* 278: 1153–1158.

Dawis, R.V. 1991. "Vocational Interests, Values, and Preferences." In *Handbook of Industrial and Organizational Psychology.* Vol. 2, eds. M.D. Dunnette and L.M. Hough. Palo Alto, CA: Consulting Psychologists Press, 833–872.

Dipboye, R.L. 1994. "Structured and Unstructured Selection Interviews: Beyond the Job-fit Model." *Research in Personnel and Human Resources Management* 12: 79–123.

Edwards, J. 1995. *When Race Counts: The Morality of Racial Preference in U.K. and America.* London: Routledge.

Elkins, T.J., and Phillips, J.S. 2000. "Job Context, Selection Decision Outcome, and the Perceived Fairness of Selection Tests: Biodata as an Illustrative Case." *Journal of Applied Psychology* 85: 479–484.

Equal Employment Opportunity Commission. 1978, August 25. Uniform Guidelines on Employee Selection Procedures. *Federal Register* 43: 38295–38309.

Gaugler, B.B., Rosenthal, D.B., Thornton, G.C., III, and Bentson, C. 1987. "Meta-analysis of Assessment Centre Validity." *Journal of Applied Psychology* 72: 493–511.

Getkake, M., Hausdorf, P., and Cronshaw, S.F. 1992. Transnational Validity Generalization of Employment Tests from the United States to Canada. *Canadian Journal of Administrative Sciences* 9: 324–335.

Gibb-Clark, M. 1996, April 24. "Drug-testing Ruling Set Aside." *The Globe and Mail,* B1, B4.

Gilliland, S.W. 1993. "The Perceived Fairness of Selection Systems: An Organizational Justice Perspective." *Academy of Management Review* 18: 694–734.

Gottfredson, L.S. 1986. "The g Factor in Employment" *Journal of Vocational Behavior* 29: 293–450.

Gruber, G.P. 2000. "Standardized Testing and Employment Equity Career Counseling: A Literature Review of Six Tests." The Employment Equity Career Development Office Public Service Commission of Canada, http://www.psc-cfp.gc.ca/eepmp-pmpee/program_overview/eecco/standardized_e.htm.

Guion, R.F. and Gibson, W.M. 1988. "Personnel Selection and Placement." *Annual Review of Psychology* 39: 349–374.

Hackett, R.D., Rose, J.B., and Pyper, J. 2000. "The Employment Interview: An Analysis of Canadian Labour Arbitration Decisions." *Labour Arbitration Yearbook,* 1: 233–250. Toronto: Lancaster House.

Harris, M.M., and Trusty, M.L. 1997. "Drug and Alcohol Programs in the Workplace: A Review of Recent Literature." In *International Review of Industrial and Organizational Psychology.* Vol. 2, eds. C.L. Cooper and I.T. Robertson. London: Wiley, 289–315.

Hogan, R.T. 1991. "Personality and Personality Measurement." In *Handbook of Industrial and Organizational Psychology.* Vol. 2, eds. M.D. Dunnette and L.M. Hough. Palo Alto, CA: Consulting Psychologists Press, 873–919.

Hogan, R.T., Hogan, M.R., and Roberts, B.W. 1996. "Personality Measurement and Employment Decisions: Questions and Answers." *American Psychologist* 51: 469–477.

Holzer, H., and Neumark, D. 2000. "Assessing Affirmative Action." *Journal of Economic Literature* 38: 483–488.

Huffcutt, A.I., and Roth, P.L. 1998. "Racial Group Differences in Employment Interview Evaluations." *Journal of Applied Psychology* 83: 179–189.

Hunter, J.E., and Schmidt, F.L. 1990. *Methods of Meta-analysis: Correcting Error and Bias in Research Findings.* Newbury Park, CA: Sage.

Huselid, M.A. 1995. "The Impact of Human Resource Management Practices on Turnover, Productivity, and Corporate Financial Performance." *Academy of Management Journal* 38: 635–672.

Jain, H.C., Piczak, M., and Zeytinoglu, I.U. 1998. "Workplace Substance Testing: An Exploratory Study." *Employee Responsiblities and Rights Journal* 11: 41–55.

Jain, H.C., Singh, P., and Agocs, C. 2000. "Recruitment, Selection and Promotion of Visible-Minority and Aboriginal Police Officers in Selected Canadian Police Services." *Canadian Public Administration* 43(3): 46–74.

Jones, T. 1996. *U.K.'s Ethnic Minorities*. London: Policy Studies Institute.

Juriansz, R.G. 1987. "Recent Developments in Canadian Law: Anti-Discrimination Law: Part II: *Ottawa Law Review* 19: 667–721.

Kanungo, S., and Mendona, S. 1994. "Culture and Performance Improvement." *Productivity* 35: 447–53.

Kraiger, K., and Ford, J.K. 1983. A Meta-analysis of Ratee Race Effects in Performance Ratings. Paper presented at the American Psychological Association, Anaheim, California.

Kuruvilla, S. 1996. "Linkage Between Industrialization and Strategy and Industrial Relations/Human Resource Policies: Singapore, Malaysia, the Philippines and India." *Industrial and Labor Relations Review* 49: 635–657.

Landy, F.J. 1989. *Psychology of Work Behavior* (4th ed.). Pacific Grove, CA: Brooks/Cole Publishing Co.

Latham, G.P., Skarlicki, D. Irvine, D., and Siegel, J. 1993. "The Increasing Importance of Performance Appraisal to Employee Effectiveness in Organizational Settings in North America." In *International Review of Industrial and Organizational Psychology*, eds. C. Cooper, and I. Robertson, 87–132.

Latham, G.P., and Sue-Chan, C. 1999. "A Meta-analysis of the Situational Interview: An Enumerative Review of Reasons for Its Validity." *Canadian Psychology* 40: 56–67.

Latham, G.P., and Wexley, K.N. 1994. *Increasing Productivity Through Performance Appraisal*. Reading, MA: Addison-Wesley.

Lawler, J.J., Jain, H.C., Ratnam, Venkata, C.S., and Atmiyanandana, V. 1995. "Human Resource Management in Developing Economies: A Comparison of India and Thailand." *International Journal of Human Resource Management* 6: 319–346.

Lin, T.R., Dobbins, G.H., and Farh, J.L. 1992. "A Field Study of Age and Ace Similarity Effects on Interview Ratings in Conventional and Situational Interviews." *Journal of Applied Psychology* 77: 363–371.

Lubinski, D., and Dawis, R.V. 1991. "Aptitude, Skills, and Proficiencies." In *Handbook of Industrial and Organizational Psychology*. Vol. 3, eds. M.D. Dunnette and L.M. Palo Alto, CA: Consulting Psychologists Press, 1–60.

Mau, W., and Bikos, L.H. 2000. "Educational and Vocational Aspirations of Minority and Female Students: A Longitudinal Study." *Journal of Counseling & Development* 78: 186–195.

Maxwell, S.E. and Arvey, R.D. 1993. "The Search for Predictors with High Validity and Low Adverse Impact: Compatible or Incompatible Goals?" *Journal of Applied Psychology* 78: 433–438.

McDaniel, M.A., and Nguyen, N.T. 2001. "Situational Judgment Tests: A Review of Practice and Constructs Assessed." *International Journal of Selection and Assessment* 9: 103–113.

McDaniel, M.A., Whetzel, D.L., Schmidt, F.L., and Maurer, S.D. 1994. "The Validity of Employment Interviews: A Comprehensive Review and Meta-analysis." *Journal of Applied Psychology* 79: 599–616.

Moscoso, S. 2000. "A Review of Validity Evidence, Adverse Impact and Applicant reactions." *International Journal of Selection & Assessment* 8: 237–247.

Mount, M.K., Barrick, M.R., and Strauss, J.P. 1994. "Validity of Observer Ratings of the Big Five Personality Factors." *Journal of Applied Psychology* 79: 272–280.

Murphy, K.R. 1994. "Potential Effects of Banding as a Function of Test Reliability." *Personnel Psychology* 47: 477–495.

Negandhi, A.R., and Estafen, B D. 1965. "Determining the Applicability of American

Management Know-How in Differing Environments and Cultures," *Academy of Management Journal* 8: 319–323.

Normand, J., and Salyards, S. 1989. "An Empirical Evaluation of Preemployment Drug Testing in the United States Postal Service: Interim Report of Findings." *National Institute on Drug Abuse: Research Monograph Series* No. 91: 111–138. Office of National Statistics. 1996. *Social Focus on Ethnic Minorities.* London: Her Majesty's Stationery Office.

Office of National Statistics. 1996. *Social Focus on Ethnic Minorities.* London: Her Majesty's Stationery Office.

Ones, D.S., and Viswesvaran, C. 1998. "Gender, Age, and Race Differences on Overt Integrity Tests: Analyses across Four Large-scale Applicant Data Sets." *Journal of Applied Psychology* 83: 35–42.

Ones, D.S., Viswesvaran, C., and Schmidt, F.L. 1993. "Comprehensive Meta-analysis of Integrity Test Validities: Findings and Implications for Personnel Selection and Theories of Job Performance." *Journal of Applied Psychology* 78: 679–703.

Parker, C.P., Baltes, B.B., and Christiansen, N.D. 1997. "Support for Affirmative Action, Justice Perceptions, and Work Attitudes: A Study of Gender and Racial-Ethnic Group Differences." *Journal of Applied Psychology* 82: 376–389.

Penn, N., Percy R., and Harold, S. 1986. "Affirmative Action at Work: A Survey of Graduates of the University of California, San Diego, Medical School." *American Journal of Public Health* 76: 1144–1146.

Principles for the Validation and Use of Personnel Selection Procedures (3rd ed.)." College Park, MD: Author.

Ratnam, V. 1995. "Economic Liberalization and the Transformation of Industrial Relations Policies in India," In *Employment Relations in the Growing Asian Economies,* ed. A. Verma, T.A., Kochan, and R.D. Lansbury. London: Routledge.

Ree, M.J. & Carretta, T.R. 1998. "General Cognitive Ability and Occupational Performance." In *International Review of Industrial and Oganizational Psychology.* Vol. 13, eds. C.L. Cooper and I.T. Robertson, 159–171.

Rosse, J.G., Miller, J.L., and Stecher, M.D. 1994. "A Field Study of Job Applicants' Reactions to Personality and Cognitive Ability Testing." *Journal of Applied Psychology* 79: 987–992.

Rosse, J.G., Stecher, M.D., Miller, J.L., and Levin, R.A. 1998. "The Impact of Response Distortion on Preemployment Personality Testing and Hiring Decisions." *Journal of Applied Psychology* 83: 634–645.

Rynes, S.L. 1991. "Recruitment, Job Choice, and Post-hire Consequences: A Call for New Eesearch Directions." In *Handbook of Industrial and Organizational Psychology,* Vol. 2, eds. M.D. Dunnette and L.M. Hough. Palo Alto, CA: Consulting Psychologists Press, 399–444.

Sackett, P.R., and Roth, L. 1991. "A Monte Carlo Examination of Banding and Rank Order Methods of Test Score Use in Personnel Selection." *Human Performance* 4: 279–295.

Sackett, P.R., and Wanek, J.E. 1996. "New Developments in the Use of Measures of Honesty, Integrity, Conscientiousness, Dependability, Trustworthiness, and Reliability for Personnel Selection." *Personnel Psychology* 49: 787–827.

Saks, A.M., Leck, J.D., and Saunders, D.M. 1995. "Effects of Application Blanks and Employment Equity on Applicant Reactions and Job Pursuit Intentions." *Journal of Organizational Behavior* 16: 415–430.

Salgado, J.F. 1999. "Personnel Selection Methods." In C. L. Cooper and I. T. Robertson, eds., *International Review of Industrial & Organizational Psychology.* New York: Wiley.

Schmidt, F.L., and Hunter, J.E. 1974. "Racial and Ethnic Bias in Psychological Tests: Divergent Implications of Two Definitions of Test Bias." *American Psychologist* 29: 1–8.

Schmidt, F.L., and Hunter, J.E. 1977. "Development of a General Solution to the Problem of Validity Generalization." *Journal of Applied Psychology* 62: 529–540.

Schmidt, F.L., and Hunter, J.E. 1989. "Interrater Reliability Coefficients Cannot Be Computed When Only One Stimulus Is Rated." *Journal of Applied Psychology* 74: 368–370.

Schmidt, F.L., and Hunter, J.E. 1998. "The Validity and Utility of Selection Methods in Personnel Psychology: Practical and Theoretical Implications of 85 Years of Research Findings." *Psychological Bulletin* 124: 262–274.

Schmidt, F.L., Hunter, J.E., and Pearlman, K. 1981. "Task Differences and the Validity of Aptitude Tests in Selection: A Red Herring." *Journal of Applied Psychology* 66: 166–185.

Schmidt, F.L., and Rader, M. 1999. "Exploring the Boundary Conditions for Interview Validity: Meta-analytic Validity Findings for a New Interview Type." *Personnel Psychology* 52: 445–464.

Sharma, R.D. 1992. "The Culture Context of Indian Managers." *Management and Labor Studies* 9: 72–80.

Shetty, R. 1970. "Apartheid in India." *The Indian Journal of Social Work,* 31, 581–598.

Society of Industrial and Organizational Psychology. 1987a. *Principles for the Validation and Use of Personnel Selection Procedures* (3d ed.). College Park, MD: Author.

Society for Industrial and Organizational Psychology. 1987b. *The Ethical Practice of Psychology in Organizations.* College Park, MD: Author.

Sparrow, P.R., and Budhwar, P.S. 1997. "Competition and Change: Mapping the Indian HRM Recipe against World-wide Patterns." *Journal of World Business* 32: 224–243.

Steiner, D.D., and Gilliland, S.W. 1996. "Fairness Reactions to Personnel Selection Techniques in France and the United States." *Journal of Applied Psychology* 81: 134–142.

Stinglhamber, F., Vandenberghe, and Brancart, S. 1999. "Les reactions des candidats envers les techniques de selection du personnel: une etude dans un contexte francophone. / Reactions of job applicants to personnel selection techniques: An investigation in a French-speaking context." *Travail-Humain* 62: 347–361.

"Storm over Drug Testing: US Style Mandatory Programs Face Heavy Weather in Canada." 1991, April 21. *Financial Post,* 19.

Taylor, M.S., and Bergmann, T.J. 1987. "Organizational Recruitment Activities and Applicants' Reactions at Different Stages of the Recruitment Process." *Personnel Psychology* 40: 261–285.

Teles, S.M. 1998. "Why Is There No Affirmative Action in U.K.?" *American Behavioral Scientist* 41: 1004–1023.

Terpstra, D.E., Mohamed, A.A., and Kethley, R.B. 1999. "An Analysis of Federal Court Cases Involving Nine Selection Devices." *International Journal of Selection & Assessment* 7: 26–34.

Tett, R.P., Jackson, D.N., and Rothstein, M. 1991. "Personality Measures as Predictors of Job Performance: A Meta-analytic Review." *Personnel Psychology* 44: 703–742.

Thornton, G.C., III, and Morris, D.M. 2001, Spring. "The Application of Assessment Center Technology to the Evaluation of Personnel Records." *Public Personnel Management,* 17–21.

Tripathi, P.C. 2001. *Human Resource Development.* New Delhi: Sultan Chaud & Sons.

Tummala, K.K. 1991. "Affirmative Action: A Status Report." *International Journal of Public Administration* 14: 383–411.

Tummala, K.K. 1999, November–December. "Policy of Preference: Lessons from India, the United States, and South Africa." *Public Administration Review* 59: 495–508.

Vining, A.R., McPhillips, D.C., and Boardman, A.E. 1986. "Use of Statistical Evidence in Employment Discrimination Legislation." *The Canadian Bar Review* 64: 660–702.

Welsh, C., Knox, J., and Brett, M. 1994. "Acting Positively: Positive Actions under the Race Relations Act." Research Series No. 31.

Zetlin, M. 1991. "Combating Drugs in the Workplace." *Management Review* 80: 17–25.

Cases

Albermarle Paper Co. v. Moody, 422 U.S. 405 (1975)

Andrews v. Treasury Board and Department of Transportation, Canadian Human Rights Commission, Ottawa: Minister of Supply and Services Canada (1994)

B.L. Mears v. Ontario Hydro, Canadian Human Rights Reporter, 5, D3433 (1984)

Brenda Patterson v. McLean Credit Union, 57 LW 4705 (1989)

British Columbia (Public Service Employee Relations Commission) v. BCGSEU, Supreme Court of Canada (1999)

Connecticut v. Teal, 457 U.S. 440 (1982)

Dattatraya v. State of Bombay, AIR 1953 Bom. 311

Fullilove v. Klutznick, 448 US 448 (1980)

Hennessey v. Coastal Eagle Point Oil Co., 37 F.E.D. 1510 (C.D.Cal., 1982)

Indra Sawhney v. Union of India, 1992 SCC (L&S) Supp. 1

Regents v. Bakke, 438 US 265 (1978)

Richmond v. Crown, 488 US 469 (1989)

State of Madras v. Champakam Dorairajan, 1951 SCR 525

Wards Cove Company v. Atonio, 57 LW 4583 (1989)

APPENDIX 1 Bias in Selection Decisions

Cascio (1992) describes differential predictor-criterion relationships that are legal and those that are illegal in the United States. His work is summarized below. Criterion validity can be represented by the relationship between a predictor of job performance (selection tool or performance appraisal) and performance criterion (some measure of job performance). Figure 3.3 represents a predictor-criterion relationship that is valid for both the designated and comparison group. In this figure, the validity for the designated and comparison (nondesignated) group is equivalent, but the designated group scores lower on the predictor and performs the job more poorly that the comparison group. The regression line overestimates the likely performance of the designated group and underestimates that of the comparison group. If this regression line were used to make hiring decisions (e.g., hire only those employees with above-average performance or scores on the predictor), the predictions of successful job performance would be biased in favor of the designated group. Nevertheless, the predictor has an ad-

Figure 3.3 **Valid Prediction with Adverse Impact**

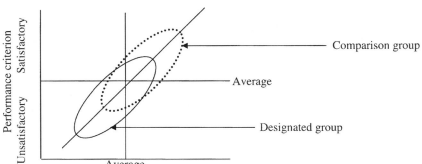

Figure 3.4 **Equal Validity, Unequal Predictor Means**

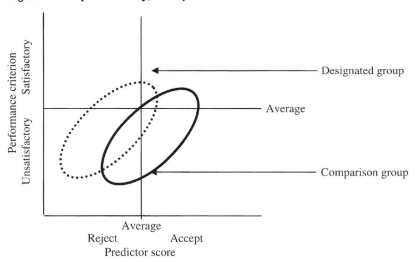

verse impact on the lower-scoring designated group members. If the predictor was used to select from the top down, there is an adverse impact that could lead to a prima facie case of discrimination. Some scholars (e.g., Cascio, 1992) have argued that in this situation, adverse impact may be defensible as long as (a) the criterion can be shown to be a bona fide occupational requirement and free from bias, (b) there is no reasonable alternative criterion that results in less adverse impact, and (c) there is no third factor that may result in the difference in job performance of the two groups (e.g., length on time on the job or training

Figure 3.5 **Unfair and not Valid**

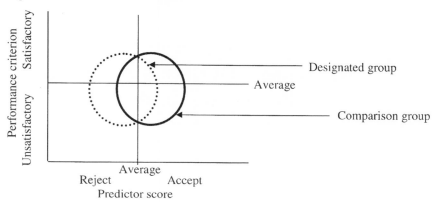

provided). That is, although there may be persistent differences between the average test scores for the designated and comparison groups, these differences do not necessarily indicate test bias. Nonetheless, although a test may be statistically free from bias, it may still be perceived as being unfair—that is, issues of fairness cannot be determined empirically. It behooves an organization to compare the fairness of a selection tool to alternatives that may be used in place of the predictor (AERA et al. 1999).

If a situation equivalent to that in Figure 3.4 exists, the predictor is valid for both groups but unfair to the lower scoring group (in this case the designated group) because their performance is as good as the performance of the higher scorers, although they score poorly on the predictor. This situation results in a larger proportion of the lower-scoring group (designated group) being rejected on the basis of their test score, even when they would have performed successfully had they been hired. One way to overcome this type of bias, called differential validity, is to generate separate regression lines for the designated and comparison groups and hence use separate cutting scores (AERA et al. 1999). If a common cutting score were used, members of the designated group would be less likely to be selected. The use of separate cutting scores rather than a common cutting score for the two groups would allow more accurate prediction of job performance for each group. In the United States, however, using different cutting scores and making adjustments to predictor scores is forbidden under provisions of the Civil Rights Act of 1991.

Figure 3.5 shows a situation in which the predictor is not valid for either group and discriminates unfairly against the lower-scoring group, but it does not help the employer to select employees from either group.

Chapter 4

Measuring Employment Equity Effectiveness: Quantitative and Qualitative Approaches

In this chapter, we examine quantitative and qualitative approaches to measuring the effectiveness of Employment Equity (EE). We propose an EE Index that is verified using Canadian data. Although the focus is on racial minorities, it may assist countries with historically disadvantaged majority groups such as Malaysia and South Africa (SA). EE approaches similar to those in Canada are found in South Africa and in other countries such as Britain, where the Commission for Racial Equality (CRE) has been authorized to do racial monitoring, and Northern Ireland, which has had the Fair Employment legislation. Northern Ireland has goals and timetables designed to proactively hire, retain, promote, and train the Catholic minority and has the authority under the FEA (see chapter 1) to monitor the progress made by employers in meeting their affirmative action goals (now the authority having been given to the Equality Commission).

Effectiveness Criteria for Employment Equity

Legislation, compliance monitoring, and good intentions are all aided by the development of effectiveness criteria. These criteria are set out in the Employment Equity Index (EEI) developed by the senior author (Jain and Hackett 1989). Employment equity/affirmative action (EE/AA) legislation in most countries, including Canada, the United States, and South Africa, embodies these factors. The EEI was later adopted in South Africa as well for the Breakwater Monitor Project (Jain and Bowmaker-Falconer 1998) at the University of Cape Town. For instance, the EEI was used in the survey of business organizations in South Africa for the South African Department of Labour to determine the state of EE in the country (Jain and Bowmaker-Falconer 1998).

In addition to the survey of organizations, the senior author was also invited to undertake a study of "good practices" in selected countries by the South African Department of Labour (SADOL), as a background study (Jain and Bowmaker-Falconer 1998) prior to passage of the EEA in South Africa. The study involved field trips to the United States, Britain, and Northern Ireland and Canada to interview officials in the Office of Federal Contract Compliance (OFCP) in the U.S. Department of Labor and the Equal Employment Opportunities Commission (EEOC) in Washington, DC; the Commission for Racial Equality (CRE) and Equal Opportunities Commission (EOC) in London; and the Fair Employment Commission (FEC) and other organizations in Northern Ireland; as well the Canadian Human Rights Commission (CHRC) and officials in the EE Branch in the Human Resources Development Canada (HRDC). The results of our studies of employer practices were widely discussed in South Africa and were partly incorporated in the EEA passed by the Parliament in Cape Town in 1998.

Identifying Employment Equity "Best Practices"

In essence, the criteria allow employers to develop "best practices" to enable, implement, nurture, and evaluate the effectiveness of EE programs. The Employment Equity Index consists of the following factors:

- Accountability
- Numerical Goals and Timetables
- Monitoring and Control Mechanisms
- Employment Practice Review
- Special Target or Designated Group Recruitment and Training Efforts
- Employment Equity Committee or Coordinator
- Resources or Budget

Accountability

Employment equity programs are more likely to succeed when line managers are incorporated into the planning and implementation of the program and held accountable for the outcomes. In this way, line managers' performance assessment and subsequent linkage of success to bonuses, salary increase, or promotion facilitate acceptance and adoption of employment equity throughout the organization.

Numerical Goals and Timetables

Numerical goals and timetables are instrumental in facilitating the effectiveness of employment equity programs. Employment equity programs should specify all the designated groups (not just one) and specific goals and timetables ranging from one to five years.

Monitoring and Control Mechanisms

Effective monitoring is necessary to the implementation of an employment equity program. Regular evaluations can indicate progress being made toward set objectives and the need for suitable corrective action or adjustment. These evaluations should include periodical reports of progress toward meeting goals, flow information on staffing; and adequate systems for human resource information management. This requires a systematic evaluation of the current environment and practices, and the development of EE indicators; these are combined in a scorecard used to evaluate progress.

On-Going Publicity

A major step in the development and implementation of an effective employment equity program is to clearly communicate company policy to employees. These communications include videos and/or memoranda sent by senior management; annual reports; workplace posters; and communication in several languages in company newsletters and other in-house organs.

Employment Practice Review

A critical requisite to an effective employment equity program is the identification and elimination of unfair discriminatory barriers to employment opportunities. These programs can include reviewing and updating job descriptions/specifications; monitoring staffing practices; ensuring job requirements are job related; conducting interviewer training; and validating tests and other staffing procedures.[1]

Special Target or Designated Group Recruitment and Training Efforts

These include making proactive efforts to recruit and train designated group members; ensuring that recruiting teams are represented by members of designated groups; making recruiting material available in several languages; mentoring programs; as well as special measures in the form of flextime, internal and external communications, work sharing, child care, and educational assistance such as bursaries.

Employment Equity Committee or Coordinator

Coordinators and committees are helpful in developing, implementing, and monitoring employment equity programs. Workplace forums with equal numbers of employee and management representatives and trade union participation where workplaces are unionized can be very helpful in this respect. However, it is important to have a full-time coordinator from senior management responsible for coordinating the work of the committee.

Resources for Budget

Most effective employment equity programs are funded from separate budgets designated solely for this purpose. Clearly, for an employment equity program to go beyond tokenism, adequate resources must be allocated. The Employment Equity Index developed by Jain (Jain and Hackett 1989) is reflected in the characteristics of "best practices."

Defining Employment Equity "Best Practices"

"Best practice" infers the concept of "better than" compliance with EE/AA legislation. It asks employers to undertake proactive initiatives. The following description is based on research into private sector organizations compiled and analyzed by the U.S. Equal Employment Opportunity Commission (Jain and Bowmaker-Falconer 1998; Jones 1997). According to the EEOC Task Force (December 1997, 25) a "best" practice has the following characteristics:

1. A "best" practice at minimum complies with the employment equity law in a country. A "best" practice is not accomplished by minimal compliance with the law since all employers must meet that standard.
2. A "best" practice promotes equal employment opportunity and addresses one or more barriers that adversely affect equal employment opportunity; A "best" practice should strive to eliminate both general (that is, societal) and specific (indigenous to the employer) job barriers. Societal job barriers include glass ceilings against designated groups that limit their advancement; perceived cultural differences, and ethnocentrism due to the "like me" syndrome; stereotyping; prejudice or outright bigotry; ignorance; and so on. Employer-specific job barriers include barriers to: (a) recruitment and hiring; (b) advancement and promotion; (c) terms and conditions of employment; and (d) termination and downsizing; and so on.
3. A "best" practice manifests management commitment and accountability; it involves commitment from top-level management to front-line supervisors. Management commitment must be a driving force. It includes management directives; communication throughout the organization indicating that it is committed to equal opportunities and will not tolerate unlawful discrimination in any form; and an integration of

equal opportunity in all aspects of an employer's policies and practices. Management must also monitor the results of its efforts and decisions. Accountability is important since it goes hand-in-hand with commitment.

4. A "best" practice ensures management and employee communication; management should participate and interact with employees and employee groups. Communication should be encouraged from the "top-down" and "bottomup," including top management speeches and letters from employees to management. Information about equal opportunities policies, programs, and practices should be distributed to all employees, informing everyone of management's positions on the various aspects of equal opportunities. This includes career opportunities to all employees, including competencies, skills, and abilities required.

5. A "best" practice produces noteworthy results. A practice may look great on paper, but without implementation and result, its value is subject to conjecture and is unrealized.

6. A "best" practice does not cause or result in unfairness; an affirmative action (AA) plan cannot unnecessarily trammel the rights of nondesignated groups. For example, it cannot require the discharge of nondesignated groups and their replacement with designated employees, nor can it create an absolute bar to the advancement of non designated groups. In addition, an individual benefiting from an AA plan must be qualified for the job at issue; an AA plan should not use inflexible quotas, but rather justifiable goals and timetables; the plan must be designed to break down patterns of segregation and to open employment opportunities for the designated groups.

Measuring EE Effectiveness

We used two approaches to measure EE effectiveness: a qualitative and a quantitative approach. The first approach was based on the EEI and best practices,

Qualitative Approach

*Measuring "Best Practices" of Employment Equity/Affirmative
Action programs*

Jain and Lawler (2002) specially designed and validated a survey instrument (see Appendix 4.1) to quantify various EE programs in organizations. They developed scales that were valid and statistically significant; these scales were used to evaluate short-term actions taken by firms to address EE issues. They found that firms that scored highly on the overall scale and/or certain of its components were more likely to have done a better job of hiring and promoting designated groups relative to others. In the latest study (Jain and Lawler, 2002), they interviewed senior managers of eighteen of the largest and most prominent organizations in the three industrial sectors: banking, transportation, and communications under the Canadian (federal) EEA (see Appendix 4.2 for a summary of narrative reports by these organizations by each sector).

In the original study, where the senior author developed the EEI (Jain and Hackett 1989), more than 200 firms throughout Canada were surveyed.

Quantitative Approach

Jain and Lawler (2002) analyzed the impact of Canadian (federal) EE legislation based on company data on the employment of racial minority or visible minority (VM) workers. Canadian EEA defines visible minorities as "persons, other than aboriginal persons, who are non-Caucasian in race or non-white in colour."

The data for this study were drawn from annual reports filed by companies under the provisions of the Canadian (federal) Employment Equity Act (EEA) over the period 1987–1999. The data came from a sample of more than 100 companies. The sample was selected from companies that filed reports in each year from 1987 to 1999. The data set contained a series of stock and flow employment measures for the organizations filing the reports.

Statistical analysis was used to identify the impact of several predictor variables on the outcome variables. The ultimate objective was to discern the effectiveness of the EEA in improving quantitative measures of employment equity outcomes. This was assessed by actual goal attainment in the analysis of the VM employment equity measure and progress toward goal attainment in the analysis of the rate of VM employment change.

Appendix 4.3 presents a conceptual framework for assessing the effectiveness of the EEA as well as data and research methods used in the Canadian study (Jain and Lawler, 2002).

This chapter has proposed a methodology and provided data substantiating the need for both a quantitative and qualitative index to evaluate employment equity progress. Additional variables could be added and validated. These relate to broader goals of economic empowerment that are especially important in developing countries such as India, Malaysia, and South Africa. Further measures could include capitalization on local stock exchanges of companies in respect of designated group or visible minority shareholding and ownership. In societies that have experienced significant and pervasive systemic discrimination, economic empowerment in terms of firm ownership and control are important indexes of the degree of progress and redistribution of opportunity, skills, and wealth in the direction of increased equality. Specifically, these measures should include financial participation such as:

- Share ownership
- Profit sharing
- Governance arrangements and representation
- Stock exchange capitalization by firm ownership in respect of designated groups or visible minorities
- Investment programs, for example, trade union-owned firms, cooperatives, and pension funds where members are predominantly from designated groups

Notes

1. For specific staffing practices that exemplify these "best practices," see Appendix 4.2.

References

Jain, Harish C., and Bowmaker-Falconer, Angus. 1998. *Employment Equity/Affirmative Action Codes of Practice and Best Practices in USA, Britain, Canada and Other Selected Countries*. Pretoria: South African Department of Labour, 1998, 84.

Jain, Harish C., and Hackett, Rick. 1989. "Measuring Effectiveness of Employment Equity Programs in Canada: Public Policy and a Survey." *Canadian Public Policy* 15: 189–204.

Jain, Harish C., and Lawler, John. 2002. *Good Practices for Visible Minorities in Canadian Workplaces*. An unpublished study with partial assistance from the Social Sciences & Humanities Research Council and Human Resources Development Canada.

Jain, Harish C., and Lawler, John. 2002. Visible Minorities under the Canadian Employment Equity Act: 1987–1999: An Analysis of Company Annual Report Data with Policy Recommendations. An unpublished study with partial assistance from Social Sciences and Humanities Research Council and Heritage Canada.

Jones, R.E., Chair. 1997, December. *Task Force Report on Best Equal Employment Opportunity Policies, Programs and Practices in the Private Sector*. Washington, DC: Equal Employment Opportunity Commission.

Leonard, Jonathan S. 1984. "The Impact of Affirmative Action on Employment." *Journal of Labor Economics* 2, no. 4: 439–463.

The South African Employment Equity Project Report. 1998. Pretoria and Cape Town: South African Department of Labour and the Graduate School of Business at the University of Cape Town, funded by USAID, 36.

Appendix 4.1 Scale Categories, Scale Items, and Reliabilities

Scale	Scale Items
Accommodation	Your organization has a written policy on accommodation of persons with disabilities. Your organization has adopted clear procedures to ensure that accommodation takes place. The policy includes accommodation of special needs for all designated groups, including VMs. *Your organization has a written policy on harassment in the workplace.*
Accountability	Your organization has a process to ensure the accountability of managers for their results in meeting goals and implementing employment equity. Your organization monitors EE plan for progress towards meeting specific goals and timetables, and any subsequent corrective action. You keep a report on your monitoring activities, results, and any subsequent action. *Your organization keeps a report describing the EE plan.*
Equity Plan	Your organization has developed an EE plan. The EE plan fully addresses all of the barriers identified through the systems review. The EE plan includes specific timetables for the implementation of each of these steps. These policies have been communicated to all employees. Your organization has a written policy on EE. Your organization provides information to your employees about the content of the EE plan; progress made towards attaining the goals and objectives of the EE plan. The information re: EE is provided on a regular and continuing basis. Your organization has separate budget designed solely for implementing EE. *Your company has developed and implemented steps to remove the identified employment barriers in all occupational groups in which under-representation was found.* *EE related materials are made available in alternate formats.*

(continued)

Appendix 4.1 (*continued*)

Scale	Scale Items
General Consultation	Consultation with one (or several) employee representatives on your company's employment equity (EE) plan or initiatives. *There is an Employment Equity committee in the organization.* Your organization has a consultation strategy for EE. You keep a record of communication/consultation activities and the documentation distributed or posted.
Proactive Initiatives	Your organization has recently undertaken a new workforce analysis. Your organization has recently undertaken new employee survey. Your organization has recently undertaken a new employment systems review. Your organization has recently undertaken a review of policies (equity, harassment, accommodation measures, other). Your organization has recently undertaken measure/s to improve corporate culture. Your organization has recently implemented a new EE plan. Your organization undertook other significant activities related to EE in 2000. Your organization has conducted a review of employment systems and related policies and practices. Your organization has a process to ensure that all new policies and procedures are reviewed and they do not create any new employment barriers. Your organization has special pro-active recruitment drive for VMs and other designated groups. *Your organization has special pro-active training programs for VMs and other designated groups.*
Union Consultation	You had a consultation meeting with union representatives on workplace equity in 2000. You have invited all bargaining agents and/or employee representatives to provide their views regarding the development, implementation and revision of the employment equity plan? Your organization has invited labour union representatives to provide assistance with respect to the communication strategy/activities. You have invited union representatives to provide assistance with the implementation of EE.

Appendix 4.2 Summary of Narrative Reports by Sector Filed by Employers under the Canadian (Federal) Employment Equity Act (EEA)

BANKING INDUSTRY SUMMARY FROM 1997–1999 NARRATIVE REPORTS	
Category	**Summary of Qualitative Initiatives for Visible Minority Members**
Employee Feedback	Open Forum available with employees.
	Employee Support Line/ Diversity phone line available for employees.
	Workforce Survey developed and implemented.
	Workplace Equality Divisional Advisory Councils established.
	Employee Opinion Survey developed and issued to all employees.
	Task Forces to find barriers and identify specific VM issues from within the workplace.
	Dispute resolution process developed for all employees.
Youth	Youth conference sponsorship and participation.
	Partner with various youth community organizations and educational institutions.
	Sponsors of various youth programs and achievement awards.
	Launching of specific VM youth programs.
	Participated in youth internship programs, on-the-job training and provide job shadowing opportunities.

(continued)

118

Appendix 4.2 *(continued)*

Summary of Qualitative Initiatives for Visible Minority Members

Category	
Youth (continued)	Participated in campus recruitment and career fairs for post-secondary students.
	Sponsored exchange program students.
Community/ Outreach	Partnership with various community VM organizations.
	Provided financial support to various VM agencies and organizations.
	In addition, also participated in traditional outreach activities such as career fairs, mentoring, job shadowing programs and community events.
	Sponsored and organized various activities for VM celebrations.
	Publicized and published information on company website.
	Worked with specific VM employment organizations.
	Printed and distributed various VM celebration and anti-discriminatory materials.
Sponsorships	Co-sponsor of the various awards such as Harry Jerome Award and others recognizing the achievements of VM Canadians.
	Creating foundations to support various VM organizations and projects.
	Sponsor for various VM events and scholarships.
Promotions	Review of internal promotion and succession planning processes.
	Proactively promote from internal VM pool of candidates.

COMMUNICATION INDUSTRY SUMMARY FROM 1997–1999 NARRATIVE REPORTS

Category	Summary of Qualitative Initiatives for Visible Minority Members
Career Development and Communications	Implemented mentoring program to target VMs.
	Developed peer support network (similar to mentoring).
	Has developed intranet site for promotion and have telephone (or other) counselling available.
Employee Feedback	Established Workplace Diversity Councils/Committees.
	Workforce/Employee survey completed.
	Developed Task Force to investigate barriers and VM issues.
	Team developed to help with workplace relationships and deal with conflict resolution.
	Focus groups conducted periodically for employee feedback.
Youth	Implemented job shadowing, internships and on-the-job training opportunities for students.
	Offered various achievement awards and scholarships for VM (some industry specific).
	Partnerships established with various community organizations.
	Mentoring available to various high-school and technical school students.
Community/ Outreach	Supported a variety of community agencies through sponsorships and participation in community events.
	Partnerships with various employment agencies.

(continued)

Appendix 4.2 *(continued)*

Category	Summary of Qualitative Initiatives for Visible Minority Members
Community/ Outreach (continued)	Developed an external toll-free job line to target and have jobs more accessible to the VM population.
	Participated in traditional recruitment methods such as job fairs to attract VM candidates.
	Produced various reports to appeal to VM group members.
	Celebrated and initiated local VM celebrations.
Sponsorships	Involved with many chartiable organizations.
Promotions	Promotion of all internal postings for access to all employees.
	Secondments available to VM employees.
	Succession planning/promotion process evaluated and new process implemented.
	Career coaching available.

TRANSPORTATION INDUSTRY SUMMARY FROM 1997–1999 NARRATIVE REPORTS

Category	Summary of Qualitative Initiatives for Visible Minority Members
Employee Feedback	Surveyed workforce.
	Formed an EE committee/group.
	Held EE information sessions (time for feedback) for employees.

Youth	Attended career and job fairs at various colleges and universities.
	Participated in various programs with community youth organizations.
	Partnered with high-schools to target students.
Community/ Outreach	Specialized recruitment to reach designated groups with advertisements in ethnic newspapers, etc.
	Worked with various VM employment agencies.
	Had ongoing liaisons with designated group organizations.
Sponsorships	Sponsored many community events that involved VM members.
Promotions	Have mentorship programs available for employees.
	In the process of evaluating current promotion policies to identify any barriers to promotion.
	Job shadowing and peer support groups in place.

Appendix 4.3   Quantitative Approach: A Conceptual Framework

As noted in this chapter, our objective was to assess the effectiveness of the EEA in improving quantitative measures of employment equity outcomes. To do this, we used data drawn from a sample of annual reports filed by companies covered under the EEA for the period 1987–1999. Our definition of the principal dependent variables in this study required that we first specify the unit of analysis. Here we used provincial-wide occupational groups from each of these companies in each year for which data were reported by the company (this data source is described in more detail below). Thus, for example, one observation may have consisted of data on professionals employed by Air Canada in British Columbia in 1997, while another might have been based on administrative and senior clerical personnel employed by the Royal Bank of Canada in Ontario in 1998, or skilled sales and service personnel employed in Nova Scotia in 1999 by Bell Canada. For simplicity we referred to a particular unit of observation as an employment group.

We focussed on two different outcome variables that served as employment equity criteria for visible minority or non-white (VM) workers. The first of these was a static measure that represented the degree to which VM workers within a particular employment group had secured parity in relation to the relevant external labor market. *Internal employment equity* was defined as the ratio of VM employment in a given employment group to total employment within the same employment group. *External employment equity* was based on corresponding data drawn from the 1996 Canadian Census and was defined as the ratio of VM employment in the corresponding occupational category and province relative to total employment in the corresponding occupational and category and province.

The composite measure of employment equity was defined as the difference of the internal and external equity measures; this was termed *VM employment equity* (see Equation 1). The value of this measure was interpreted as the percentage adjustment that would have to be made in the employment group's relative headcount in order to achieve equity in comparison to the relevant external labour market for the year in question. A value of zero indicated that the firm had achieved, at least in a technical sense, employment equity for VM employees for that particular group. Positive values indicated the firm exceeded objectives defined by the Census data for the employment group in question and negative values indicated VM employees were underrepresented in the firm for the occupation and province in question.

$$VM\_EE_{c,p,i,t} = (VM_{c,p,i,t}/N_{c,i,p,t}) - (VM_{c,p}/N_{c,p}) \tag{1}$$

$VM\_EE_{c,p,i,t}$ = measure of VM employment equity in occupational category c in province p for company i at time t;

VM = number of VM employees in category defined by subscripts;

N = number of all employees in category defined by subscripts.

We recognized that the attainment of employment equity objectives would require time, and continual adjustment and readjustment as a function of variations in economic activity and shifting demographics, a *dynamic* (i.e., change) *measure* represented another, and equally important, indicator of a firm's employment equity performance. Here we focussed on the overall annual change in VM employment within an employment group. This was the most comprehensive of possible dynamic measures, as it captured all aspects of employment change (terminations, hirings, promotions, demotions, attrition). Thus, our dynamic measure was the annual *rate of VM employment change* within an employment group. The dynamic measure was defined as indicated in Equation (2):

$$VM\_CH_{c,i,p,t} = (VM_{c,i,p,t} - VM_{c,i,p,t-1})/VM_{c,i,p,t-1} \tag{2}$$

where:

$VM\_CH_{g,c,i,t}$ = rate of change in VM employment in occupation c in company i in province p between periods t and t−1.

Regression analysis was used to discern the impact of several predictor variables on the outcome variables described above. The ultimate objective was to discern something about the effectiveness of the EEA in improving quantitative measures of employment equity outcomes. One major limitation in this work was that we only had data on organizations covered by the EEA and thus were required to have active employment equity programs in place. Similar research conducted in the United States on affirmative action (i.e., employment equity) programs (Leonard 1984) benefited from the fact that not all companies studied were required to have affirmative action programs in place, so it was possible to contrast companies with affirmative action programs to those without such program within the same economic sectors. Therefore in this study we were not able to observe directly the impact of the presence of a legally mandated program on the achievement of employment equity objectives. However, we could observe the impact of several context variables on employment equity outcomes to discern within the set of covered firms conditions under which the EEA had been more versus less effective.

The explanatory variables in the analyses of both the static and dynamic employment equity measures included time, occupational categories, geographical location (i.e., province), organizational size, employment group size, and industrial sector. Time was measured by the difference of the year of the observation from the year of EEA implementation (1986). EEA reports are filed annually, so there were separate observations for a given employment group for each year in which the firm has had to provide data relevant to the group. The temporal measure is very important as it assesses changes in employment equity over time.

An upward trend in employment equity suggests that the EEA may have the desired consequences. It certainly is a necessary condition to establish the effectiveness of the law, but since we were not able to make direct comparisons to similar companies without employment equity provisions, we could not rule such changes to be rooted in broader social change in Canada. However, if the trend was negative, or only weakly positive, then we could conclude that the EEA is having no substantive effect on employment equity. In other words, progress over time with regard to employment equity was a necessary condition to establish EEA effectiveness, though was not alone sufficient to warrant such a conclusion. There were other time-related confounds as well, as will be discussed later.

The total size of the employer within Canada, along with the size of the employment group, were also included in our analysis as explanatory variables. Prior research on the effectiveness of affirmative action in the United States have shown associations between organizational size and various indicators of affirmative action effectiveness. Overall organizational size might be expected to impact employment equity in a couple of ways. Large companies are more visible to both the public and government regulators. Thus they may be inclined to pursue more aggressive employment equity efforts to avoid adverse publicity and excessive attention from the government. Also, larger organizations typically have more slack resources and thus may be better able to absorb the costs of making employment adjustments.

We anticipated that firm size was positively related to employment equity attainment. We also saw the size of the employment group as highly relevant. Larger units would attract more attention and changes and larger units would also have a bigger effect on overall firm employment equity. Larger units would normally have a higher turnover, allowing the firm to make employment adjustments more easily by responding to attrition. Finally, there might be social constraints imposed on change by close-knit groups in smaller units. We would anticipate that employment group size to be positively related to employment equity attainment.

Data and Research Methods

Sample

The data used in this analysis were derived from information provided from annual employment equity reports submitted to Human Resource Development Canada (HRDC) by business firms for the period 1987–1999. The dataset contained a series of stock and flow employment measures for the organizations filing the reports. However, the study was based on the broadest measure contained in these reports: total headcount in each of the company's employment groups (as we have defined above) and VM headcount in these units. Static and dynamic employment equity indicators were derived from these data according to the formulas provided in Equations 1 and 2. Our sample consisted of the 116 companies that filed EEA reports in each year from 1987 either through 1999 or the last year the company was an independent entity, for companies that went out of business, were acquired, or otherwise changed organizational identity.

As we have noted, the unit of observation was the employment group (defined previously), not the company as a whole. So although there were 116 companies in our sample, each company consistsed of a large number of employment groups. Thus the actual sample size depended on the number of employment groups in each company and number of years in the analysis. As there are different types of analysis, the realized sample size ranged from 7000 to 20,000 cases, depending on the nature of the analysis.

Predictors

Several observed predictor variables were used in the study; the rationales for inclusion of these variables have been presented. All of these variables were obtained from the

HRDC database as they are included in the annual EEA reports. The predictor variables include:

1. A set of dummy variables representing the *major occupational* categories contained in the dataset.
2. A set of dummy variables representing *all provinces*. Only provincial data were analyzed, as the number of cases and units sizes for territorial data were quite small.
3. A set of dummy variables used to indicate *the year of the EEA report*. This variable allowed us to assess variations in VM employment equity.
4. *Organizational size.* This is a measure both by the total size of the company's Canadian operations and the size of the specific employment group. As both measures had quite skewed distributions, we used the logarithm of the total number of Canadian employees in the company in the year of observation (overall company size) and the logarithm of the total number of employees in the employment group (e.g., sales workers in British Columbia) for the year in question (group size).
5. *Dummy variables indicating industrial sector.* The EEA applies to three industrial sectors: communications, banking, and transportation. Dummy variables were included to discern sectoral variations in EEA goal attainment. (*Source:* Jain, Harish C. & Lawler, John, *Visible Minorities under the Canadian (Federal) Employment Equity Act: 1987–1999: An Analysis of Company Annual Report Data.* 2002. Unpublished paper.)

Chapter 5

Fair Pay

Nan Weiner

The concept of fairness is a social construct that is affected by cultural values and that changes over time. Fairness in pay is no exception. All the countries discussed in this book have, at one time, linked pay to characteristics such as gender and race. As early as the 1950s, international conventions and some national legislation recognized the potential of gender wage discrimination. Wage discrimination is complex and multifaceted; since wages are set at the organizational level (for the most part) in the six countries studied in this book, firm-level discrimination is the focus of this chapter. Specifically, three kinds of wage discrimination—general, equal work, and equal value—are discussed. It is necessary to understand something about different aspects of wage setting at the firm level in order to understand how the different kinds of discrimination operate. Compensation models differ across countries; a model that is more reflective of North America is presented here since the most extensive work to remove discrimination in pay systems is found in Canada.

In North America, most large organizations have an established compensation system that institutionalizes at least some of the variables on which pay is based. Typically, there is some relationship between one's pay and the job one does or the organizational level at which one works. For some kinds of work, typically craft and some blue-collar jobs, everyone is paid the same rate regardless of their individual characteristics (i.e., experience). However, in many other jobs there is a salary range bracketing the minimum and maximum pay that incumbents can earn for a particular job. Within this range, individual employees are paid differently based on individual characteristics such as performance, seniority, number of university courses, years in profession, and so on. The process of determining pay for work or level can be referred to as the "wage determination" process, while "salary administration" refers to the setting of salaries for individuals such as the hiring salary, the basis for salary increases, and so on. In addition, employees' wealth is affected by the benefits they receive from their employer. Most of the focus of this chapter will be on wage determination and salary administration policies. Even when compensation decisions are made at the level of the firm, there are often some legal requirements, for example, minimum wage legislation and pay equity legislation.

The aspects of compensation identified above are useful in distinguishing between different kinds of wage discrimination. Such a distinction is important because the remedies for redressing each type of discrimination differ. Discrimination against individuals because of gender or race can be found in salary administration policies or practices—for example, hiring an equally qualified woman or man of color at a lower salary, or consistently rating performance lower and thus providing lower merit increases to women and to men of color. North American women have historically been denied the same benefits as men, notably, pension. Two kinds of discrimination are linked to the wage determination process—unequal pay for *equal work* and unequal pay for work of *equal value*.[1] Wage determination links pay to job content—typically measured in terms of factors such as skill, effort, responsibility, and working conditions. Both "equal work" and "equal value" are concerned with job content and the characteristics (gender, race) of the people who typically perform the work. Historically, certain jobs have become associated with members of certain groups— for example, secretarial jobs are typically seen as female in Western countries, whereas manual jobs are regarded as male. The "designation" of the job (female or male) rather than the characteristics of those actually performing the job (e.g., some men are secretaries and some women do manual work) is of concern.

Equal pay for equal work requires that jobs that are substantially the same be paid the same. Substantially similar jobs are similar on skill, on effort, on responsibility, and on working conditions. Correcting unequal pay for equal work addresses the situation of stewardess and stewards on airplanes, and nurse aides and orderlies in hospitals. Although the job titles denoted gendered jobs, the work was (and remains) substantially the same, warranting the same pay. The same thing was found among the Chinese and white workers on the railroads in Canada in the 1800s—although they did the same work, the whites were paid more. Concerns about unequal pay for equal work do not eliminate all unfair pay because of occupational segregation. Occupational segregation is the association, stereotypically and/or in practice, of certain kinds of work with particular kinds of workers (e.g., based on gender or race). For example, in Canada, until relatively recently, the job of train porter was staffed exclusively by black men. Exactly which gender or race predominates in particular occupations may differ in different countries; for example, dentists tend to be female in Eastern Europe and male in North America. However, the link between members of a certain gender or race with a particular kind of work defines occupational segregation. Occupational segregation can be either horizontal or vertical. Men in blue-collar jobs and women in pink-collar jobs reflect horizontal occupational segregation. Women's predominance in bookkeeping and men's in controllerships is vertical segregation. Equal value can only redress horizontal segregation.[2] To achieve equal pay for work of equal value, it is necessary to compare jobs that are dissimilar in content but potentially similar in their value to the employer. In assessing comparable value, it is the total value (or composite) of skill, effort, responsibility, and working conditions of jobs that is compared. So one job might require more skill than the other, but the jobs can still be of comparable value because the second job has more value in one of the other factors. Jobs that are of "equal work" will also be of "equal value"; but jobs can be of "equal value" without being "equal work."

A key component of achieving equal value is job evaluation (JE), a compensation technique developed in the 1930s in North America. The purpose of JE is to assess the relative worth of jobs within an organization based on their content. The goal is to achieve "internal equity" within an organization—to develop a ranking of jobs in terms of their values to the organization. However, because JE has typically been done within job families (groups of occupations), it has been affected by the traditional gender/race of the incumbents of specific occupations; in addition, other kinds of gender bias have historically been part of JE (see Weiner and Gunderson 1990 and Weiner 1991 for a critique of JE systems). Although JE has tended to be biased in the past, it is still seen as a key tool to achieve equal pay for work of equal value. It is the technique by which the value of jobs can be measured. JE requires job information that describes each job in terms of the criteria on which the job will be assessed (evaluated). For pay equity purposes, four overall factors (criteria) have been required to be measured—more than one subfactor can be used to measure each of these criteria. The four criteria (or factors) are skill (e.g., education, interpersonal skill), effort (e.g., physical, mental), responsibility (e.g., human resources, scope and impact, financial), and working conditions (e.g., disagreeable and hazardous situations). The actual subfactors selected are those valued by a particular organization. Typically, a JE committee is used to apply the criteria in a systematic fashion to the job information. In the most common type of JE system, the point factor method, jobs are given points based on their level of each criterion—the total JE points reflect the jobs' value to the organization. Moving from JE points to salaries typically involves a salary survey[3]—identifying what similar jobs are paid by other employers. Where job evaluation is concerned with internal equity—fair relationships between jobs within the organization—salary surveys are concerned with external equity—paying competitive salaries.

International Conventions Against Discrimination Based on Gender and Race

As will be seen, in the countries studied, the three kinds of discrimination discussed typically form a hierarchy—with individual pay discrimination (salary administration) being addressed first, then equal pay for equal work, and finally equal value concerns. For the most part, national policymakers did not recognize the need for equal value until the 1970s (Eyraud 1993). This makes it particularly interesting that international conventions have been more advanced than even the industrialized countries, calling specifically for equal pay for work of equal value for women in 1951 in the International Labor Organization (ILO) convention 100 (reinforced by the 1966 Covenant of Economic Rights and the 1979 Convention on the Elimination of All Forms of Discrimination Against Women). In 1958, Convention 111 (Discrimination [Employment and Occupation]) prohibited individual discrimination in terms and conditions of employment—which obviously includes compensation issues—based on either gender or race. Prohibition of racial discrimination in terms of equal work is found in the 1965 United Nations Convention on the Elimination of all Forms of Racial Discrimination, while reference to equal value is made for all workers in the 1966 Covenant of Economic Rights. The key sections of the ILO and the United Nations conventions are provided in Table 5.1; in addition, this figure provides the date of ratification by any of the six countries discussed here. For the most part, these countries have ratified these conventions with the following exceptions—the United States has not ratified Conventions 100 and 111, and Malaysia has only ratified Convention 100 and the Convention on the Elimination of All forms of Discrimination Against Women.

Although international bodies recognize that countries differ in their wage determination mechanisms and so the solutions will differ (see Equal Remuneration Recommendation (ILO 1951, R90), it is interesting that commitment to international conventions is only moderately related to the passage of national legislation. As seen in Table 5.1, of the six countries discussed in this chapter only the United States has not signed the Equal Remuneration Convention (100) and Discrimination Convention (111), but, as discussed,later, federal legislation has been passed prohibiting discrimination in salary administration and equal work legislation, and equal value issues have been at least raised. On the other hand, both conventions have been signed by India (1958) and Convention 100 by Malaysia (1997), and they do not have specific legislation against the various kinds of wage discrimination.

Comparison of Six Countries

Before discussing fair pay issues in the six countries, it is useful to compare a few related labor force statistics. Figure 5.1 indicates the labor force participation rate of men and women in these six countries. The countries with the highest male participation (India, Malaysia, and South Africa) tend to have the lowest female participation. This may say something about household decisions related to total financial needs. Alternatively, it may reflect the invisibility of women's

Table 5.1
International Conventions Requiring Fair Pay and Status of Ratification by Six Countries

ILO and UN Covenants and Conventions (Emphasis added in bold)			Date Ratified					
Title (ordered by date open for ratification)	Dates • Open for ratification • In force	Fair pay provision (emphasis added)	Canada	India	Malaysia	South Africa	United Kingdom	United States
Equal Remuneration Convention (Convention 100) Equal Value	June 1951 May 1953	Article 1: For the purpose of this Convention: (a) The term "remuneration" includes the ordinary, basic or minimum wage or salary and any additional emoluments whatsoever payable directly or indirectly, whether in cash or in kind, by the employer to the worker. . . (b) The term **"equal remuneration for men and women workers for work of equal value"** refers to rates of remuneration established without discrimination based on sex.	1972	1958	1997	2000	1971	Not ratified

(continued)

	Article 2: 1. Each Member shall, by means appropriate to the methods in operation for determining rates of remuneration, promote and, in so far as is consistent with such methods, ensure the application to all workers of the principle of equal remuneration for men and women workers for work of equal value. 2. This principle may be applied by means of: (a) National laws or regulations; (b) Legally established or recognised machinery for wage determination; (c) Collective agreements between employers and workers; or (d) A combination of these various means.

Table 5.1 *(continued)*

ILO and UN Covenants and Conventions (Emphasis added in bold)			Date Ratified					
Title (ordered by date open for ratification)	Dates • Open for ratification • In force	Fair pay provision (emphasis added)	Canada	India	Malaysia	South Africa	United Kingdom	United States
Discrimination (Employment & Occupation) Convention 111 General	June 1958 June 1960	1. For the purpose of this Convention the term "discrimination" includes: (a) Any distinction, exclusion or preference made on the basis of **race**, colour, **sex**, religion, political opinion, national extraction or social origin, which has the effect of nullifying or impairing equality of opportunity or treatment in employment or occupation; (b) Such other distinction, exclusion or preference which has the effect of nullifying or impairing equality of opportunity or **treatment in employment** . . .	1964	1960	Not ratified	1997	1999	Not ratified

133

		3. For the purpose of this Convention the terms *employment* and occupation include access to vocational training, access to employment and to particular occupations, and terms and conditions of employment.	Oct. 1970	Dec. 1968	Not ratified	Dec. 1998	March 1969	Oct. 1994
Convention on the Elimination of all Forms of **Racial** Discrimination Equal Work	Dec. 1965 Jan. 1969	Article 5: . . . to eliminate racial discrimination in all its forms and to guarantee the right of everyone, without distinction as to race, colour, or national or ethnic origin, to equality before the law, notably in the enjoyment of the following rights: Economic, social and cultural rights, in particular:						

(continued)

Table 5.1 *(continued)*

ILO and UN Covenants and Conventions (Emphasis added in bold)			Date Ratified					
Title (ordered by date open for ratification)	Dates • Open for ratification • In force	Fair pay provision (emphasis added)	Canada	India	Malaysia	South Africa	United Kingdom	United States
		The rights to work, to free choice of employment, to just and favourable conditions of work, to protection against unemployment, to **equal pay for equal work**…						
Covenant on Economic, Social and Cultural Rights / Equal Work / Equal Value	Dec, 1966 / Jan 1976	Article 7: (a) Remuneration which provides **all workers**, as a minimum, with: (i) Fair wages and **equal remuneration for work of equal value** without distinction of any kind, **in particular women** being guaranteed conditions of work not inferior to those enjoyed by men, with **equal pay for equal work;**	May 1976	April 1979	Not ratified	Oct. 1994	May 1976	Oct. 1977

			Dec. 1981	July 1993	July 1995	Dec. 1995	April 1986	July 1980
Convention on the Elimination of All forms of Discrimination against **women** Equal value	Dec 1979 Sept 1981	Article 11 1. States Parties shall take all appropriate measures to eliminate discrimination against women in the field of employment. . . . in particular: . . . (d) The right to **equal remuneration, including benefits, and to equal treatment in respect of work of equal value**, as well as equality of treatment in the evaluation of the quality of work; (e) The right to **social security**, particularly in cases of retirement, unemployment, sickness, invalidity and old age and other incapacity to work, as well as the right to paid leave.						

Source: Taken from ILO and United National conventions found at http://ilolex.ilo.ch:1567/english/iloquery.htm.

Figure 5.1 **Female and Male Labour Force Participation**

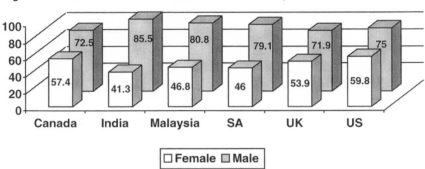

Source: Table 1a *Yearbook of Labour Statistics*. Geneva: International Labour Organization, 2001.

work; Maatta (1998) notes that women's work is more invisible in developing countries than in developed countries because a larger number of women work in the informal sector.

When discussing unfair pay, the statistic typically quoted is the wage ratio—the proportion that women's wages are of men's, or the proportion that people of color's wages are relative to those of whites. Since governments often publish the average wages for men and women, it is possible to calculate the female-male ratio; racial wage differentials tend to be available only through academic research studies. Figure 5.2 shows the female-male wage differential for the six countries, though these figures may not be exactly comparable—some are for full-time, full-year employees only, others for all workers, plus they are based on data from different years. The UK (82 percent), South Africa (80 percent), and the United States (75 percent) have the highest ratios (women's earnings are closest to men's), while Canada (69.9 percent), India (52.7 percent), and Malaysia (52 percent) have the lowest.

In trying to comprehend issues of fair pay, interpretation of these wage ratios is not straightforward. Some of the ratios could be due to valid differences in human capital investment. For example, in South Africa, whites have a higher level of education than Africans and hold more responsible jobs. Greater education leading to higher salaries is seen as a valid reason for part of any wage differential, as is performing more responsible jobs. However, the greater educational level of whites is due to past (nonmarket) discriminatory practices against Africans. Furthermore, part of the wage differential could be due to direct wage discrimination—the three kinds discussed in this chapter. Academic researchers try to determine what proportion of the wage differential is due to (1) valid factors (e.g., education, experience) and other explanatory variables (even if some of these are due to nonwage discrimination) and (2) discrimination and

Figure 5.2 **Female-Male Wage Ratio**

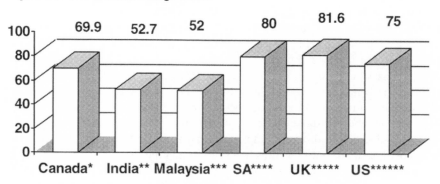

*1999, Full-time workers, Statistics Canada.

**1995, Maatta (1998), for non-agricultural sectors, 1995.

***1991, Asian Development Bank Country Briefing: Women in Malaysia, 1998.

****2000, Commission on Gender Equality, *http://www.cge.org.za/* Retrieved January 23, 2002.

*****2001, New Earnings Survey Streamlined Analysis GB, Full-time workers Tables A16 (male) and A17 (female) *http://www.statistics.gov.uk/statbase/Product. asp?vlnk=5749&More=N.*

******1995, Altonji and Blank, 1995.

unexplained factors. Researchers try to measure as many valid/explanatory factors as they can (i.e., human capital, number of young children [for women], geographic area, industry). What these variables do not explain is assumed to be due, at least in part, to discrimination, though it is recognized that there are likely to be unexplained factors that were not examined. Some of the unexplained factors could be valid but difficult to measure; for example, education is typically measured in terms of the number of years of schooling, but the quality of the education (e.g., university attended) is not measured and could make a difference in pay.

Of concern with regard to issues raised in this chapter is the way occupation is measured in the research. Given the importance of occupational segregation to equal value issues, using occupation to try to understand wage ratios is important. However, occupation data can be very broad (i.e., professional) or more specifically defined (i.e., nurses and engineers or hospital nurses and electrical engineers). Occupational segregation is more likely to be detected when more narrowly defined occupations are used. In fact, Levine (2001, 9) notes that studies that use detailed occupational classifications are better able to explain wage differences than those that use broader occupations. Some broader occupations tend to be very gender specific—for example, clerical work is seen as female in North America, even though some particular jobs within this occupation (e.g., Computer Operator, Mailroom Clerk, Shipping and Receiving Clerk) are typically male. For instance, the broad occupation, professional, has many narrower occupations which are gender specific, for example, elementary teachers compared to university professors. Since this chapter is concerned with firm-level discrimination, it is really jobs, not occupations, that are of interest. However, the data available for most studies of wage ratios tend to be aggregated across different jobs, across different employers, and across different industries, so it is impossible to separate out firm-level discrimination, let alone whether it has to do with salary administration discrimination, or unequal pay for equal work or for equal value concerns. One very unique study focusing on gender (Schumann et al. 1999) collected individual characteristics for employees in different jobs and organizations but evaluated all the jobs on the same set of criteria (factors). They found only a small relationship between the human capital, characteristics of job incumbents, and the total job points of their jobs (p. 498).[4] Thus, although some research studies on gender and racial wage ratios are reported in this chapter, they should be used cautiously in terms of the main concern of the chapter—firm-level wage discrimination.

In the remainder of this section, first gender and then racial issues related to fair pay are discussed. Table 5.2 summarizes the legislation found in each country addressing various aspects of pay. Minimum wage legislation is included in Table 5.2 since in a number of the countries (both developing and developed) it is seen as an important contribution to helping women, concentrated in low paying jobs, begin to receive fair pay. Four of the six countries have minimum wage legislation—Malaysia and South Africa do not. A general prohibition against discrimination based on gender and race covering all employment functions (and thus the compensation function) is found in all countries except India and, for gender, the United Kingdom, though the UK has legislation requiring equal work and equal value for women. A specific requirement for equal pay for equal work for women is found in four countries, but not in Malaysia or South Africa; no country specifically requires equal work based on race. Specific, clearly designed equal value legislation related to gender is found in Canada and the UK. Related to equal value issues, South Africa requires data collection and redressing of wage differentials on the basis of both gender and race within occupations in its Employment Equity Act. The United States has some proposed legislation and some regulations requiring data collection based on gender and race that could be used to begin to redress equal value issues. No country has the full range of legislation necessary to fulfill the international conventions they have signed (except the United States which has not ratified the equal pay for work of equal value convention).

Table 5.2
Legislation Related to Fair Pay in Six Countries

Country	Minimum wage	General prohibition including salary administration		Equal Work		Equal Value	
		Gender	Race	Gender	Race	Gender	Race
Canada	Canada Labour Code	Canadian Charter of Rights & Freedoms, 1985 Canadian Human Rights Act, 1976		Canadian Labour Code Canadian Human Rights Act, 1976		Canadian Human Rights Act, 1978 (9 of 10 provinces have either legislation or program)	
India	Minimum wage, 1948			Equal Remuneration Act, 1976 (as amended 1987)			
Malaysia		Constitution—gender added August 2001. Islamic laws only apply to Muslims; Employment Act (1955) covers wages and benefits [only applies to Peninsular Malaysia while Sabah and Sarawak have their own legislation]					

(continued)

Table 5.2 (continued)

Country	Minimum wage	General prohibition including salary administration		Equal Work		Equal Value	
		Gender	Race	Gender	Race	Gender	Race
South Africa		Constitution (1996) Employment Equity Act 1998, S.5 (unfair discrimination) Labour Relations Act, 1995 (unfair labour practices) Promotion of Equality & Prevention of Unfair Discrimination Act, 4 (2000) Wage Act				Employment Equity Act (S.27)	Employment Equity Act (S.27)
U.K.	Minimum Wage Act, 1999		Race Relations Act (1976, amended 2000)	Equal Pay Act (1970, amended 1983)		Equal Pay Act (1970)	
United States	Fair Labor Standards Act	Civil Rights Act (1964)		Equal Pay Act (1963) S 703(a) of 1964 Civil Rights Act 42 States have legislation		Regulatory agencies may use Title VII (EEOC) and Contractors Program (OFCCP) to collect salary information to compare between women and men, and people of colour and whites 20 out of 50 state governments have some legislation or voluntary program (Hartmann and Aronson 1994)	

Source: Compiled by author.

First, gender issues and then race is discussed for each of the six countries. Each section begins with the countries that are redressing the more difficult pay discrimination—equal value. The discussion of each country typically provides some brief background and relevant research on the wage gap, a detailed discussion of the most advanced legislative response and any research relevant to the legislation's effectiveness follows.

Fair Pay and Gender

More has been done to redress gender pay discrimination than racial. Canada has the most extensive record in this regard, followed by the UK, South Africa, and the United States. India is addressing equal pay for equal work, while Malaysia has neither minimum wage legislation nor legislation beyond a general requirement not to discriminate.

Countries That Are Attempting to Remove Unequal Pay for Equal Value

Canada

Fifty-seven percent of women (compared to 73 percent of men) are in the labor force; the gender wage ratio provided by Statistics Canada is 69.9 percent for full-time, full-year workers. Canada is highly unionized (about 40 percent of the workforce), particularly in the public sector which employs a large proportion of women. A recent study (Drolet 2001,14) found that the gender wage gap has declined over time with an unexplained gap (some of which can be attributed to discrimination) of 11 percent to 16 percent (the lower gap controls for occupation and industry). In Drolet's (2001) review of the literature, she notes that none of the research can account for a substantial portion of the gap using human capital and job-related responsibilities (e.g., supervision)—leading to the conclusion that discrimination still exists, though it has been declining. In her particular study, Drolet (2001, 14) is unable to explain a half to three-quarters of the gap. Gender occupational segregation is also declining but is still present. Although there has been a recent trend of women entering into careers typically associated with men, it has not eliminated gender-based occupational segregation. For example, among forty-six occupations listed[5] in order of their proportion of female incumbents, the top five (secretaries, nurses, child care and home support, cashiers, and health-assisting occupations) each had at least 85 percent women; the proportion for secretaries was 98 percent women. Conversely, the bottom five occupations (senior management, professions in natural and applied sciences, protective services, technical occupations in natural and applied sciences, and trades) each had less than 21 percent women; there were only 6 percent women in the trades (Statistics Canada 1996).[6] These ten occupations constitute 30 percent of the Canadian labor force.

Canada has legislation covering all the current fair pay issues. Since Canada has the most extensive equal value legislation, this is the focus of this section. Canada is a federation where, in labor matters, both the federal government and the provincial (and territorial) governments can enact their own legislation covering different sets of employers.[7] The federal government and all but one of the provinces have a commitment to equal value. Equal value was initially incorporated into human rights legislation in the 1970s by the Province of Quebec and the federal government. Inclusion in human rights legislation meant that a complaint-based (compared to proactive) system was used to redress discrimination. In effect, only when there is a complaint is equal value enforced for those jobs involved in a proven complaint.[8] In the mid-1980s, provinces began passing proactive legislation. This placed a positive obligation on employers to examine their wage determination systems for all their female jobs—not just jobs for which there had been a complaint. Quebec has since changed to a proactive approach. The pay equity provision of the Canadian Human Rights Act is currently under review, and its complaint-based nature has been questioned by the Canadian Human Rights Commission that implements the Act (Canadian Human Rights Commission 2001). A proactive approach is consistent with the systemic nature (rather than interpersonal discrimination) of equal value discrimination. Systemic discrimination is (unintentionally) built into a neutral employment system (i.e., compensation system) that is not designed to discriminate but has this unintended effect. Proactive legislation assumes that discrimination may be found in compensation systems against female jobs and requires an assessment to determine whether it exists within organizations, and if it is found it must be redressed. Regardless of the jurisdiction, achieving pay equity, proactively, basically follows the same steps:

- **Definition of employer:** Female and male jobs are considered within the same establishment. Establishments can be subsets of organizations based on geography, for instance. Establishment was the issue in the *Air Canada* case (*Canadian Union of Public Employees v. Canadian Airlines International Ltd.*, [2000] F.C.J. No. 1258), which to date has come up with a complicated determination of establishment, which, in this case, basically finds each bargaining unit to be an establishment. This decision is being appealed.
- **Gender predominance:** Female-predominant and male-predominant jobs are identified. Typically, a cutoff of 60 percent or 70 percent is used to determine gender predominance (see Weiner and Gunderson, 1990 for a summary of cutoffs used in various Canadian jurisdictions).
- **Job evaluation:** A gender-neutral job evaluation system must be used to ascertain the value of female and male jobs measuring skill, effort, respon-

sibility, and working conditions. The gender neutrality of the Willis job evaluation system was an issue in the federal government case (Treasury Board Secretariat) involving two of its unions (Public Service Alliance of Canada and Professional Institute of Public Service of Canada). The tribunal found the system to be gender-neutral, given the state of knowledge of gender neutrality, when it was used (1996 Joint Union Management Initiative (JUMI) decision–*PSAC (No. 2) v. Canada (Treasury Board)* 29 C.H.R.R. D/349 (Can. Trib.)).

- **Equal pay:** Female jobs found to be of equal (comparable) value to male jobs must be paid the same (it is typically the maximum of the salary ranges that must match). The most typical mechanism to determine whether equally valued female and male jobs are paid fairly is to draw a male wage line (least-squares regression line of maximum salary for male jobs and their job evaluation points) and either moving female jobs below the line, up to the line (job-to-line approach) or moving the female wage line up to the male wage line (line-to-line approach). To be clear, when ensuring "fair pay," both men and women in female jobs benefit if their job is found to be underpaid relative to its value, while neither men nor women in male-dominated jobs benefit. (Methodology was a major issue in the *JUMI* case; the tribunal decision (*PSAC (No. 3) v. Canada (Treasury Board)* (1998), 32 C.H. R.R. D/349 (Can. Trib.) was judicially reviewed, and the court in its 1999 decision stated that the Act should result in applying approaches that remedy systemic dissemination and so unduly restrictive methodologies should be avoided.

- **Allowable differences**[9]: Individual men and women working in jobs of equal value can be paid differently owing to such factors as seniority, merit, temporary skill shortage, and red-circling (which partially freezes employees' wages because their job has been found to be less valuable to the organization than its current pay warrants) (see Weiner and Gunderson, 1990, for the allowable exceptions in various jurisdictions).

- **Adjustments:** Pay equity adjustments are made differently under complaint-based and proactive approaches as follows:

  a. Complaint-based (federal): retroactive pay back to one year prior to the complaint.
  b. Proactive: 1 percent of the organization's total previous year's payroll (for all jobs, not just female-dominated jobs) becomes a "pool" of money that must be spent on pay equity adjustments each year. One percent of payroll continues to be paid out each year until pay equity is achieved, or, in some jurisdictions, a time limit is set, for example, four years.

- **Maintenance:** pay equity must be maintained.

Given the greater experience of pay equity in Canada, some research has been done to ascertain its effects. Weiner (1995) looked at various outcomes for five Canadian provinces and one U.S. state (Minnesota). She found that the Canadian jurisdictions had a higher average annual adjustment ($2,520 in New Brunswick to $3,600 in Manitoba) than did the state of Minnesota ($1,600). The costs of pay equity as a percentage of payroll ranged from 2.5 percent in Ontario (before amendments to their Act) to 4.9 percent in Prince Edward Island. Pay equity removed approximately a third of the organizational wage gap in Minnesota, Manitoba, and Nova Scotia, 42 percent in British Columbia, and 52 percent in Prince Edward Island. Ontario's legislation covers the largest number of employers—some 7,000 to 8,000. Because employers are not required to report their pay equity results, there is no comprehensive database of all outcomes. However, the Ontario Pay Equity Commission surveyed employers to determine some of the effects of pay equity (Canadian Facts 1992 and 1993; Institute of Social Research 1994; SPR 1991). These studies have been summarized in Gunderson (1995, Table 4). Average pay equity adjustments ranged from 6.7 percent (private sector organizations with 500 to 999 employees) to 19.8 percent (public sector employers with 100to 499 employees). The cost, as a percentage of an organization's payroll, varied from 0.6 percent (private sector with 500 or more employees) to 2.9 percent (public sector with 100 to 499 employees). However, these data do not provide a full picture for two reasons. First, many employers had not completed their pay equity plans when they were surveyed, and second, the surveys were conducted before the 1993 amendments to the Act. The amendments added the job-to-line and line-to-line means of determining equal pay[10] and provided the ability to make comparison across organizations in the broader public sector. Both of these changes are likely to have increased the coverage and the costs of the adjustments. Second, Gunderson (1995) looked at a hodgepodge of employers, and since there is a tendency to report "success stories" the data are likely to be upwardly biased. Still he reports a trimmed average adjustment of about $4,000 or a 22 percent increase for those jobs that received an adjustment. He tentatively concludes that adjustments were larger in the union sector and in the public sector. McDonald and Thornton (1998) looked at twenty-seven private sector organizations, primarily large firms in Toronto. Most provided small adjustments (about 5 percent of base salary) costing less than 1.5 percent of payroll (p. 192). They found that administrative costs were larger than the adjustments. Interestingly, most firms, 59 percent, rated their pay equity experience as a positive one. Baker and Fortin (2000) have conducted a research study specifically meant to determine whether pay equity has had an impact in Ontario (after ten years of pay equity) as compared with Quebec before it had proactive legislation. They found no evidence of any impact. However, their study was not done within individual employers, so their finding may be due to a lack of sustained impact or because their measurements were too macro. While taken together, these data appear to indicate that pay equity has had an effect on providing wage increases, but the lack of comprehensive data makes it difficult to draw clear conclusions. No Canadian research has looked at the employment effects (whether higher wages for female jobs leads to less employment), but U.S. studies indicate that there are few effects (Hartmann and Aaronson 1994; review in Gunderson 1995).

United Kingdom

The UK has a higher rate of labor force participation by women (72 percent) than other European Union (EU) countries (though they have a higher proportion of women working part-time) and one of the widest hourly gender pay gaps (18 percent) within the European Union (EU) (twelfth out of fifteen) (Kingsmill 2001, 6, 20).[11] Thirty percent of all women work in the public sector compared to less than 20 percent of men. The public sector is most highly unionized in a country where 40 percent of workers are unionized. Still, 31 percent of working women hold low-wage jobs compared to 13 percent of men. The government's position is that a quarter to a half of the 18 percent wage gap is due to discrimination (Employment Minister at launch of Equal Opportunities Commission's Taskforce report, April 2001). The public sector has a smaller wage gap (14 percent) than the private sector (22 percent) (Kingsmill 2001, 25). Occupational segregation results in over 60 percent of women working in ten occupations (out of a total of seventy-seven).[12]

The European Community (EC) has required equal pay for equal value (consistent with ILO Convention 100) since the late 1970s. Great Britain had legislation at that time which covered both the public and private sectors and included homeworkers, part-time workers, and casual workers in addition to regular, full-time employees. However, this legislation did not fulfill the equal pay for work of equal value requirement as defined in Convention 100 and was amended.[13] Half the equal value cases within the EC have been from the UK. The original British legislation, Equal Pay Act, 1970, came into full force at the end of 1975. In 1982, the European Court of Justice ruled against the UK in an equal value case; this led to the Equal Value (amendment) Regulations of 1983, adding a broader requirement for equal pay for work of equal value. Before the amendment, a woman could file a complaint of unequal pay for work of equal value *if* the employer had already conducted a job evaluation study. With the amendment three kinds of wage discrimination complaints could now be brought (McCrudden 1993):

- Equal work[14]—job evaluation *may* be used to resolve issue.
- Equivalent work—where job evaluation had been voluntarily undertaken by an employer.

- Equal value—where employer does not have a JE system; JE *must* be used to ascertain if jobs are of equal value.

The processes for proving a case are somewhat different under each of the above. All are complaint-based, but unlike Canada's complaint-based legislation where a union can bring a complaint on behalf of numerous female jobs and/or a human rights commission could pursue a case, in Great Britain only an individual employee can pursue complaint. It is the individual claimant's duty to choose the comparator and to prove that equal value exists. To aid in comparing the UK and Canadian processes for pay equity, the same headings that outlined the Canadian process are used in the following. In a number of places, the legislation in Great Britain is significantly different.

- **Definition of employer:** The jobs must be part of the same or an associated employer.[15] Associated employers are those where one employer has direct or indirect control over the other, or both are controlled by a common third party. Court decisions have defined "associated" broadly; for example, two different organizations were defined as associated because the same government ministry regulated them. If the female and male jobs are within the same employer, it is assumed that the terms and conditions of employment are the same. This assumption is not made if the two jobs are employed by associated employers.
- **Gender predominance:** This is not an issue since complaints are on an individual basis—one person identifies another (of the opposite gender), and their two jobs are compared.
- **Job evaluation:** If an organization has a *gender-neutral* job evaluation system that shows the two jobs *not* to be of equal value, then equivalent value is not established. If there is no job evaluation system, then the industrial tribunal engages the services of an independent expert to determine equal value; the expert selects the factors (criteria) on which to assess the value of the jobs. Since the 1983 amendments to the Act, JE has become more important.[16] The JE system must consider effort, skill, and decision, and the Equal Opportunities Commission recommends also using responsibility and working conditions.
- **Equal pay:** Pay is defined comprehensively under the Equal Pay Act to include bonuses, overtime, holiday pay, sick pay, performance-related pay, or occupational pensions. Where potential male (female) comparators are paid different rates, the woman (man) can choose the highest one to compare to. With respect to what constitutes "equal pay," the House of Lords (which hears appeals) decided that it is not a matter of comparing total compensation to total compensation (e.g., wages plus benefits) but that if any term of the woman's (man's) employment contract is less favorable

than that of the male (female) comparator, it should be made equal to the comparator's terms.[17]

- **Allowable differences (material differences):** Can include individual success, for example, commission or bonus. Alternatively, the employer can argue that there is a business necessity, for example, labor shortage. Material difference has been found to include market forces.[18] In another case [*Mrs. E. Rainey v. Greater Glasgow Health Board* (1987 IRLR 26) (House of Lords)], a man was paid a higher salary because he was recruited from the private sector—this was seen as a justifiable reason for a pay difference.
- **Adjustments:** Compensation must be made equal; there can be back pay for up to two years.
- **Maintenance:** Equal pay must be maintained for the individual who successfully showed that the jobs were of equal value. However, there is no requirement to provide equal pay to others in a similar situation (e.g., same job but different position).

The Equal Opportunities Commission (EOC) oversees the Equal Pay Act and has developed a Code of Practice on Equal Pay (May 1997). The EOC (and unions) can aid employees but cannot bring cases before a tribunal (EIRO 2002; UK report, item 3.2). In 1994–1995, 418 cases before tribunals were disposed of as follows—286 (68 percent) were withdrawn, 98 (24 percent) were settled by conciliation, 17 (4 percent) were dismissed by tribunal, nine (2 percent) were otherwise disposed of, and seven (less 2 percent) were successful in proving unequal pay for equal value (Maatta 1998). The 1983 amendments revived the legislation since the number of equal pay claims before industrial tribunals in Great Britain fell from 1,742 in 1976 to 39 in 1982 (EMIRE 2002).

How effective is the Equal Pay Act? The Trades Union Congress (TUC) has criticized the legislative process because it is complex and unclear, resulting in long delays; furthermore, they do not feel that an employer's existing JE study should be allowed to be used in equivalent value cases, and they decry the fact that an equal pay decision cannot be extended from an individual applicant to all employees in the same establishment who do the same or broadly the same work (ILO 1994). In 2001, two reviews of the Equal Pay Act were published, one by a Task Force of the Equal Opportunities Commission (EOC 2001) and one by a consultant hired by the government (Kingsmill 2001). The EOC Equal Pay Task Force set a "goal that the gender pay gap caused by discrimination should be reduced by 50 percent within the next 5 years and eliminated entirely within 8 years" (Equal Pay Task Force 2001, ix). Others have estimated that at its current rate of change it will take 20 years to close the gender wage gap (EIRO 2002: UK report, comment section). The government has rejected the Equal Pay Task Force's recommendation for mandatory equal pay reviews for the private sector and is going to work toward voluntary reviews (EIRO 2002: UK report, items 3.4, 3.5). Some of the key recommendations made by the government's consultant are as follows (Kingsmill 2001, 12–13, 15–16):

- Employers should be required to disclose relevant information before an application is made to an industrial tribunal (e.g., provide employees with confirmation whether he/she is receiving remuneration equal to a named colleague).
- Mandatory pay equity audits should be required for the public sector and voluntary audits for private sector. (The government has funded the EOC to prepare a model for voluntary pay reviews.)
- Government should monitor voluntary efforts for the private sector to determine whether legislation is needed.

Some research has examined the gender wage gap and the effects of the Equal Pay Act. The Act's impact on employment was studied by Manning (1996), which did not find an adverse employment effect. Joshi and Paci (1998) examined wage effects by comparing two cohorts, both in their 30s—one born in 1946 and the other in 1958. So the first cohort was in its 30s just after the Equal Pay Act became effective, and the second cohort was in their 30s after the Act had been in place for ten years, and after the critical 1983 amendment. There are some differences between the two cohorts—the latter has a higher level of education and greater incidence of full-time employment, later childbearing, and fewer interruptions in their work history. As expected, the wage gap was smaller for the later cohort, dropping from a little over 30 percent to 16.7 percent. The authors conclude that virtually all of the smaller gap is due to unfavorable treatment of women workers in the full-time labor market, compared to only two-thirds of the larger (earlier) gap. In other words, the part of the gap that is due to human capital differences has disappeared as human capital differences have disappeared, but the majority of the gap due to discrimination remains. They examined the effects of the legislation and concluded that equal pay legislation seems to have improved the treatment of the majority of women working full-time (though not at a statistically significant level). A study by Dolton et al. (1996) concluded that the decrease in the wage gap in the early 1970s was due to gender-specific forces, either the impact of equal pay legislation or a convergence in unobservable skills, rather than income policies (government limitations on wage inflation).

The government has also undertaken efforts other than the Equal Pay Act to decrease the gender wage gap within the public sector. In March 2001, the central government committed to a proactive review of pay and to prepare action plans within two years for departments and agencies in order to close the gender wage gap (Kingsmill 2001, 9). Since 30 percent of women are employed in the public sector, this is expected to have an impact. Furthermore, the government introduced a statutory national minimum wage for all workers (full, part-time, permanent, temporary, and casual) in 1999 which gave over one million women an immediate pay raise (Cabinet Office undated). Women are twice as likely as men to be affected by minimum wage legislation; with half of all part-time women workers being affected (EIRO 2002: UK report, item 3.6).

Countries Responding to Potential Equal Value Discrimination with Data Collection Response

South Africa

In South Africa, women and Africans, particularly in rural areas, disproportionately comprise the poor. Only 46 percent of women are in the labor force. Women earn 80 percent of what men earn, though this is highly influenced by race—many Asian and white women are earning more than African and coloured men (Bhorat 2001). A comparison of educational levels and wages shows that that African women have two more years of schooling than African men but the same average pay when domestic workers are excluded (Maharaj 1999). When domestic workers, most of whom are women, are included, there is a gender wage gap. Seventeen percent of South African women with jobs are domestics—most are African women (Itano 2001). Even though men's and women's educational levels are equal, women earn only 67 percent of what men do (Maharaj 1999). Indian women have both lower education and lower wages than Indian men, earning 74 percent of what Indian men do; for coloured women the ratio is 82 percent. Interestingly enough, while average educational attainment differs by race,[19] women's average educational level is 1.2 years greater than men's (Maharaj 1999). The wage gap exists even though a higher proportion of women (21 percent) works in professional jobs (teaching and nursing) compared to only 12 percent of men in professional jobs (Maharaj 1999). Erichsen and Wakeford (2001), in one of the few research studies that examined gender in addition to race, found similar patterns in explaining the gender and the racial wage differentials. Whites and men are overpaid relative to their productivity characteristics. Above-average productivity characteristics of white women accounted for 71 percent of the wage differential in 1993 and 66 percent in 1995. About a third of nondomestic workers are unionized, compared to 35 percent of men and 29 percent of women (Canadian International Development Agency 2001).

South Africa is clearly a country in transition. Its Constitution and labor legislation are relatively new (since 1996). As noted in Table 5.2, there are a number of pieces of legislation promoting fairness, of a general nature. With respect to equal value, the Employment Equity Act requires organizations to report on wages and reduce differentials based on gender and race—more is said about this topic in the next section covering racial issues since there are few legislative responses related to race. Furthermore, the government is considering basic income grants as a form of minimum wage. In addition, the Promotion of Equality and Prevention of Discrimination Act (2000) and the Labor Relations Act (1995) also prohibit discrimination. The former prohibits discrimination by government, individuals, and organizations whether such discrimination is intended or unintended. The Labor Relations Act prohibits discrimination by an employer against an employee. Moreover, the government is considering a basic income grant as a form of minimum wage.

United States

Of the six countries studied, the United States has the highest labor force participation rate of women, 59.8 percent (compared to 75 percent for men). Women are disproportionately employed in the public sector, and it has been public sector unions that have tended to push for equal value—at both the federal and state level. While overall unionization is about 13 percent, public sector unionization rate is about 40 percent and only about 10 percent of the private sector is unionized. Occupational segregation for women has declined, though it still remains, and job characteristics are found to explain a substantial part of the male-female wage differential (Altonji and Blank 1999, 3220). The national female-male ratio is 75 percent. Researchers find that the aggregate male-female wage ratio was relatively stable between the post–World War II era and the late 1970s, and since then there has been a major decline in the gap (Altonji and Blank 1999, 3240). This is consistent with women's human capital increases during this period, though women's return on education is less than men's (Altonji and Blank 1999, 3241). Changes in experience have been more important than changes in education in closing the male-female gap. Almost all studies indicate that comparable worth policies raise women's wages relative to men's (Altonji and Blank 1999, 3247)—though the employment effects are less clear. From a review of the literature Altonji and Blank (1999, 3249–3250) conclude that there is still a substantial gender wage gap, even though it has been declining over the last two decades, and that a large share of gender differential remains unexplained even after controlling for detailed measures of individual and job characteristics. (This is unlike the black-white wage differential where there is little unexplained variance once skill is included.)

The United States has never ratified ILO conventions 100 or 111 dealing with equal value and gender prohibitions, respectively. In 1980, the U.S. ratified the UN Convention on Elimination of All forms of Discrimination against Women—

this convention may guarantee women equal pay for equal value, but it does not state this explicitly as Convention 100 does. In terms of their own legislation, in 1963 the Equal Pay Act (an amendment to the Fair Labor Standard Act) provided for equal pay for equal work within the same establishment, allowing differences due to seniority, merit, or productivity, or any factor other than gender. This legislation passed the year before the more general antidiscrimination legislation—the 1964 Civil Rights Act, of which Title VII prohibits discrimination in all areas of employment including compensation. Women were not initially included in the Civil Rights Act when it was proposed, and, in fact, women were added in an attempt to defeat the bill (Bellace 1993).

The history of comparable worth or pay equity in the United States has not been as clear-cut as in Great Britain. During World War II, the National War Labor Board used a comparable worth standard, but this did not continue to influence human rights thinking after the war. Because of a link between the Equal Pay Act and Title VII, it was unclear whether Title VII could be used to redress equal value situations. In the 1981 *Gunther* decision, the Supreme Court stated that Title VII should be broadly interpreted as prohibiting a broad spectrum of sex-based practices, but the Court did not specifically address the issue of equal value cases. In the 1980s, comparable worth was not of interest at the federal level, so pay equity proponents turned to the state level.[20] Hartmann and Aaronson (1994) note that twenty states have some level of involvement in pay equity.[21] The state of Minnesota's legislation was the most extensive covering the public service and the broader public sector (i.e., universities, county and municipal governments).[22]

At the federal level efforts have been made along two fronts for equal value—first, to use current legislation and the federal contractors' program, and second, to try to introduce new legislation. The federal contractors' program covers both gender and race and requires affirmative action programs as a condition of doing business with the federal government for employers with at least fifty employees and with a single contract of $50,000.[23] This program is overseen by the Office of Federal Contract Compliance Programs (OFCCP). Recent regulations require the OFCCP to collect data, within nine occupational groups, on average salaries by race and gender—more is said about data collection in the section on race.

Two pieces of legislation related to wage discrimination have been introduced but have not passed. In 1995, the Fair Pay Act was introduced to provide for equal pay for equal value based on both gender and race. Some support for this legislation comes from a Department of Labor (undated) study that found that since 1979, the contribution of occupational segregation to the pay gap jumped from explaining 18 percent to 46 percent of the gap. The Fair Pay Act would allow exceptions for different wage rates based on seniority, merit, or quantity or quality of work. In 1999, the Paycheck Fairness Act was introduced seeking to strengthen the Equal Pay Act of 1963 which requires equal pay for equal work. The bill would expand damages under the Equal Pay Act and would amend its very broad exception of "factors other than sex"[24] and make it easier to bring class action suits. In addition, the Paycheck Fairness Act proposes that the Department of Labor develop voluntary guidelines to show employers how to evaluate jobs with the goal of eliminating unfair disparities (National Committee on Pay Equity, undated; National Women's Law Center, 2002). It is unlikely that these pieces of legislation will pass under a republican president (Bush), especially since their passage failed passage under a democratic president who supported them (Clinton).

In a particularly interesting study, because both job value and human capital characteristics were included, Schumann et al. (1999, 498) found that the gross gender wage gap was 34 percent in the sample of jobs examined. When JE points were used to explain wages, the gap was reduced to 24 percent; with just human capital characteristics the gap was about the same, 26 percent. When both JE and human capital characteristics were used, the gap was lowered to 16 percent, about half of the gross gap. This is one of the only studies that used firm-level data and included job evaluation point-values as a variable; thus, it is particularly relevant to measuring the need for equal value efforts. Gunderson (1995, 233–236) reviewed the U.S. literature in terms of pay equity outcomes. Based on simulations, the earning gap could be closed by somewhere between 8 and 50 percent, with estimates for the average increase of 16 to 34 percent and the cost of payroll being 8 percent. Gunderson's review of the actual U.S. results showed that the gap was closed by about a third and that the costs were 4 to 8 percent of payroll. Hartmann and Aaronson (1994) report on twenty U.S. states. The costs of adjustments for sixteen states on which there was data ranged from 1 percent of payroll to 11.8 percent (which involved total revision to the compensation system rather than just pay equity) (p.79). Classical economic analysis maintains that as wages go up, employment goes down. The research indicates no effect (Hartmann and Aaronson 1994) or small employment effects due to pay equity (Kahn 1992). For example, in Minnesota it was found that women on the state payroll increased by 17.2 percent rather than the 20 percent expected if there had not been pay equity adjustments; while men's employment rose 2.9 percent rather than 3.9 percent, it would have without pay equity. The literature generally finds evidence that antidiscrimination laws have made a difference, particularly in the 1960s and 1970s (Altonji and Blank 1999, 3246). Chen et al. (1999), however, raise a concern about measurement error in job evaluation. Their examination of the state of Iowa's pay equity process estimated that 34 percent to 44 percent of the discrimination found was due to measurement error. This study was conducted at the level of the firm.

Blau and Kahn (1999), looking at the broader economy, have determined that one reason for the gender wage gap is the large wage inequity between jobs (not just gendered jobs) within the U.S. labor market. This explains why, despite the high qualifications of women in the United States and stronger anti-discrimination laws compared to those in other countries, the United States has such a large wage gap. As the authors note, "gender-specific factors, including differences in qualifications and the impact of labor market discrimination, may be regarded as determining the percentile ranking of women in the male wage distribution, while the overall wage structure (as measured by the magnitude of male wage inequality) determines the wage penalty or reward associated with this position in the wage distribution" (p. 632).

Countries with Equal Work Legislation

India

Women's labor force participation in India is 41.3 percent, the lowest of any of the countries studied, though this figure understates the proportion of working women since it misses those in the informal sector. Women's labor force participation rate is unevenly divided between rural (27 percent of women in labor force) and urban (9 percent) (Dunlop and Velkoff 1999, 2). Looking at the kind of work women do in the formal sector, we find that the largest proportions, about 20 percent each, are concentrated in clerical/computer work, some of which is relatively high paying, and stitching, which is low paying; an additional 10 percent work in production/manufacturing and in patient care, of which nursing work is highly paid (SARDI 1999, 9).

The gender wage gap is 47.3 percent. The Indian economy is characterized by diverse wage-setting forces such as minimum wage legislation, wage boards, court adjudications, and collective bargaining (in the public sector, guidelines affect wage negotiations). Women's lower wages are probably a combination of lower skill level,[25] occupational segregation, assumptions that women are supported by men, family responsibilities, and lack of enforcement of minimum wage legislation, particularly for women. Furthermore, women's earnings are less because they are restricted from working overtime and night shifts (SARDI 1999, 5, 6, and 8). As in many developing countries, most women work in the informal sector; some estimates range as high as 90 percent (Dunlop and Velkoff 1999, 2); this sector includes domestic services, small traders, artisans, or field laborers on family farms. Women's work in the informal sector has a profound effect on their earnings: the average wage in this sector was found to be three times lower than in the formal sector. Moreover, unionized women earn twice as much as unorganized women (SARDI 1999, 12). Unlike some other countries (i.e., North America), public sector wages for women are *less* egalitarian, though the public sector is where many women work (Dunlop and Velkoff 1999, 3).

India's legislative response includes minimum wage legislation and the Equal Remuneration Act (passed in 1976 and amended in 1987). Given that women's wages are low, payment of the minimum wages would often provide *de facto* equal wages (Maatta 1998). However, the minimum wage legislation is not always enforced; this appears to be more of a problem for women than men (SARDI 1999, 11, and a study by the Ministry of Labor reported in ILO, CEACR 1992). The Equal Remuneration Act requires equal pay for equal work. The 1987 amendments to this Act increased the penalties, expanded coverage (promotions, training, transfer), and made the complaint process more extensive (allowing advocacy organizations to file complaints). The Act covers all industries and public and private sectors, organized and unorganized work, including permanent, temporary, and causal work, but it excludes women who are in agriculture, or domestic workers (Maatta 1998). which is the majority of the female labor force. Equal work needs to be achieved within an establishment.

The Supreme Court has noted that equal work should be defined to be "broadly similar," but this interpretation is still short of Convention 100's requirement of equal pay for work of equal value (*Mackinnon* case reported in Jain and Ratnam 1996, 5–6; and ILO CEACR 1999). The Centre for Indian Trade Unions (CITU) feels that there is a lack of serious effort on the part of the government with respect to the Act, that the powers to grant exemptions are grossly misused (ILO, CEACR 1991, 1992, 1997), and that the enforcement is effective in the public sector but not in other parts of the formal and informal sectors (ILO CEACR 1999). In 1993–1994, inspections rectified more than 3,500 violations of the Equal Remuneration Act (ILO CEACR 1997); in 1995, 37,323 state inspections were carried out, finding 5,543 violations, while the central government carried out 4,468 inspections that detected 4,373 violations (ILO CEACR 1999). The ILO reports do not indicate the rate of prosecution and convictions, which Jain and Ratnam (1996, 11) conclude are low. But these figures need to be put into context. The findings of irregularities in Equal Remuneration Act (ERA) comprise only 1 percent of all irregularities found in labor legislation; irregularities in minimum wage account for 50 percent (Maatta chapter VIII(D) 1998). Jain and Ratnam (1996, 5–6 and citations in Table 8, pp. 15–18) highlight a number of cases under the Equal Remuneration Act. They found that of the twenty cases between 1987 and 1995, in eight the employee's case was upheld, in nine it was not upheld, and in two the decision was withheld. (In one additional case there was no indication of outcome.) Only one case involved a private sector organization; the others were government or broader public sector organizations.

Jain and Ratnam (1996, 2–3) note the following barriers to the application of the equal pay concept: problems in the definition of pay (e.g., should benefits be included); lack of familiarity with JE;[26] bias in JE; emphasis on multi-skills and compensation for additional skills; linking of pay to individuals' qualifications; two-tier wage systems; shift from full-time to part-time and short-term contracts, with women more likely to be employed in the short term; and shifts from collective bargaining to individual contracts. Maatta (VIII:E 1998) reports that the effectiveness of the Equal Remuneration Act is limited by the difficulty of getting the necessary information in some sectors (e.g., garment packing and pharmaceuticals). This leads unions to enter into bilateral negotiations rather than using the legislation; in some industries, use of piece-rate systems makes it difficult to ascertain whether there is equal pay for equal work. Finally, women's organizations have not made equal pay a priority and have instead focused on other issues.

A study examining the gender wage differential (Duraisamy and Duraisamy 1996) finds that 67 to 77 percent of the differential is due to discrimination rather than to valid productivity differences between men and women. Other studies noted in SARDI (1999, 11) also support the presence of discrimination. Because of the extreme gender occupational segregation, (SARDI 1999, 10) and the lack of enforcement of the 1948 Minimum Wage Act, both equal work and equal value discrimination are present. Considering equal pay for equal work, women who occupy similar positions and have the same education only earn 80 percent of what men do (Dunlop and Velkoff 1999, 3). If discrimination were removed, it is estimated that rural women would earn 40 percent more, while women in urban areas could earn 20 percent more (Bagga 1998).

Countries with Only General Prohibitions Against Gender Pay Discrimination

Malaysia

Women's labor force participation is 46.8 percent, representing "36 percent of the Malaysian workforce, though half of this comprises women working as unpaid, family members" (WAO 2001). With respect to fair pay issues, women are often paid less than men in the private sector, while in government women are paid the same as men for the same work. The latter is due to a female cabinet minister who insisted that the first women to join the Judicial and Legal Services be paid the same salary as men. Before this time, women in government were paid lower salaries than their male counterparts (Haskim 2000).

Prohibition against discrimination on the basis of race was found in Article 8(2) of the Constitution (1957), but "sex" was only added in August 2001. Though currently the Constitution is interpreted to cover only intentional discrimination, some activists are calling for the Constitution to cover the effect of discrimination regardless of the intent (Netto 2001). This means that currently the Constitution is inconsistent with the United Nations' Convention on the Elimination of All Forms of Discrimination Against Women, which Malaysia ratified, with reservations, in 1995. Forty years earlier, in 1955, the Employment Act was passed, which covers wages and benefits (this applies only to Peninsular

Malaysia, while Sabah and Sarawak have their own legislation). Certain parts of the Employment Act, such as contracts of service, wages, rest hours, hours of work holidays, annual leave, sick leave, and termination and layoff benefits, apply equally to men and women (Asian Development Bank 1998). The Malaysian Truce Union Congress has been pushing for minimum wage legislation. The government has agreed in principle but has not yet passed the legislation. There is, however, a Wages Council Act which provides for statutory wage-setting bodies that establish a minimum wage (and conditions of employment) in industries where workers are not adequately organized to negotiate effectively.[27]

In 2001, Malaysia established a Ministry of Development of Women and Family. The first minister, Datuk Shahrizat Abdul Jalil, noted that with "more than 50 percent of the workforce being women, we have to pay more attention to them" (Star Online, 2001). At this time, however, nothing specific was said about the needs to redress wage discrimination. In fact, Ms. Shahrizat noted, in her list of areas of concern, the need to reinforce the "women's basic and traditional functions like cooking and caring for the household."[28] Finally, the Ministry of Human Resources has presented Guidelines on Wage Reform adopted by the National Labor Advisory Council, which talks about linking wages and productivity but nowhere mentions any issues related to equality (www.jaring. my/ksm/bulle1.htm, 8/1/02). Clearly, wage discrimination is not a strong agenda item. However, Malaysia has committed to the Beijing Platform for Action at the UN Fourth World Conference on Women (1995), which included the removal of legal obstacles and gender discriminatory practices. The platform specifically requires enactment and enforcement of legislation to guarantee the rights of women and men to equal pay for *equal work* or equal pay for work of *equal value* (WAO 2001).[29]

Fair Pay and Race

There is considerably less of a legislative response for racial pay gaps than for gender, even though there is evidence that racial pay gaps exist. The ordering of these countries in terms of their legislative response related to fair pay and race differs from the ordering related to gender and fair pay. First, South Africa, as part of its Employment Equity Act, has a requirement to collect information on wage differentials by race and to correct them (the same is required for gender). Second, the United States has proposed legislation that requires equal pay for work of equal value based on race (though it is unlikely to pass) and has regulations requiring the collection of some data that might be used in this area. Third are countries that have antidiscrimination legislation, covering race and compensation, but that do not specifically require equal work or equal value; this includes Canada, Malaysia, South Africa and the UK. India is the only country with no legislation related to racial discrimination in compensation.

Data Collection Required

South Africa

In 1948, the apartheid system was introduced into South Africa linking economic and social situations to skin color; apartheid was not abolished until 1991–1992. The residue of this system means that most unskilled workers are Africans (blacks) and that Africans are found at the lowest salary levels (Horwitz et al. 2000, 3). Africans form the majority of the population and the labor force. In all, four racial groups are recognized in South Africa—Africans, Asians, coloureds (people of mixed races), and whites. Skilled and unskilled Africans earn less than whites with the same skill level; for example, a white professional earns 2.83 times what a black professional earns (Bhorat 2000). Numerous research studies (Allanson et al. 2000, 2001; Erichsen and Wakeford, 2001; Hicks and Watson 2001; Jenkins and Thomas 2000; Knight and McGrath 1987; Moll 1998; Sherer 2000; Treiman et al. 1966) have looked at wage differentials. Although there are some inconsistencies, some overall trends are apparent:

- The racial wage differential is substantial; in 1991, African men earned 19 percent of what white men earned (Treiman et al. 1996).
- The racial wage differential between Africans and whites is due to both the lower productivity characteristics of Africans and positive discrimination toward whites (Allanson et al. 2001; Erichsen and Wakeford 2001). Whites and Asians experienced *positive* wage discrimination and Africans *negative* discrimination between 1995 and 1997, and this has continued in the post apartheid period (Allanson et al. 2001, 21).
- Over the long term, 1980 to 1995, the wage hierarchy was compressed significantly due to compression of productivity differentials and reduction in discrimination (Allanson et al. 2001, 21).
- There was a narrowing of the racial wage hierarchy through the period just prior to the end of apartheid, (Moll 1998, 2000; Treiman 1996; van der Berg 2001), while the post-apartheid era has been less favorable (Allanson et al. 2001, 23; Erichsen and Wakeford 2001; Rospabe 2001).
- In 1997, discrimination resulted in whites earning 47 percent more and Africans 12 percent less than they would in a nondiscriminatory market (Allanson et al. 2001, 22).

The reasons for the lower racial wage gap include increased within-group inequity, especially for Africans during the 1970s and 1980s (Jenkins and Thomas 2000) and unionization. Union membership provides a greater premium for Africans than for whites, though there is disagreement about how much—Butcher and Rouse (2001) identify 20 percent for Africans compared to 10 percent for whites, while Rospabe (2001) identifies the premium as 13 to 20 percent for

Africans and zero for whites. Working in the public sector had a negative wage effect for whites but little or no impact on the other groups (Treiman 1996). Education has a stronger effect for whites and Asians than for coloureds and Africans, the coloureds and Africans showing no returns for education (Treiman 1996).

In terms of a legislative response[30] to the racial wage gap, Section 27 of the Employment Equity Act requires employers to submit, in their employment equity plan, data on compensation and benefits received for each occupational category (and level) by race and gender. The Act requires that where disproportionate income differentials exist, the employer must take measures to progressively reduce such differentials using collective bargaining, compliance with sectoral pay determinations of the Ministry of Labor, benchmarks set by the Employment Conditions Commission (which researches norms and benchmarks for proportionate income differentials), and relevant measures in the Skill Development Act (1998) (Horwitz et al. 2000, 7). However, the legislation does not set a standard as to exactly what an appropriate income differential is. Still, Horwitz et al. (2000, 13) note that it is difficult to prove pay discrimination, even though the onus is on the employer to prove that differences are justified. Currently, there are few pay discrimination cases before the Commission for Conciliation, Mediation and Arbitration or the courts (Horwitz et al. 2000, 7, 13–14), though the first employment equity plans were only submitted in 2000. There has been one significant court case where an African alleged that he was paid less than a white colleague because of race. In *Louw v. Golden Arrow Bus Services* ([PTY] LTD LLR[2000] 1CC), Mr. Louw alleged that a white in the same job was paid more and that when this individual was promoted into the supervisory position, he was paid more than he should have been, given the differences in the work. The Labor Court found that Mr. Louw had failed to prove, on a balance of probabilities, that the wage differential was due to race (February and Abrahams undated).

Data Collection Proposed

United States

Occupational segregation related to race is assumed to be due to discriminatory barriers and human capital differences, which are often due to nonmarket discrimination; unlike the case with women, there is no assumption that members of minority groups make a free *choice* to work in low-paying jobs. Bayard et al. (1999) examined race-gender interaction related to wages and occupational segregation. They found larger racial and ethnic wage gaps for men than for women; they also found greater racial segregation between men than women for both Hispanics compared to whites and for blacks compared to whites. Although

segregation accounted for almost all of the of wage differential between Hispanics and whites, for blacks they accounted for only a third to a half. Segregation is a major factor in racial wage differentials—where individual
characteristics are similar. The wage implication of this finding was examined
by Mason (1999) who looked at both black-white and Hispanic-white wage
differentials. Regardless of race, getting a job typically filled by white men
increased wages for those from minority groups. Browne et al. (2001) found
that blacks employed in predominantly black jobs are paid lower wages compared to blacks employed in predominantly white jobs. A study examining men
in public and private sector organizations looked at income inequality operating
both within and between occupations. Grodsky and Pager (2001) found that
within the private sector racial disparities increase in both absolute and percentage terms as one moves up the occupational earnings hierarchy, unrelated
to individual or occupational characteristics. In the public sector, earnings differences are more closely linked to individual human capital and occupational
characteristics.

Title VII of the 1964 Civil Rights Act covers race, in addition to gender.
Research clearly shows that occupational segregation declined in the 1970s and
1980s (King 1992) and that wages declined until the mid-1970s. There was a
significant and sustained decline in the black-white earnings differential following passage of the Act (Altonji and Blank 1999; Darity and Mason 1998; Donahue and Heckman 1991). For instance, Smith (1993, 80) found that in 1968,
blacks earned 45 percent less than white men, whereas by 1977 the difference
had dropped to 29 percent. This decrease is due to affirmative action. Smith
(1993, 83) observed that the wage gains made by blacks are too large to be
explained by the more slowly evolving historical process of racial skill convergence. For instance, the almost complete racial wage parity for new college
graduates in the early 1970s and the speed at which this parity was reached
means that it could not be exclusively due to additional skill increases. Beginning
in the mid-1970s, the gap ceased to decrease and stagnated. More recently, the
black-white earnings gap has decreased (Harrison and Bennett 1995), while the
human capital of blacks has increased. By 1988, the black-white wage ratio was
66 percent, increasing to 73 percent by 1998 (Couch and Daly 2000). This
change is due to less concentration of black men in low-paying industries and
occupations, though Couch and Daly (2000) estimate that based on human capital factors black men should be earning 85 percent of white men rather than
the 73 percent they are—thus, discrimination still exists. One study looked at
the return of unionization to minority members and women and found that union
wage premiums were greatest for men of color, followed by white women, white
men, and women of color (Wunnava and Peled 1999).

As noted earlier, the OFCCP, which oversees the federal contractors' program, is required by regulations to collect salary data on race and gender within

nine occupational groupings. The nine occupational groupings are too broad to determine if equal pay for work of equal value is achieved. Rather, these data were to be used to identify which employers would be audited and asked to provide more detailed data so that a better assessment could be made to determine whether bias existed (Fay and Risher 2000). Data have been collected from half the employers covered by the contractors' program via the Equal Opportunity Survey. However, the OFCCP has not analyzed the data they have collected, nor have they followed up by surveying the other half of the employers (though they have committed to this, and it is required by regulation). The data collected allow comparison of the organization's average salary for employees of color (and gender) to white (male) average salary within occupations (also collect average seniority of each group as a possible explanation for wage differences).

Racial wage discrimination is explicitly prohibited in the proposed Fair Paycheck Act (equal work) and Fair Pay Act (equal value). These are the only pieces of legislation in any of the six countries that address fair pay for race so specifically. However, neither act is likely to pass under the conservative Bush administration when they did not make it under the supportive Clinton administration.

General Prohibitions Against Pay Discrimination

Canada and the United Kingdom

The United Kingdom has the Race Relations Act 1976 (amended 2000) in place, but this Act does not deal specifically with equal pay for either equal work or equal value. It does, however, provide a gender prohibition against discrimination, and it focuses primarily on recruitment and hiring. In Canada, human rights legislation prohibits racial discrimination in all employment areas; thus, compensation matters are covered, but there is no specific reference to equal work or equal value issues.[31]

In Canada, the UK, and the United States, for that matter, immigrants are assumed to be people of color. However, not all people of color are immigrants. Still, studies of wage differentials often combine race, immigrant status, and gender. Studies in the UK that have looked at wage differentials among immigrants find a racial component. That is, immigrants of color are discriminated against more than white immigrants (Bell 1997; Blackaby et al. 1994; Chiswick 1983; McNabb and Psacharopoulos 1981; Stewart 1983).A recent review of the literature in Canada, that also included Aboriginal Peoples (Finnie and Meng 2001), finds the following:

- There is a wage gap of 8.2 percent between Canadian-born men of color and Canadian-born white men; the gap between Canadian-born white men and immigrant men of color is 15.8 percent.
- For men, the racial wage gap is found for immigrants but not the Canadian-born populations (though one study found that blacks were an exception);
- There is a 11 percent wage gap between male Aboriginals who are off-reserve and outside of the territories, working full-time year round, and white men; the Aboriginal-white wage gap for women is 6.5 percent. Half the gap or less is due to discrimination.

Malaysia

Prohibition against discrimination on the basis of race is covered in the Constitution (1957). Occupational segregation in Malaysia affects racial groups, though as yet nothing has been proposed to directly redress any wage discrimination separate from the issue of employment discrimination.

No Antidiscrimination Legislation Related to Compensation

India

In India, castes and occupations are intertwined. Thus, occupational segregation is linked to the caste system, which was established by the seventh century before the common era. Caste is not linked to race or skin color per se, but is determined by heredity and could be said to represent ethnic groups. Each caste traditionally had a common occupation, and like some Western European names (Barber, Baker, Cooper, Smith), caste names refer to occupation. Although affirmative action is being used to redress caste inequities, no efforts have been made to date to directly redress unfair pay.

Conclusion

Unfair pay is only one kind of employment discrimination, and it is typically not the first type to be addressed. Removing barriers to employment precedes a focus on fair pay. When fair pay is specifically required, the focus tends to be on women before people of color. This is true for both international conventions and national legislation. This chapter has focused on two kinds of wage discrimination that are linked to occupational segregation at the level of the firm—equal work and equal value. It appears that gender occupational segregation is harder to remove than racial. For instance, in the United States in the 1940s, the degree of racial and gender segregation was similar; by the early 1980s, racially based occupational segregation had decreased by more than 70 percent, while for women it had decreased by 11 percent for white women and 33 percent for black women (Reskin and Hartmann 1986). When wage discrimination is addressed, there appears to be something of a hierarchy in how it is approached—first, minimum wage, then general prohibition against discrimination in employment functions, including compensation, followed by requirement for equal pay for equal work and then equal pay for work of equal value. These six countries, however, provide numerous exceptions to this general rule. It is also true that one kind of discrimination is not "resolved" before another is begun. Rather, they all work simultaneously redressing different problems. For example, in the United States concurrent legislation has been proposed to strengthen the 1963 equal work legislation and to introduce pay equity at the federal level. The role of unions in fair pay has not been explicitly discussed in this chapter because of space constraints. It is clear that unions, often public sector unions, have been important in pushing for fair pay issues to be on the agenda, for legislation, and for the enforcement of legislation. In many countries, women's groups have also been an important social force.

This chapter has focused on wage discrimination as if it were separate and distinct from other discrimination—employment and societal. This distinction is useful for understanding the workings of pay discrimination, but not for fully comprehending how things actually happen. The real situation is, of course much more complex. A study conducted for the Equal Opportunities Commission in the UK (Morrell et al. 2001) found that human resource managers are far more comfortable dealing with hiring issues and presuming that the pay gap will resolve itself. When asked about the fairness of their compensation systems, 93 percent of the organizations were very or fairly confident that their pay systems were fair to both men and women. The authors of the study speculate that this level of confidence may be inappropriately limiting the amount of action organizations are taking. For example, 98 percent of manufacturing firms surveyed were confident in their pay systems, but this sector, compared to the service and the public sectors, was doing the least to ensure gender equality in pay. Only 59 percent of employers had carried out any type of audit to ascertain fair pay.[32] The study concluded that employers do not take ownership of equal pay issues.

Legislation is a necessary, but not sufficient, condition for redressing wage discrimination. In addition, all the various aspects of wage discrimination need to be understood and redressed in an appropriate manner. Two aspects of legislation are particularly important in redressing the kinds of wage discrimination discussed in this chapter. First, the legislation needs to be specifically designed to redress particular wage discrimination (equal work or equal value). It must set out a set of steps for employers to ascertain whether the discrimination exists, and if so, how to correct it over time. Second, the legislation needs to be proactive since this is best for redressing the systemic nature of such wage discrimination. Proactive legislation compels employers to make the necessary assessment (and corrections) rather than relying on complaints. Ontario's Pay Equity Act, though far from perfect, is the best example of such legislation (see Gunderson, 2002 for more details). Legislation that is not proactive but relies on complaints (e.g., UK's Equal Pay Act) is less effective since it requires employees to know more about the workings of the compensation system than can be reasonably expected. General prohibitions against wage discrimination, such as those dealing with race in Canada, Malaysia, the UK, and the United States have been little used since they are not proactive. Even the proactive requirement to collect general information in order to obtain the desirable objective of "reducing wage differential" (i.e., South Africa's Employment Equity Act covering both gender and race) is likely to prove ineffective, since it is not specific enough.

Notes

1. Also referred to as pay equity or comparable worth.
2. Affirmative action or employment equity are strategies to affect vertical occupational segregation.
3. In reality, current market rates may, inappropriately, affect job evaluation ratings.
4. Interestingly, there was a stronger relationship between gender and job evaluation points than between human capital attributes and JE points (Schumann et al. 1999, 498).
5. *Source*: Statistics Canada Labor Force 15 Years and Over by Broad Occupational Categories and Major Groups Based on the 1991 Standard Occupational Classification and Sex, for Canada, 1991 and 1995 Censuses (20 percent sample data). Data from catalogue No. 93F0027XDB96007 in the Nation Series. Retrieved April 10, 2000 at http://www.statcan.ca/english/census96/mar17/occupa/table2/t2p00.htm.
6. *Source*: Statistics Canada Labor Force 15 Years and Over by Broad Occupational Categories and Major Groups Based on the 1991 Standard Occupational Classification and Sex, for Canada, 1991 and 1996 Censuses (20 percent sample data) Data from Catalogue No. 93F0027XDB96007 in the Nation Series, also found at (April 10, 2000): http://www.statcan.ca/english/census96/mar17/occupa/table2/t2p00.htm.
7. Private sector employers operating in different provinces must comply with different laws in different jurisdictions. About 90 percent of the workforce is covered by provincial legislation and about 10 percent by federal. Six of the provinces have passed pay equity legislation; three other provinces have negotiated with their unions for pay equity in the public service and require it for other broader public sector organizations. Typically, pay equity requirements cover the public sector (though different jurisdictions differ on the degree to which the broader public sector is covered). The federal government, Ontario and Quebec, covers private sector organizations.
8. Where pay equity is included in human rights legislation, it also covers male jobs. In practice, there have been virtually no cases where the issue has been the underpayment of male jobs.
9. If the jobs are found to be of equal value and the pay is unequal this is not deemed

to be discriminatory if there is a valid material difference that justifies the pay difference.

10. This aspect of the amendments was needed to deal with the between 6.4 percent and 43.0 percent of the jobs within organizations where it was impossible to determine whether a female job was underpaid based on the original methodology that required each female job to find a specific male comparator job (job-to-job methodology) (Gunderson 1995, Table 4).

11. The UK's wage gap is the lowest of the six countries discussed here. Since 1995, the gender wage gap has decreased in seven of thirteen EU countries, including the UK (Kingsmill 2001, 22). In the UK the female-male wage ratio rose from 64 percent in 1973 to 82 percent in 2000 (Kingsmill 2001, 24).

12. These ten occupations are: sales assistant and checkout operators (10.2 percent); other sales and service (7.5 percent);, numerical clerk (6.8 percent); secretaries, personal assistants, and typists (6.3 percent); health related (6.0 percent); teaching professionals (5.8 percent); health associate professionals (5.4 percent); clerks not classified elsewhere (4.7 percent); child care (4.2 percent); and catering occupations (3.6 percent) (reported in Kingsmill 2001, 19)

13. There is separate legislation in Great Britain and Northern Ireland; only the British legislation will be discussed in detail. The legislation for Northern Ireland is: Equal Pay Act (Northern Ireland) 1971, amended by the Sex Discrimination (Northern Ireland) order 1976; the Equal Pay (Amendment) Regulations (Northern Ireland) 1984; Sex Discrimination (Northern Ireland) Order 1976; and Sex Discrimination (Northern Ireland) Order 1987

14. Interestingly, in equal pay for *equal work* situations, a woman can compare her job to that of a male who previously or subsequently performed her job and was paid more. (Relevant decisions are: *Diocese of Hallam Trustee v. Miss J. Connaughton* (1996 IRLR 505) (Employment Appeal Tribunal) and *Macarthys Ltd. v. Smith* (1980 IRLR 209).) Further, Palmer et al. 1997, 365, sustained the claim that, even though a male had never performed this or like work, the female should be paid the rate that a male *would have been paid.*

15. The European Court of Justice is clarifying whether equal pay comparisons across employers is allowed in certain circumstances.

16. JE is being more widely used as a compensation tool, particularly by large employers (Maatta 1998). Virtually all 470,000 civil service jobs are covered by a JE scheme, and the National Health Service is using a national JE scheme.

17. In July 2002, the Prevention of Less Favorable Treatment Regulations for part-time workers came into force. Based on the European Council Directive, the Regulations give part-time workers the right to receive the same hourly pay rates as comparable full-timers. However, given that large numbers of part-time workers do not have a male full-time comparator in an identical job, this is unlikely to have any impact on the gender wage gap (EIRO 2002; UK report, item 3.1).

18. In a European Court of Justice decision, *Enderby v. Frenchay Health Authority* (1993), the Court noted that market forces could be justification for a material difference in pay if statistics relied on cover sufficient numbers, were not a short-term phenomenon, and were of significance (ILO 1994).

19. Educational attainment is under six years for Africans, eight years for Indians, and almost ten years for whites (Maharaj 1999)

20. If the federal government does not act, states may. If Congress does act, federal regulations may coexist with state regulations, or it may displace state regulations. In the antidiscrimination area, states may legislate alongside the federal government.

21. Some states conducted a full pay equity process for all female jobs, others targeted only a few jobs, and some did pay equity within the context of a comprehensive revision of their compensation system.

22. Minnesota has two acts, Pay Equity Act of 1982, which covers state employees, while local governments and other broader public sector organizations are covered by the Pay Equity Act of 1984.

23. The Federal Contractors Program was put into place by presidential Executive Order 11246 in 1965 under the Democratic administration of Lyndon Johnson.

24. Currently, employers can argue that men's stronger bargaining power is an allowable reason for pay differentials. In addition, the Act would eliminate the establishment requirement, which has been used to prohibit the comparison of jobs in different facilities of the same employer.

25. Almost 40 percent (38 percent) of women compared to 66 percent of men are literate (Menon-Sen, undated: 4th chapter). Still, many women are underemployed (i.e., have higher level skills than their jobs demand) (Dunlop and Velkoff 1999, 3).

26. The Court requires that job evaluation (measuring skill, effort, responsibility, and working conditions) be used to determine whether there is equal value; then it can be ascertained if there is another basis, other than job content, for the differential pay, such as productivity differences.

27. Currently, there are four wage councils for (1) shop assistants, (2) cinema workers, (3) stevedores and cargo handlers, and (4) catering and hotel workers.

28. The priorities include: upward mobility, giving credit for work done in the home, good work environments (e.g., eliminate sexual harassment), improving employment status of workers, including domestic workers, and ratifying global labor conventions related to collective bargaining, for example (Third World Network—twnside.org.sg/title/nst-cn.htm. Retrieved January 4, 2002).

29. Strategic Objective F.1, Article 165(a), Fourth World Conference on Women, Beijing, September 1995 (www.un.org/womenwatch/daw/beijing/platform/economy.htm).

30. There are also general statements against discrimination in the Constitution (sections 9(1 and 2)) and Section 7 of the Labor Relations Act (1995).

31. Equal value issues linked to race are just beginning to be thought of (personal conversation with Manager, Equal Pay Unit, Canadian Human Rights Commission, March 2002).

32. Forty percent had undertaken an assessment of how the value of jobs is determined; 35 percent had undertaken an analysis of basic pay by gender; and 15 percent had reviewed the access to pay benefits of employers.

References

Allanson, Paul, Atkins, Jonathan P., and Hinks, Timothy. 2000. "A Multilateral Decomposition of Racial Wage Differentials in the 1994 South African Labor Market." *Journal of Development Studies* 37: 93–120.

Allanson, Paul, Atkins, Jonathan P., and Hinks, Timothy. 2001, April 5–7. Did the End of Apartheid Spell the Beginning of the End for the Racial Wage Hierarchy in South Africa? A Multilateral Analysis of Racial Wage Differentials in the Early Post-Apartheid Period. Presented at DESG-IESG Annual Conference, University of Nottingham.

Altonji, Joseph G., and Blank, Rebecca M. 1999. "Race and Gender in the Labor Market." In *Handbook of Labor Economics.* Vol. 3, eds. Orley Ashenfelter and David Card. Amsterdam: Elsevier, chapter 48.

Asian Development Bank. 1998. "Country Briefing Paper: Women in Malaysia." www.adb.org/documents/books/country-briefing-papers/women-in-malaysia/ (December 12, 2001).

Baker, Michael, and Fortin, Nicole M. 2000. "Does Comparable Worth Work in a Decentralized Labor Market?" Cambridge, MA: National Bureau of Economic Research Working Paper 7937. http://www.nber.org/papers/w7937 (November 16, 2000).

Bagga, Kamaljit. 1998, April 17. "The Myth of Equal Remuneration in India: Sorting Fact from Fiction about Working Women in the World's Largest Democracy." *Chicago Business* 36(8). http://gsbwww.uchicago.edu/student/chibus/articles/980417/980417027.html (February 21, 2002).

Bayard, Kimberly, Hellerstein, Judith, Neumark, David, and Troske, Kenneth R. 1999. "Why Are Racial and Ethnic Wage Gaps Larger for Men Than for Women? Exploring the Role of Segregation Using the New Worker-Establishment Characteristics Database." http://econwpa.wustl.edu:8089/eps/ab/papers/9902/9902002.pdf (April 3, 2002).

Bell, Brian D. 1997. "The Performance of Immigrants in the United Kingdom: Evidence from the GHS." *Economic Journal* 107(2): 333–344.

Bellace, Janice R. 1993. "Equal Pay in the United States." In *Equal Pay Protection in Industrialised Market Economic: In Search of Greater Effectiveness,* ed. F. Eyraud. Geneva: International Labor Organization, 159–174.

Bhorat, Haroon. 2001. "How to Reduce South Africa's Wage Gaps." In *Essays on the South African Labor Market,* Development Policy Research Unit (DPRU) University of Cape Town. http://www.uct.ac.za/depts/dpru/essays.pdf (February 5, 2002).

Blackaby, David; Clark, Ken; Leslie, Derek; and Murphy, Philip. 1994. "Black-White Male Earnings and Employment Prospects in the 1970s and 1980's: Evidence from Britain." *Economic Letters* 46: 273–280.

Blau, Francine D., and Kahn, Lawrence M. 1996. "Wage Structure and Gender Earnings Differentials: An International Comparison." *Economica* 63(250): S29–S62.

Blau, Francine D., and Kahn, Lawrence M. 1999. "Analyzing the Gender Pay Gap." *The Quarterly Review of Economics and Finance* 39: 625–646.

Browne, Irene, Hewitt, Cynthia, Leann Tigges, and Green, Gary. 2001. "Why Segregation Leads to Wage Inequity. Person, Place, Sector or Skill?" *Social Science Research* 30(3): 473–495.

Butcher, Kristin F., and Rouse, Cecilia Elena. 2001. "Wage Effects of Union and Industrial Councils in South Africa." *Industrial Labor Relations Review* 54(2): 349–374.

Cabinet Office (UK). Undated. "The Gender Pay Gap." Retrieved March 13, 2002 from http://www.womens-unit.gov.uk/pay percent20gp/introduction.htm.

Canadian Facts. 1992. "Outcome of Pay Equity for Organizations Employing 100 to 499 Employees in Ontario." Toronto: Report for Pay Equity Commission.

Canadian Facts. 1993. "Outcome of Pay Equity for Organizations Employing 50–99 Employees in Ontario." Toronto: Report for Pay Equity Commission.

Canadian Human Rights Commission. 2001. "Time for Action: Special Report to Parliament on Pay Equity." Ottawa: Public Works and Government Services. At http://www.chrc-ccdp.ca/pe-ps/TFA-LTD/SRPE_TC_TDM_RSPS.asp?l=e.

Canadian International Development Agency. 2001."Gender Profile in South Africa" Retrieved December 12, 2001 from http://www.acdi-cida.gc.ca/cida_ind.nsf/vLUallDocByIDEn/0EAE7AB371AFD86885256B57007112D4?OpenDocument.

Chen, Shih-Neng, Orazem, Peter F., Mattila, Peter J., and Greig, Jeffrey J. 1999. "Measurement Error in Job Evaluaiton and the Gender Wage Gap." *Economic Inquiry* 37(2): 181–194.

Chiswick, Barry R. 1983. "The Earnings of White and Colored Male Immigrants in Britain." *Economica* 47(1): 81–87.

Couch, Kenneth, and Daly, Mary C. 2000. "Black-White Wage Inequality in the 1990s: A Decade of Progress." *Economic Inquiry* 40: 31–41.

Darity, William, Jr., and Mason, Patrick. 1998. "Evidence on Discrimination in Employment: Codes of Color, Codes of Gender." *Journal of Economic Perspectives* 12: 63–90.

Dolton, Peter, O'Neill, Donal, and Sweetman, Olive. 1996. "Gender Differences in the Changing Labor Market: The Role of Legislation and Inequality in Changing the Wage Gap for Qualified Workers in the United Kingdom." *Journal of Human Resources* 31(3): 549–565.

Donahue, John, and Heckman, James. 1991. "Continuous vs. Episodic Change: The Impact of Civil Rights Policy on the Economic Status of Blacks." *Journal of Economic Literature* 29: 1603–43.

Drolet, Marie. 2001. "The Persistent Gap: New Evidence on the Canadian Gender Wage Gap." Ottawa: Statistics Canada Analytical Studies Branch—Research Paper Series, no. 11F0019MPE No. 157.

Dunlop, John E., and Velkoff, Victoria A. 1999. "Women at Work: Women and the Economy in India." Washington, DC: Bureau of the Census. Retrieved November 30, 2001 at http://www.census.gov/ipc/prod/wid-9802.pdf.

Duraisamy, Malathy, and Duraisamy, P. 1996. "Sex Discrimination in Indian Labor Markets." *Feminist Economics* 2(2). Retrieved February 21, 2002 at http://www.ruf.rice.edu/ femec/contents/22duraisamy.html.

EIRO (European Industrial Relations Observatory). 2002, January. "Gender Pay Equity in Europe." Retrieved February 5, 2002 from www.eiro.eurofound.ie/2002/01/study/TN0201101s.html (whole report); or for UK report: www.eiro.eurofound.ie/2002/01/study/index.html (UK report).

EMIRE (European Foundation for Improvement of Living and Working). 2002. United Kingdom Report: Equal Pay Act 1970. Retrieved April 2, 2002 at http://www.eurofound.ie/emire/UNITEDpercent20KINGDOM/EQUALPAYACT1970EQPA! (&)-EN.html.

Erichsen, Gaute, and Wakeford, Jeremy. 2001. "Racial Wage Discrimination in South Africa: Before and After the First Democratic Elections." Development Policy Research Unit (DPRU) Working Paper No. 01/49.

Equal Pay Task Force. 2001. "Just Pay," Manchester, UK: Equal Opportunities Commission. Retrieved January 19, 2002 from http://www.bt.com/equalpaytaskforce.

Equal Opportunities Commission. 1997. "Code of Practice of Equal Pay" Manchester, UK: EOC. Retrieved February 28, 2002 at http://www.eoc.org.uk/EOCeng/EOCcs/Legislation/code_of_practice_equal_pay.asp.

Eyraud, F, ed. 1993. *Equal Pay Protection in Industrialised Market Economic: In Search of Greater Effectiveness.* Geneva: International Labor Organization.

Fay, Charles H., and Risher, Howard W. 2000. "Contractors, Comparable Worth and the New OFCCP: Déjà vu and More." *Compensation & Benefits Review* 32(5): 23–33.

Finnie, Ross, and Meng, Ronald. 2001. "Minorities, Measured Cognitive Skills and the Earnings of Canadian." Kingston, ON: Queen's University School of Policy Studies, Working Paper 26.

Grodsky, Eric, and Pager. Devah. 2001. "The Structure of Disadvantage: Individual and

Occupational Determinants of the Black-White Wage Gap." *American Sociological Review* 66(4): 542–567.

Gunderson, Morley. 1995. "Gender Discrimination and Pay Equity Legislation." In *Aspects of Labor Market Behaviour: Essays in Honor of John Vanderkamp,* eds. L. Cristophides, E.K. Grant, and R. Swidinsky. Toronto: University of Toronto Press, 225–247.

Gunderson, Morley. 2002. "The Evolution and Mechanics of Pay Equity in Ontario." *Canadian Public Polic,* 28(supplement 1), forthcoming.

Harrison, Roderick, J., and Bennett, Claudette E. 1995. "Racial and Ethnic Diversity." In *State of the Union: America in the 1990s,* ed. R. Farley. Vol. 2, *Social Trends.* New York: Russell Sage Foundation.

Hartmann, Heidi, and Aaronson, Claudette E. 1994. "Pay Equity as a Remedy for Wage Discrimination: Success in State Government." *Duke Journal of Gender Law and Policy* 1: 69–87.

Haskim, Harun. 2000, September 14. "Malaysian Women Have Come into Their Own." *New Straits Times.* Kuala Lumpur.

Hicks, Timothy, and Watson, Duncan. 2001. "A Multinomial Logit Nondiscriminatory Approach to Estimating Racial Wage and Occupational Discrimination." *Applied Economics* 33(5): 605–612.

Horwitz, Frank M., Jain, Harish, and Steenkamp, Anton J. May-June, 2000. "Pay Discrimination in South Africa: Overcoming the Apartheid Legacy." International Industrial Relations Association 12th World Congress, Tokyo, Japan.

Institute of Social Research. 1994. "Pay Equity Survey of Private-Sector Organizations Employing 10–49 Employees in Ontario." Toronto: Report for Pay Equity Commission.

International Labor Organization (ILO), CEACR (Committee of Experts on Application of Convention and Recommendation), Individual Observation concerning Convention No. 100, Equal Remuneration, 1951; India published 1991, 1992, 1997, and 1999; United Kingdom published 1990, 1992, 1994, and 1999. Retrieved November 30, 2001 at http://ilolex.ilo.ch:1567/ilolex/pqconv.pl?host=status01&textbase=iloen g&chspec=30&hitdirection=1&hitstart=0&hitsrange=999&highlight=&context= &query=percent28C100percent29+@ref+percent2B+percent28Indiapercent29+@ ref+percent2B+percent28percent23classificationpercent3D02_03_02*percent29+ @ref+percent2B+percent23YEARpercent3E1990&chspec=5percent2C6&query0 =C100&query1=India&query2=percent23classificationpercent3D02_03_02*&year =percent3E1990&title=&query3=&sortmacro=sortconv&submit=Submit+query.

International Labor Organization. 1951. "R90 Equal Remuneration Recommendation." Geneva. Retrieved November 30, 2001 from http://ilolex.ilo.ch:1567/english/ recdisp2.htm.

Itano, Nicole. 2001, July 19. "Turning the Tables on Apartheid: A Proposed Law to Protect South Africa's Exploited Domestic Workers Should be Approved by Year's End." Boston, MA: Christian Science Monitor, 6.

Jain, H.C., and Ratnam, C.S. Venkata. 1996, November–December. "Pay Equity in India." Indra-Dhanush, New Delhi: International Management Institute, 1–18.

Jamaludin, Farid. 2001. "Bringing Women's Issues to the Fore." Star Online, January 19, 2001. Retrieved November 10, 2001 from http://thestar.com.my/services.

Jenkins, Carolyn, and Thomas, Lynne. 2000. "The Changing Nature of Inequality in South Africa." Helsinki: United Nations University WIDER (World Institute for Development, Economic Research) working paper 203. Retrieved February 21, 2002 at http://www.wider.unu.edu/publications/wp203.pdf.

Joshi, Heather, and Paci, Pierella with Makepeace, Gerald and Waldfogel, Jane. 1998. Unequal Pay for Women and Men: Evidence from the British Birth Cohort Studies. Cambridge, MA: MIT Press.

Kahn, Shulamit. 1992. "Economic Implications of Public Sector Comparable Worth: The Case of San Jose, California," *Industrial Relations* 31(2): 270–291.

King, Mary. 1992. "Occupational Segregation by Race and Sex, 1940–88." *Monthly Labor Review* 115: 30–37.

Kingsmill, Denise. 2001, December. "Women's Employment and Pay." Report to Government. Retrieved April 2, 2002 from http://www.kingsmillreview.gov.uk.

Knight, John, and McGrath, Michael. 1987. "The Erosion of Apartheid in the South African Labor Market; Measures and Mechanisms." Institute of Economics and Statistics Applied Economic Discussion Paper No. 35, University of Oxford.

Levine, Linda. 2001. "The Gender Wage Gap and Pay Equity: Is Comparable Worth the Next Step?" Washington, DC: CRS (Congressional Research Service). Report for Congress. Retrieved November 30, 2001 at http://www.mjfreedman.org/98-278.pdf.

Libeson, Sandra J. 1995. "Reviving the Comparable Worth Debate in the United States: A Look Toward the European Community." *Comparative Labor Law Journal* 16(3): 538–398.

McCrudden, Christopher. 1993. "Equal Pay in the United Kingdom." In *Equal Pay Protection in Industrialised Market Economies: In Search of Greater Effectiveness*, ed. F. Eyraud. Geneva: International Labor Organization, 141–158.

McDonald, Judith A, and Thornton, Robert J. 1998. "Private Sector Experience with Pay Equity in Ontario." *Canadian Public Policy* 24:2: 185–208.

McNabb, R., and Psacharopoulos, George. 1981. "Racial Earnings Differentials in the UK." Oxford Economic Papers 33: 413–425.

Maatta, Paula. 1998. *Equal Pay Policies: International Review of Selected Developing and Developed Countries.* Geneva: International Labor Organization. Retrieved February 21, 2002 from http://www.ilo.org/public/english/dialogue/infocus/papers/equalpay.

Maharaj, Zarina. 1999. "Gender Inequality and the Economy: Empowering Women in the New South Africa." Keynote speech at Professional Women's League of KwaZuluNatal, August 9, 1999. Retrieved November 30, 2001 at http://womensnet.org.za/news/speech.htm.

Manning, Alan. 1996. "The Equal Pay Act as an Experiment to Test Different Theories of the Labor Market." *Economica* 63: 191–212.

Mason, Patrick L. 1999. "Male Interracial Wage Differentials: Competing Explanations" *Cambridge Journal of Economics* 23(3): 261–299.

Menon-Sen, Kalyani. Undated. "Moving from Policy to Practice: A Gender Main Streaming Strategy for India." New York: United Nations Development Programme. Retrieved March 5, 2002 from http://www.undp.org.in/report/gstrat/Default.htm.

Moll, Peter G. 1998. "Primary Schooling, Cognitive Skills and Wages in South Africa." *Economica* 65: 263–84.

Moll, Peter G. 2000. "Discrimination Is Declining in South Africa But Inequality Is Not." *Studies in Economics and Econometrics* 24(3): 91–108.

Morrell, J., Boyland, M. Munns, G., and Astbury, L. 2001. "Gender Equality in Pay Practices." Manchester, Equal Opportunity Commission. Retrieved January 24, 2002 from www.eoc.org.uk/EOCeng/dynpages/research_pay.asp.

National Committee on Pay Equity (U.S.). Undated. Retrieved January 21, 2002 from http://www.feminist.com/fairpay/legislation.htm.

National Women's Law Center. 2002. "The Paycheck Fairness Act: Helping to Close the

Women's Wage Gap," Washington, DC. Retrieved January 21, 2002, from http://www.nwlc.org/display.cfm?section=employment#.

Netto, Anil. 2001. "Rights-Malaysia; Government Takes a Step Toward Gender Equality." Retrieved November 30, 2001 from http://www.globalinfo.org/eng/reader.asp?ArticleId=8603.

Palmer, C., Moon, G., and Cox, S. 1997. *Discrimination at Work: The Law on Sex, Race and Disability Discrimination.* London: LAG (Legal Action Group).

Reskin, B.F., and Hartmann, H.I., eds. 1986. *Women's Work, Men's Work: Sex Segregation on the Job.* Washington, DC: National Academy Press.

Rospabe, Sandrine. 2001. "How Did Labor Market Racial Discrimination Evolve after the End of Apartheid?" Presented at ESSA (Economic Society of South Africa) 2001 conference as noted at http://www.essa.org.za/download/papers2001.htm. Retrieved November 30, 2001 from http://www.essa.org.za/download/papers/008.pdf.

SARDI (South Asian Research and Development Initiative). 1999. "Report of the Survey of Women Workers' Working Conditions in Industry: Women Workers Inequalities at Work." New Delhi.

Schumann, Paul L., Ahlburg, Dennis A., and Mahoney, Christine Brown. 1999. "The Effects of Human Capital and Job Characteristics on Pay." *Journal of Human Resources* 29(2): 481–503.

Sherer, George. 2000. "Intergroup Economic Inequality in South Africa: The Post Apartheid Era." *The American Economic Review* 90(2): 317–321.

Smith, James P. 1993. "Affirmative Action and the Racial Wage Gap." *The American Economic Review* 83(2): 79–84. Retrieved April 3, 2002 from http://www.jstor.org/.

SPR Associates. 1991. "An Evaluation of Pay Equity in Ontario: The First Year." Toronto: Report for the Ontario Pay Equity Commission, April.

Stewart, Mark B. 1983. "Racial Discrimination and Occupational Attainment in Britain." *Economic Journal* 93: 521–541.

Treiman, Donald J., McKeever, Matthew, and Fodor, Eva. 1996. "Racial Differences in Occupational Status and Income in South Africa, 1980 and 1991." *Demography* 33: 111–132.

U.S. Department of Labor. Undated. "Equal Pay Matters!" Retrieved March 4, 2002 from http://www.dol.gov/wb/public/gils/records/000105.

Van der Berg, Servaas. 2001, November 15–16. "The Role of Education in Labor Earnings, Poverty and Inequality." DPRU/FES Conference on Labor Market and Poverty, Johannesburg.

WAO (Women's Aid Organization). 2001, March. "Women's Equality in Malaysia—Status Report." Retrieved December 17, 2001 from http://www.wao.org/my/news/20010301statusreport.htm.

Weiner, Nan. 1991. "Job Evaluation Systems: A Critique." *Human Resources Management Review* 1(2): 119–132.

Weiner, Nan. 1995. "Workplace Equity." In *Public Sector Collective Bargaining in Canada,* eds. G. Swinner and M. Thompson. Kingston, ON: IRC Press, 78–102.

Weiner, Nan, and Gunderson, Morley. 1990. *Pay Equity: Issues, Options and Experiences.* Toronto: Butterworths.

Wunnava, Phanindra (with Noga O. Peled). 1999. "Union Wage Premiums by Gender and Race: Evidence from PSID 1980–1992." *Journal of Labor Research* 20: 415–423.

Chapter 6

Trade Unions and Discrimination

Introduction

Trade unions may have a negative or a positive effect on the employment of minority groups. Discriminatory behavior could arise because white males who form the majority of union members dislike associating with black employees or women in the workplace, particularly where such workers are placed in supervisory positions. Alternatively, such minority groups may be seen as a potential threat to employment and wages through their potential for increasing substantially the overall supply of labor.

Unions may, however, offer minority workers some protection against discriminatory acts by employers inasmuch as unions are generally founded on the basis of an egalitarian ideology. Thus, Ray Marshall (1965) reports that early in the history of the union movement in the United States Samuel Gompers and other leaders of the American Federation of Labor were committed to the organization of workers regardless of race or religion. In Britain, the Trades Union Congress also had a number of resolutions concerning equal pay for women from the late nineteenth century onwards. Northrup (1971) and others, however, have argued that unions have been little more than passive recipients of the prevailing industrial climate. Yet, we must remember in general that unions raise wages and compress the wage structure. To the extent, therefore, that minority workers gain entry into unions and they are disproportionately concentrated among the relatively unskilled they may benefit from both of these effects. If, however, by raising wages unions reduce the level of employment, it may become more difficult for members of minority groups to find gainful employment.

Relevant Legislation

In the United States, Title VII of the Civil Rights Act of 1964 forbids employment discrimination by labor unions regardless of size. Therefore, individual discrimination complaints and class action lawsuits alleging "a pattern and practice" of discrimination against individuals protected by Title VII can be brought against labor unions. In addition to the Civil Rights Act, as amended by the Equal Employment Opportunity Act of 1972 and the Civil Rights Act of 1991, unions are affected by labor relations statutes as well as by the administrative decisions of the National Labor Relations Board, which administers these statutes. In addition, the National Labor Relations Act imposes certain duties on trade unions to represent all union members fairly in cases where exclusive bargaining rights have been obtained. The extent to which unions can adopt a positive approach to employment equity is, however, constrained by the fact that employers with fifteen or fewer workers, comprising about 20 percent of the private sector workforce, are not covered by the Civil Rights Act and noncontractors with fewer than 100 workers—a group including about half that workforce, do not regularly submit reports monitored by officials of government agencies with the authority to file lawsuits.

In Canada, the Labor Code, as amended in June 1978, prohibits trade unions from discriminating with respect to membership, referrals for employment, and a variety of other actions. The code requires trade unions to observe the duty of fair representation for all employees within a bargaining unit. Otherwise the union may be refused certification or be decertified and face the possibility of its collective agreements being annulled. The code also provides that unions which operate a hiring hall must establish rules regarding the assignment of work to employers via that hiring hall and display these rules at the hiring hall. Similar provisions apply in several provincial labor relations statutes.

Employment equity (the term used in Canada for affirmative action) legislation was enacted by the federal government in 1986 and was also subsequently introduced in Ontario.

In Britain, the 1975 Sex Discrimination Act and the 1976 Race Relations Act make it unlawful for a trade union to discriminate against anyone who is not a member on account of their sex, marriage, or race, in the terms under which it is prepared to admit persons into membership, or by refusing or deliberately omitting to accept an application for membership. Furthermore, it is unlawful for a trade union to discriminate with regard to denial of access to benefits, deprivation of membership, or any other detriment. Both the Commission for Racial Equality and the Equal Opportunities Commission are empowered to carry out formal investigations of organizations, including trade unions, if they believe there are indications of discriminatory behavior with regard to particular groups.

In each of these three advanced industrialized countries, legislation has followed the particular industrial relations traditions and practices pertaining to each country. Thus, explicit provision has been made to protect the seniority provision in the United States and to enforce rules relating to hiring halls in Canada. In contrast, in Britain, the legal framework has been more restricted in line with that nation's tradition of voluntarism, which is underpinned by the belief that agreements are better arrived at through negotiation between employers and unions than imposed through legislation.

The Employment Equity Act (1998) in South Africa aims to achieve equality in the workplace by eliminating unfair discrimination and implementing positive measures to redress disadvantages experienced by designated employees, notably blacks, women, and the disabled. Chapter 11 of the Act prohibits unfair discrimination, and Section 5.3 states that harassment, either sexual or racial, is considered a form of unfair discrimination. Section 5 (i) refers to direct and indirect discrimination. The Act requires a designated employer (i.e., an employer with fifty or more employees or employers who may employ fewer, by linking designation to turnover) to prepare an employment equity plan. This includes targets and timetables aimed at achieving "equitable representation" based on national and regional demography. The Act is complemented by the Skills Development Bill (1997) which requires a payroll levy of 1 to 15 percent for training and development. The Employment Equity Act, controversially requires employers to disclose remuneration information on managerial/executive pay levels. Although the Act is largely an enabling one, there are penalties under Chapter 11 with punitive damages in the form of R500,000 to R900,000 fines for failure to comply. The Act's dispute resolution procedures are complemented by Schedule 7 of the Labour Relations Act, which it will likely replace. This requires discrimination disputes to be referred to the Commission for Conciliation Mediation and Arbitration (CCMA) for conciliation and then to the Labour Court for subsequent arbitration. The CCMA arbitrates certain disputes surrounding the duties of designated employers, in terms of S. 24 (Horwitz 1998).

Prior to the Labour Relations Act of 1995, registered unions with racially exclusive constitutions were permitted in South Africa. Historically, most artisan unions served to protect the interests of skilled and semiskilled white workers. Job reservation on the basis of race was permitted by the Industrial Conciliation Act (1953) and the Mines and Works Act until the Wiehahn Commission reforms of 1990 abolished these clauses. Access to skilled work and apprenticeship training was denied to black workers by law until the 1990s. White unions perpetuated legal discrimination by ensuring that job reservation on the basis of race remained a high priority until these practices were outlawed. Legislated affirmative action in favor of white, coloured, and Asian workers dates back to the exclusion of African workers from joining registered unions by the Industrial Conciliation Act of 1924. They were denied access to industrial council collective bargaining. An "apartheid wage gap" was consequently created, which the new Employment Equity Act (1998) seeks to address. In the *SA Chemical Workers Union v. Sentrachem Industrial Court* case (1988), pay discrimination against black workers at the same job level, doing work of comparable worth, was ruled an unfair labor practice. The White workers were members of the conservative Mineworkers' Union. The Labour Relations Act (1 995) disallows the registration of trade unions with discriminatory constitutions. This does not mean that trade unions are immune from internal practices that discriminate *de facto* against officials, for example, on the basis of gender. While the South African Constitution permits affirmative action programs, unfair discrimination is unlawful in terms of Section 8 (2). In the case of sixteen white state attorneys, who had been overlooked for promotion, the Pretoria High Court ruled that there had been unfair discrimination. The men who were potential candidates for promotion were not called before a selection panel. Leave to appeal was granted. Few have been brought before the Labour Court dealing with unfair discrimination within trade unions. The Commission for Conciliation Mediation and Arbitration (CCMA) is required by the Labour Relations Act (1995) to attempt to resolve such a dispute, failing which an employee may then refer it to the Labour Court for adjudication.

Affirmative action in Malaysia followed the 1948 Federation of Malay agreement which entrenched the "special position" of a Malayan majority over Chinese and Indian groups. Provision for affirmative action is contained in the Malaysian Constitution and extends to institutions at all levels of society, for example, education, land ownership, and licensing of a business and public trusts, and not just to the employment relationship. Affirmative action tends to be defined in ethnic rather than racial terms. Statutory policies favor Malays who constitute 55 percent of the population of 17 million, over Chinese (35 percent) and Indians (10 percent). Religious differences also coincide with ethnic ones, and class stratification occurs within each of these groups, reflecting a complex ethnopolitical situation (Castle 1995; Faaland et al. 1990; Jesudason 1990). Quotas are set in the Constitution. South Africa has no constitutional quotas or targets.

In Malaysia and South Africa, diversity policies deal with majority communities, unlike the notion of visible minorities in Canada (Jain and Verma 1998, 4–8). In India, the government's task is to address inequalities for a significant number of minorities, such as for scheduled castes and tribes. Both groups in India constitute 26 percent, or more than 200 million people. Levels of unionization are proportionally lower in Malaysia and India than South Africa. Similarly to South Africa, in both of these countries, almost 45 percent of the workforce are women. The Indian experience is characterized by affirmative action reservations and quotas for state posts in favor of backward classes. Constitutional safeguards and affirmative action programs for the socially and economically depressed classes occur. Affirmative action in India has strengthened because of popular support, although exclusion of higher castes has led to periodic conflict and progress has been slow. The emphasis has been on middle management, professional, and governmental positions rather than on the working class. The pressure for affirmative action emanates from the government in both India and Malaysia rather than from trade unions and direct negotiation between employers and trade unions, as preferred in South Africa. Slower progress in India, according to Jain and Ratnam (1994), has been due to low economic growth, high unemployment, and scarcity of resources available for education and training. In Malaysia, quotas were used extensively in the public sector. High economic growth of between 6 and 7 percent per year over the past two decades, with cabinet-driven affirmative action, has resulted in a Malay middle class and a more affluent Malay community. Internal monitoring and implementation of affirmative action programs in India is done through liaison officers and not necessarily through trade unions. Unlike South Africa, there is also no affirmative action in private sector employment. Occasionally, interest groups such as nongovernmental organizations (NGOs) have raised demands for its extension to this sector. Employees' associations of scheduled castes and scheduled tribes, akin to parallel trade union structures, often pursue the interest of their candidates in taking fuller advantage of constitutional provisions and affirmative action programs. Mobilizing popular political support has been a more distinctive feature of the Indian experience than trade union initiatives.

Types of Union and Minimum Group Representation

Trade union density in the United States peaked in the late 1960s at around 25 percent of the civilian workforce. By 1997, trade union membership had declined, according to the Bureau of Labor Statistics, to 14.2 percent of the nonagricultural workforce and coverage to 15.8 percent. However, in the public sector membership and coverage remained relatively high at 37.2 and 42.3 percent, respectively, contrasting sharply with the figures for the private (nonagricultural) sector of 9.8 and 10.8 percent, respectively.

Ashenfelter and Godwin (1972) showed that up to 1930 the percentage of black workers who were unionized was negligible, but subsequently the figure grew to equal that of white workers by 1967 and they predicted that it would exceed that of white workers by a third by 1980. Furthermore, since the bulk of unionization was craft-related prior to 1930, this outcome is consistent with the view that industrial unions discriminate less than do craft unions as far as entry into membership is concerned. Ashenfelter's predictions were not widely off the mark. By 1990, according to *Employment and Earnings,* January 1991 (p 228), collective bargaining coverage for black males was 27.5 compared to 20.8 percent for white males and 18.0 percent for Hispanic males. The corresponding figures for women were 21.2 percent for blacks, 14.0 percent for whites, and 14.2 percent for Hispanics. This left a total collective bargaining coverage figure for men of 21.4 percent compared to 14.9 percent for women. These gender differences do not necessarily imply discrimination, however. Antos, Chandler, and Mellow (1980) found, for example, that almost 57 percent of the male-female unionization differential was eliminated when occupation and industry were accounted for.

It is important to distinguish between unions that attempt to influence pay and conditions by limiting the available supply of labor (e.g., craft unions) and those that attempt to do so by a bargaining settlement based on the strike threat (e.g., industrial unions). In the former case, a union must determine the basis for exclusion from the union, and an obvious way to do so is on the basis of race and gender. This may be achieved indirectly by limiting membership predominately to friends and relations of incumbent members. In the alternative case, where power depends on the ability to organize a substantial proportion of the total workforce, any attempt to limit membership will weaken the potential of the strike threat, so that discrimination is more costly to implement. Here minority groups are dependent on the strength of the employers' motives to hire them and on their ability to threaten the wage rates and job control procedures of unionists. The conflict between improved pay and conditions for union members and the organization of minority groups is greatest when unemployment is high, since then unemployed, nonunion, minority workers can be more easily substituted for union members in the event of a strike. Historically in the United States, many such examples can be found of blacks being employed as strikebreakers in industries such as automobiles, coal, iron and steel, and clothing.

In certain industries, such as construction, printing, and transportation, employers have depended primarily on the unions for recruitment through hiring halls which are limited to union members. Therefore, refusal of union membership is tantamount to denial of employment opportunities and may impact particularly badly on minority workers. An EEOC study, for example, based on an historical analysis of the position of blacks and women in unions, concluded that only minimal progress had been recorded for blacks entering into unions representing the skilled building trades. It is in this area that discrimination had been rife for most of the twentieth century and still today harbors considerable sex segregation among union members. Furthermore, representation of minorities and women in the government of unions remains severely limited for the most part.

In Canada, trade union membership and collective bargaining coverage are more than twice as high as in the United States. In 1999, total membership was 30.1 percent, and coverage was 32.6 percent (Akyeampong 1999). Again, the public sector is much more heavily unionized—70.9 percent membership and 75.1 percent coverage compared to 18.2 percent and 20.2 percent, respectively, in the private sector. The gender gap is relatively small—30.9 percent male membership compared to 29.3 percent for females and 33.5 percent male coverage compared to 31.6 percent for females. The gender gap has in fact narrowed substantially over recent years. Doiron and Riddell (1994) reported that in the late 1960s males were more than twice as likely to be union members as females. Thus, in 1966, male unionization was over 38 percent compared to 16 percent for women. The change, therefore, represents both a decline in male unionization and a substantial growth in female unionization. Unfortunately, there are no comparable data on union membership by race for Canada. However, Reitz and Verma (1999) provide data on immigrants. They report that, overall, recent immigrants (defined as those who arrived during 1980–1994) and also visible minorities have lower unionization rates. For racial minorities, the percentage unionization is 31.0 percent compared to 35.6 percent for the majority group. There are gender differences with hardly any differential for women—33.5 percent for the racial minority compared to 34.9 percent for whites, while the corresponding figures for men are 28.6 percent and 36.3 percent, respectively. Moreover, immigrants arriving earlier are more highly unionized, suggesting an assimilation process with respect to union membership and one that is faster for women than for men. Finally, they report that racial minorities born in Canada have a 9 percent lower rate of unionization than those who are not members of a racial minority.

In Britain, unionization peaked in 1979 at 50.5 percent of employment according to Labour Market Trends and has subsequently declined in every year to only 31.3 percent by 1996. The decline was particularly marked in the private sector where unionization was only 23 percent by 1996. Collective bargaining coverage remained significantly higher but itself declined from 70 to 47 percent.

The degree of unionization in Britain is lower for women than for men; for example, in 1992, the female density figure was 32 percent compared to 39 percent for men, but the gap has narrowed as female unionization has remained fairly static while that of males has declined. Female unionization is highly concentrated, reflecting the degree of gender segregation in the labor force and a number of major unions such as the Union of Shop, Distributive and Allied Workers (USDAW), Confederation of Health Service Employees (COHSE), National Union of Public Employees (NUPE), and National Union of Teachers (NUT) which have a majority of female members. However, women's representation as full-time union officials is much lower than would be expected on the basis of their share of total union membership. Trade union membership is, if anything, higher among minority groups than among the white population. A 1984 Political Studies Institute (PSI) Survey showed that in 1982 56 percent of Asian and West Indian employees were union members compared with 47 percent in the case of white employees. Although this difference was partly explained by the overrepresentation of minority workers in industrial sectors with above-average union density, correcting for this still leaves a residual higher union representation among minority workers. More than ten years later, a 1993 PSI Survey confirmed this result for Afro Caribbean and Indian employees, who had unionization rates of 44 percent and 38 percent, respectively, compared to

35 percent for white employees. In contrast, Pakistani and African Asian employees had lower unionization rates than whites (33 percent and 28 percent, respectively) and Bangladeshi employees substantially lower (14 percent). Wrench and Virdee (1995) suggest that the black workers' above-average propensity to join unions is now declining. They attribute this change both to the disillusionment experienced by some first-generation migrant workers over their treatment by unions and to the fact that second-generation minority employees do not necessarily have an ideological sympathy toward unions.

Therefore, both similarities and differences are evident across these three industrialized countries in relation to the representation of minorities within unions.

Total union membership in South Africa is 3.2 million; this is approximately 22 percent of the economically active population. Contrary to international trends, union membership in South Africa increased by 127 percent between 1985 and 1997, although the rate of increase declined in the period 1992–1996 to 4 percent (Sidiropoulos et al. 1998). The 1995 October survey of the Central Statistical Service found that approximately one-third of the 10.2 million people working in South Africa belonged to trade unions. Some 39 percent of African men and 36 percent of African women working belong to unions. Union membership is lowest amongst white working men (28 percent) and white working women (17 percent). The Bureau of Market Research estimates that only 2.5 percent of African workers in urban areas were unionized in 1975, 5.5 percent by 1980, and 19 percent by 1985 (Moll 1993). In 1993, 37 percent of African workers were unionized.

Some traditional artisan/craft unions became nonracial before the reforms brought in by the new Labour Relations Act (1995)—for example, the South African Boilermakers Society, the South African Electrical Workers Association, and the Artisan Staff Association. Several craft unions transformed themselves into industrial-craft unions by opening their membership to all workers on a non-racial basis. Some such as the South African Typographical Union and National Union of Furniture and Allied Workers Union did so in 1980. But the top structures of several of these unions are still dominated by white male artisans (von Holdt 1993). One of the two largest unions in South Africa, the traditionally black National Union of Mineworkers (NUM), has over 2,000 white skilled workers. As the skill profile of workers has changed with increasing numbers of black artisans and as the appeal of racially based unions reinforced by legislative provisions for nonracialism in registered unions has declined, the racial mix of union members has started to change. "However, craft unions will have to shed their history of paternalism and racism if they wish to attract increasing numbers of Black artisans. Whether Black artisans are attracted towards Congress of SA Trade Union (COSATU) affiliates or towards craft unions will depend on the extent to which either meet their needs. Black artisans may feel their position is compromised by COSATU affiliates which put forward demands to close the wage gap and increase the skills of all workers." (von Holdt 1993, 34).

Apartheid ensured that, by 1986, 68 percent of South Africa's artisans were still white. Only in the building and furniture industries were black artisans a majority (von Holdt 1993, 29). Increasing white-collar unionization, such as the banking employees union, the South African Society of Bank Officials (SASBO), has also seen a growing deracialization of the union movement, with SASBO formerly a conservative staff association joining COSATU (Baskin 1996, 12). According to Baskin, union densities for white males are not substantially lower than those of black workers. White unions have been recognized since 1924 and for many years were encouraged by the apartheid state. In recent years there has been a resurgence of white workers joining unions. Some have joined predominantly black unions (e.g., in the auto industry), which are seen as more effective (Baskin 1996, 12). With the mediating structures of patriarchy and experience with the cheap labor system and racist state, women were also marginalized throughout the existence of one of the early and most powerful black unions in the 1920s, the Industrial and Commercial Workers' Union of Africa (ICU) (Bradford 1988). Female participation in the ICU was very low. From its early judgments, the industrial court in South Africa has ruled against racism, including discriminatory trade union practices. In *Chamber of Mines v. Council of Mining Unions*, the court ruled that the Council's refusal to agree to remove racially discriminatory provisions in the Mine Employees' Pension Fund was an unfair labor practice (Mphelo, Grealy, and Trollip 1991). In *Chamber of Mines v. Mineworkers' Union*, the Mineworkers' Union, an exclusively white workers' union, refused to allow its members to train workers of a different race group to become winding engine drivers. This was held to be an unfair labor practice for it unfairly prejudiced the employment opportunities of coloured workers and had an adverse impact on the employment relationship. These decisions suggest that trade unions are under a duty not only to refrain from hampering the removal of discrimination, but also to cooperate positively in its elimination (Mphelo et al., 23). In South Africa, trade unions are designated employers in terms of the Employment Equity Act 1998 and therefore are subject to its antidiscrimination provisions. In Malaysia and India, there is no statutory requirement to consult trade unions regarding affirmative action. Employment equity is not a significant item for unions internationally, including South Africa.

Following the African National Congress (ANC) Charter, COSATU trade unions are non-racial, and in several sectors, including auto, mining, and engineering, have recruited white workers. The National Council of Unions (NACTU) has held an Africanist ideology aimed at developing black leadership, although its membership is open to workers of all ethnic groups. In the 1990s, increasing numbers of white workers joined more powerful COSATU unions. In the longer run, class solidarity could become more prominent than racial differences in the South African union movement.

Malaysia is a multi-ethnic country. In 1990, 57.6 percent of the labor force was Malaysian, 32.9 percent Chinese, 8.5 percent Indian, and 0.8 percent other. However, the agricultural population was 76.8 percent Malay as opposed to 15.8 percent Chinese. The situation is also complicated by illegal immigrants, mainly Indonesian, whose population was estimated to amount to no less than 1.2 million in 1992 and is roughly one-fifth of the labor force. This is largely unrecorded. According to Jomo and Todd (1994), union membership grew from 425,000 to 668,000 in 1991, and by 1996 another estimate suggests a figure of 728,000. While in 1964 almost 50 percent of union members were employed in agriculture, by 1991 this figure had dropped to 14 percent, while over the same period the percentage of union members in manufacturing increased from 4 to 22 percent, in commerce from 4.7 to 9.3 percent, and in services from 30 to 39 percent. The ethnic composition of union membership has changed equally dramatically, with Malays replacing Chinese and Indians as the majority of union members, with their percentage rising from 13 percent in 1949 to 59 percent in 1988. The proportion of Chinese dropped from 24 percent in 1949 to 18 percent in 1988, and the percentage of Indians from 58 percent to 22 percent over the same period. Female trade union membership has lagged considerably behind the increased participation of females in the labor force, with 29 percent of women being union members in 1990. Only 5 percent of principal trade union officials are female. The degree of unionization has also been generally greater in the public sector than in the private sector.

In India, there are five major national trade union centers, with a membership in excess of half a million and with a women's wing dealing with gender issues. Less than 8 percent of the 380 million workforce is unionized. According to Ratnam and Jain (2001), unions have largely remained indifferent to issues of gender equality. Many women are, however, employed in the informal sector in casual construction and contract employment. Female unionization is low for a number of reasons, including not only family responsibilities, but also traditional roles and stereotypes and job segregation.

Trade Union Perspectives on Discrimination

Historically, in the United States certain unions have excluded non-whites from membership by means of limitations in their constitutions. Norgren and Hill (1964) report that in 1930 at least twenty-two national unions, predominantly railroad unions, barred blacks from membership by such means. After World War II, such practices gradually disappeared, though some may have continued on through informal means. Furthermore, partly in response to court cases and affirmative action measures, construction industry unions and employers in particular have been forced to adopt more objective apprenticeship standards and selection procedures.

By the 1940s, a majority of U.S. labor unions affiliated to the AFL had organized segregated locals or all-black auxiliary units, which had the effect of excluding black workers from certain job classifications. Auxiliary locals were subordinate to their white local's union officials and only nominally enjoyed equal status within the national union. In some cases, blacks were opposed to integration because they felt that segregated locals gave them a measure of job security. Nonetheless, their effect was to limit blacks to a narrow range of unskilled, low-paying jobs with minimum promotion prospects.

In Canada, a number of court cases have concerned union attempts to exclude workers on the basis of race, creed, nationality, ancestry, or place of origin, which suggests that the situation there has historically not been very different from that in the United States. One means of restricting the supply of labor, which has also been an issue in Canada, is the exclusion of women from employment upon marriage. Thus, in 1971, the Manitoba Human Rights Commission had to act to abolish a collective agreement between a union and a municipality which permitted termination of employment under such circumstances.

More recently, a more positive attitude at least toward women's issues has been detected among Canadian unions (Kumar and Acri 1992). This can be seen in two policy documents—*The Equality Challenge: Taking Hold of Our Future* (Canadian Labour Congress 1988) and *Taking Stock and Moving Forward: Union Women in the 1990s* (Ontario Federation of Labour 1990). Key clauses have been inserted into collective bargaining agreements relating to gender-neutral language, no discrimination clauses, sexual harassment, affirmative action/employment equity, family-related leave, child care, job protection in the event of technological change, and part-time workers' rights. However, Kumar and Acri conclude that success has been somewhat mixed in that progress has been slow in regard to some of these issues and the performance of individual unions varies markedly with public sector unions being more successful than private ones.

In both the United States and Canada, seniority provisions are the norm. These provisions may slow down or prevent the integration of black workers or women in the workplace by ensuring that recently hired employees from these groups will be the first to go in times of layoffs. In the United States, following the adoption of Title VII of the Civil Rights Act of 1964, there were innumerable lawsuits on the issue, culminating in a series of Supreme Court decisions in the late 1970s and early 1980s. Yet in Canada, Dulude (1995) reports that there has not been a single case of direct challenge to seniority systems.

In Britain, the union response to the waves of immigrant workers from the new Commonwealth in the 1950s and 1960s was significant. In many industries, white workers insisted on a quota system restricting black workers to a maximum of generally 5 percent, and there existed understandings with management that the principle of "last in first out" would not be implemented if it were to mean the departure of white workers before blacks (Wrench and Virdee 1995). In the 1950s, transport workers engaged in strike activity and overtime bans in protest against the employment of black labor. It was not unusual to have motions at annual union conferences asking for black workers to be excluded from particular sectors.

In this period, the Trades Union Congress (TUC) took the view that to implement special policies for minorities would be tantamount to discrimination against the white majority. But in the 1970s this picture gradually changed, and in 1981 the TUC published a charter for black workers, revised seven years later, which encouraged unions to be more proactive on this issue. There is evidence that individual unions have reacted positively to this initiative.

Similar trends can be detected in the unions' policies toward women. When modern unions developed in the nineteenth century, they tended to be craft-based and male-dominated. The general strategy was to keep women out of better paying jobs (Cunnison and Stageman 1993). As a consequence, separate trade union organizations for women developed in the 1870s, and rights to send delegates to the TUC conference were eventually conceded. In 1977, the TUC drew up a charter for women suggesting reserved seats. This was updated in 1990 to include commitment to a policy of proportionality—that is, women were to be represented on all committees in proportion to their representation in union membership.

Thus, both in North America and Britain there is evidence that unions have excluded minority workers from membership, limited apprenticeships in such a way as to favor the majority group, failed to represent adequately the interests of these minority workers who have gained entry, enforced discriminatory seniority systems in collusion with the employers, and on occasion operated segregated locals and branches. However, over time this stance has changed, and a more positive attitude toward minorities has developed.

In South Africa, COSATU, the largest union federation, holds that the economic power structure of South African society requires fundamental change. Redressing past discrimination will occur through legislation such as the Employment Equity Act (1998), but workplace programs negotiated directly with workers and trade unions are preferred. These should then be integrated with national measures such as reforming the education and training system (Collins 1994). Collins argues that for COSATU, employment equity or affirmative action is part of a wider process in providing basic and technical skills to workers. COSATU's policy on employment equity considers it necessary for workers to be integrated into a broader human resource policy. Elements of this policy include an integrated certified education and training system linked to economic planning and restructuring; paid education and training leave; retraining; skill-based pay with training linked to grading and pay; recognition of acquired skills; and career-pathing through training. The Skills Development Act (1998) seeks to promote human resource development especially of those previously discriminated against. It sets a levy of 1 to 1.5 percent on an employer's payroll to subsidize training initiatives, including industry/sectoral training boards. The South African Clothing and Textile Workers Union argues that effective affirmative action will involve the extension of collective bargaining beyond the agenda of wage rates and conditions of employment (Patel 1994). Democratization of the workplace is seen as an important process for eliminating discrimination.

COSATU believes that the state should play an important role in employment equity and in eliminating discrimination through a combination of measures. Among these measures are passing appropriate legislation; using the new South African Constitution, which outlaws discrimination and permits special measures (employment equity programs); addressing workplace discrimination; and making the commissioning of goods and services by the state from private sector companies, as well as state funding or subsidies, conditional on the supplier showing satisfactory progress in implementing employment equity. Such implementation is indeed increasingly happening. COSATU also believes that public sector employment practices should set an example for the private sector and that the labor market should be evaluated and monitored to ensure that historical racial disparities in pay and income differentials are addressed. South Africa is in this regard considered to have one of the highest Gini coefficients in the world. Nearly 75 percent of middle and senior managers are white, with capitalization of the Johannesburg Stock Exchange in terms of black-owned firms beginning to increase to around 8 percent. Although collective bargaining began to erode earnings differentials in the 1980s, the impact of globalization and increased competition has seen employers arguing strongly to maintain high pay differentials in order to retain managerial and professional staff in an increasingly open and mobile international labor market. An important priority for the trade unions is, however, to reduce the apartheid wage gap, which they believe is a legacy of pay discrimination in the past.

The Chemical Workers' Industrial Union, in its strategy for affirmative action, puts strong emphasis on a negotiated policy. Bird (1994) argues that while comprehensive guidelines exist for improving the position of women workers, little progress has been made. Major worker federations such as COSATU and the National Council of Unions (NACTU) have campaigned for equal representation of women in union structures, but union congress resolutions have had only a small effect in addressing gender imbalances within trade unions (Horn 1995, 33). Black women are the most discriminated against and are more highly represented than men in the ranks of part-time, casual, and homeworkers. A Self-Employed Workers Union was formed in 1994 (Horn 1995). At its 1997 congress, COSATU rejected a quota system to ensure women were elected to structures of the federation and affiliates, in favor of setting targets for electing women leadership and employing women organizers. Von Holdt (1997) argues that the federation ignored evidence by the September Commission showing that it had made no progress in this regard.

It is an offense, under the Sedition Act in Malaysia, to discuss any form of amendment to the positive discrimination provisions of the Constitution (Thompson 1993, 39). Contesting workplace discrimination is made more difficult by the tightly circumscribed capacity of the workforce union. The workforce in the export-led production of textiles and electronics is largely composed of women. Malaysia's trade unions have not played a role in integrating ethnic groups, apparently because the Indian origins of trade union leaders are not conducive to Chinese membership, and because the Malay working class was not in any case engaged in wage labor (Jesudason 1990, 40). Imposition of quotas has arguably reinforced ethnic divisions, and income disparities are greater within the Malayan community than within other ethnic groups (Plant 1992, 22; Wentzel 1996, 25). However, with high economic growth, unlike India and South Africa, the Malaysian experience shows success in that poverty has decreased and education and employment for Malays have improved.

Patterns of Union Discrimination: Empirical Studies

Most empirical work has concentrated on the effect of trade unions on the majority/minority relative wage rate. This effect will be determined by three factors: the difference in the percentage of each group which is unionized or subject to collective bargaining coverage; the difference, if any, in the percentage union wage markup across groups; and the depressing effect of unionization on the wages of nonunionists. The union effect on relative employment is more problematical. Kuhn (1998), for example, argues that union effects on employment are theoretically ambiguous and there is almost no empirical evidence to support the claim that unions reduce employment.

In the United States, there have been a number of time-series analyses focusing on these issues. Thus, Rapping (1970) attempted to estimate the impact of unions on the percentage change in nonwhite male employment relative to the total change in male employment and unionization in the periods 1910–1930 and 1930–1960, but was unable to find conclusive evidence that the presence of unions had increased racial barriers. Ashenfelter and Godwin (1972) were able to confirm the hypothesis, for the period 1900–1967, that industrial unionism had a less discriminatory effect on the black-white wage ratio than did craft-unionism. Moore and Raisian (1980) showed that over the period 1967–1974 union-relative wage effects were subject to considerable cyclical fluctuations, but the fact that their results differ for blue-collar and white-collar workers suggests that factors other than cyclical forces were at work.

The cross-sectional results for the United States are not entirely consistent. Oaxaca (1965) found that wage differentials were highest among black males and white females within occupational/regional subgroups, while Ashenfelter (1976) found that females and white males obtained roughly the same wage advantages from union membership and black males significantly more. Ashenfelter estimates that overall unionization may narrow white/black wage differentials by 2.3 percent but widen male/female differentials by 2.9 percent.

In both Canada and Britain, empirical studies of the effects of unions on racial differentials are notable by their absence. However, there are a number of studies of the impact of unions on gender differentials. For Canada, Gunderson (1975) found a substantial effect in raising the wages of women relative to men from a ratio of 0.82 to 0.90, but since women are much less likely to be unionized the total impact of unions favors male wages. Since then, however, the gap in male and female unionization rates has narrowed. Doiron and Riddell (1994) conclude that male-female earnings differences in the nonunion sector make a substantially larger contribution to the gender earnings gap than do male-female earnings differences in the union sector. This result is consistent with unions reducing the impact of gender discrimination on earnings in net terms. We should also bear in mind that unions tend to narrow wage dispersion. Lemieux (1998) suggests that for Canada unions reduce overall wage inequality for men but not for women (because it is predominantly high wage women who tend to be unionized in Canada and their wages are raised by unions).

For Britain, Nickell (1977) found that the union markup for women was 14 percent in 1966 compared to 5 percent for men, and 19 percent in 1972 compared to 18 percent for men. Joshi and Paci (1998) found that the positive wage premium for women applied only to part-timers, not full-timers, and suggested that this might be accounted for by the coverage of nonmembers by union agreements being limited to full-time jobs. However, this result contrasts with that of Main and Reilly (1992), who allow for the simultaneous determination of union and employment status, where employment status is defined in terms of the full-time/part-time employment split. The mean differential reported for full-time workers suggests a markup of 14.6 percent and for part-time workers of 15.3 percent, substantially higher estimates than found for male employees.

To conclude, it does appear on balance that unions change the relative wage differential in favor of black workers and against women in the United States, but in favor of women in Canada and Britain. However, the overall impact is quantitatively small.

Wage inequality is more extreme in South Africa than in the vast majority of countries. According to Schultz and Mwabu (1998), the average wage of a white worker is five times as great as the average for an African, although half the difference is explained by differences in education and location. Their regression analysis suggests that an African union worker receives a wage that is 60 percent higher than that of a nonunion worker with the same observed characteristics, while a white union worker receives a wage that is 5 percent lower than that of a comparable nonunion worker. Clearly, therefore, unions have considerable potential for reducing racial wage inequality. However African union workers only represent one in seven of the African workforce. The estimated union racial wage effect dwarfs that found in the industrialized countries, including the United States, Canada, and Britain. These results are more substantial than those of Moll (1993) for 1985. He found that the union wage effect for black male and female blue-collar workers in 1985 was around 24 percent. This compared with a union wage effect of 13 percent for white skilled and semiskilled male workers.

For both whites and Africans male unionization is much higher than for that of women (21.6 compared to 10.8 percent and 36.8 compared to 22.0 percent in 1993), but for coloured and Asians the figures are substantially higher and much closer.

Of 25,000 shop stewards in COSATU in 1991, some 14 percent (3,500) were women (Nyman 1996). Nyman's research shows that the unavailability of women for shop steward elections is the largest reason for their low representation in shop steward ranks. The reasons for their nonavailability for election include lack of time because of family commitments, single parenthood, lack of childcare facilities, and combining homework, job and the extensive responsibilities of shop stewards. Other factors found include not being taken seriously by male members and leaders, sexual harassment, and a "glass ceiling" in terms of union leadership positions (Nyman, 32). Perhaps even lower on the industrial relations agenda of both unions and employers is the question of gay and lesbian rights. The National Coalition for Gay and Lesbian Equality launched an Equal Rights Project to work with trade unions, workers, and employers on educational programs aimed at building awareness, tolerance, and action programs on gay and lesbian issues in the workplace (Jara 1996).

Women are underrepresented in COSATU (Orr, Daphne, and Horton 1997). A study by the National Labour and Economic Development Institute (NALEDI) indicated that, while some 36 percent of total COSATU membership are women, women occupy 15 percent of regional leadership positions and 8 percent of national leadership positions in the union federation (Filita 1997; Orr et al. 1997). Some unions outside COSATU have a better gender balance (Baskin 1994, 4133). While adherence to the principle of nonsexism is officially espoused, equal participation of women in union structures has not occurred. Participation of women in the South African economy has increased to over 40 percent of people in formal employment. Table 6.1 shows the representation of

Table 6.1
Role of Women in COSATU Affiliates

Union	Est. female membership (%)	Female regional leadership (%)	Female national leadership (%)
Sadwu	80%	100%	100%
Nehawu	62%	41%	0%
Sactwu	65%	21%	33%
Fawu	-	21%	0%
Ppwawu	8%	14%	0%
TGWU	45%	9%	0%
Saccawu	70%	7%	33%
CWIU	-	5%	0%
Sadtu	Over 50%	4%	20%
Numsa	15%	2%	0%
Sarhwu	1%	0%	0%
Samwu	15%	0%	0%
Potwa	7%	0%	0%
NUM	-	0%	0%
Cawu	2%–3%	0%	0%
COSATU	36%	12%	17%
Total		**13%**	**13%**
Total (excl Sadwu)		**8%**	**8%**

Source: Baskin, J. *Unions in Transition NALEDI.* Johannesburg, 1994: 42.

women in COSATU affiliates. The largest representation occurs in unions within industries employing large numbers of women, such as commercial, catering, retailing, clothing and textiles, domestic works, health, and education. In South Africa, employment equity programs are preoccupied with racial discrimination, neglecting gender issues, which are lower on the agenda of both trade unions and employers.

Gender issues remain outside the mainstream activities of unions, although some unions such as the National Union of Metalworkers in the Western Cape

Table 6.2
COSATU and Affiliates Occupational Positions According to Gender

Current position	Male	Female	Total (M&F)	Females as % of total
Local administrator	2	32	34	94
Branch administrator	1	24	25	96
Regional administrator	3	48	51	94
H/O administrator	5	53	58	91
Local organiser	79	7	86	8
Branch organiser	33	8	41	20
Regional organiser	46	6	52	12
National organiser	24	3	27	11
Branch secretary	17	4	21	19
Regional secretary	23	1	24	4
General secretary	10	0	10	0
Research officer	6	3	9	33
Legal officer (regional)	14	3	17	18
Legal officer (national)	2	3	5	60
Education officer (branch)	4	0	4	0
Education officer (regional)	12	0	12	0
Educational officer (national)	11	3	14	21
Media officer	5	0	5	0
Other	43	40	83	48
Total	**340**	**238**	**578**	**41%**

Source: Union officials survey, Buhlungu (1997).

have taken initiatives, including campaigns and organization of strategies and workshops to address this concern (Jantjies and MacQuene 1998, 67–69). Like both India and Malaysia, South African society remains extremely patriarchal, creating a glass ceiling that prevents women from progressing through trade union ranks to high positions. Within COSATU over 90 percent of the clerical and administrative positions are held by women. Women fare better in specialist positions that require professional qualifications, such as national legal officers (60 percent women) and research officers (33 percent); but women occupy less than 20 percent of core posts of union organizers at local, branch, and regional and national levels (Buhlungu 1998, Table 6.2).

Unions consider home-based workers, for example, as exploited, push for enforcement of labor laws, and sometimes attempt to organize them. Cases exist in India of home-based microenterprise development and union organization through the Self-Employed Women's Association (SEWA) (Prugl and Tinker 1997). Home-based workers are not easily identified as either self-employed or dependent workers because their employment status fails to capture gender subordination salient in home-work. Bhatt (1995) and Jhabvala (1995) refer to examples of the manifest solidarity of female Indian homeworkers through SEWU, a large regional organization aimed at improving their plight. Economic development through irrigation schemes in south India has led to positive attitudes among rural women toward modernization and active participation in trade unions (Satyanarayana, 1994). Studies of the relative deprivation of women in Indian tea plantations refer to the role of unionization as a form of empowerment and education with respect to labor rights in a patriarchal environment (Balagopal 1990). Similarly to South Africa, social, occupational, and familial constraints account for the very low or even nonparticipation of Indian women in unions. Workplace segregation and fear of job loss are also important factors (Sharan 1986).

A self-employed women's association the Gauteng African Self Employed Women's Association (GASEWA) was formed in the Gauteng Province of South Africa in 1994 in order to develop the basis for a trade union for self-employed women (Masangwane 1998). These developments are a response to the frequent marginalization of women in unions and other organizations. In several sectors where women are highly represented, their working hours are longer; examples of such sectors include clothing and retailing. Most casual (over 70 percent), part-time, and home workers are women. These workers are difficult for unions to organize (Budlender and Theron, 1995; Horwitz, Brosnan, and Walsh 1998). According to Rees (1998), "there is a view inside COSATU that a domestic workers' union is not a viable option" (p. 52). At the end of 1996, the South African Domestic Workers' Union (SADWU) resolved to dissolve itself. This move was supported by COSATU office bearers. Domestic work is done almost entirely by women, and they have struggled to find a home in the union movement. Several unions have challenged discrimination against women and have taken up cases of sexual harassment. COSATU unions such as the CWIU and NUMSA have adopted employment equity policies. In addition, some bargaining councils have adopted codes of practice to end unfair discrimination. Within some trade unions, such as the South African Clothing and Textile Workers' Union (SACTWU), women are proportionately represented on negotiation teams (Dove 1993). Several COSATU congresses have debated and taken resolutions on the role of women in the organization. Strong differences of opinion have been expressed, especially in congresses held in the 1980s (Baskin 1991). A resolution referring to incidents of sexual harassment, which called for "tighter sexual discipline," was passed in the 1980s (Baskin 1991, 356).

Economic inequalities between ethnic groups in Malaysia have been contained, though not significantly reduced, while inequalities in each community have widened (Faaland et al. 1990). After 1970, Malay leaders took on an interventionist role in the economy under the banner of the "New Economic Policy." This policy was introduced to transfer wealth to Malays and to prevent erosion of their already established political position. Targets were set in respect of corporate ownership. This created a Malayan bourgeoisie (Castle 1995, 22). The Constitution was amended to ban public debate on "sensitive" issues such as language, citizenship, and the special provisions favoring Malays.

Policy Implications

The extent of unionization in the six countries considered in this work varies significantly, with Britain, Canada, and South Africa having average levels of unionization by international standards and the United States, Malaysia, and India low levels. Public policy revolves around state-created constitutional and legislative measures to prohibit discrimination in organizations, and such policy varies in the six countries studied. As employers in their own right, trade unions are not exempt from discrimination prohibitions and affirmative action legislation. Within unions, minority representation and gender equity remains a problematic area. In a number of countries (i.e., Britain, the United States, Canada, and South Africa), some unions have instituted policies that deal with this issue. In other countries, women are almost totally excluded, to the extent that they prefer to voice their grievances through separately established associations or unions. Trade unions have to deal with discrimination and equitable representation internally, as well as in grievance disputes with employers. It is unlikely that additional public policy will focus specifically on gender discrimination in unions. Thus, it is clearly left to the unions themselves to address these issues. In the case of ethnic minority representation, statutory provisions do play an important role, but these statutes are more robust in some sectors (e.g., the public sector in India) than in others.

What seems clear is that unions have tended to follow changes in society with respect to the treatment of minority groups rather than acting as catalysts for change.

References

Akyeampong, E.B. 1999, Autumn. "Unionisation—An Update." *Perspectives,* Statistics Canada: 45–65.

Antos, J.R., Chandler, M., and Mellow, W. 1980. January. "Sex Differences in Union Membership." *Industrial and Labor Relations Review* 33(2): 162–169.

Ashenfelter, O. 1976, August. "Union Relative Wage Effects: New Evidence and a Survey of Their Implications for Wage Inflation." Princeton University Working Paper No. 89, Industrial Relations Section,

Ashenfelter, O., and Godwin, L.I. 1972. "Some Evidence on the Effect of Unionism on the Average Wage of Black Workers Relative to White Workers, 1900–1967." In

Proceedings of the 24th Annual Winter Meeting, IRRA, December 1971, Madison, ed. G. Somers.

Balagopal, G. 1990, September. "Women in Tea Plantations." *Indian Journal of Social Science* 3(3): 431–442.

Baskin, J. 1991. *Striking Back: A History of COSATU*. Johannesburg: Ravan Press, 354–356.

Baskin, J. 1996. "Unions at the Crossroads." *South African Labour Bulletin* 20(1): 12.

Baskin, J., ed. 1994. *Unions in Transition*. Johannesburg: NALEDI, 41–44.

Bhatt, E. 1995. In *Women in Micro- and Small-Scale Enterprise Development*, eds. L. Dignard and J. Havet. Boulder, CO: Westview Press, 86–100.

Bird. 1994. In Collins, D. "Affirmative Action Tokenism or Transformation?" *South African Labour Bulletin* 18(4): 48.

Bradford, H. 1988. *A Taste of Freedom: The ICU in Rural South Africa*. Johannesburg: Ravan Press, 90, 110.

Brown, C. 1984. *Black and White Britain: The Third PSI Survey*. London: Heinemann.

Budlender, D., and Theron, J. 1995. "Working from Home." *South African Labour Bulletin* 19(3): 16–17.

Buhlungu, S. 1998. "Full-time Officials in COSATU and Its Affiliates." In "In the Union–Women Union Officials Speak Out," ed. M. Tsolaedi. *South African Labour Bulletin* 22(2): 54–58

Canadian Labour Congress. 1988. *The Equality Challenge: Taking Hold of Our Future*.

Castle, J. 1995. "Affirmative Action in Developing Countries." *SA Journal of Labour Relations* 19 (1): 19–30.

Central Statistical Service. 1995, March. *October Household Survey*, P0317, 30.

Collins, D. 1994. "Affirmative Action Tokenism or Transformation?" *South African Labour Bulletin* 18(4): 40–44.

Cunnison, Sheila, and Stageman, Jane. 1993. *Feminising the Union*. Aldershot: Avebury.

Doiron, Denise J., and Riddell, W. Craig. 1994, Spring. "The Impact of Unionisation on Male-Female Earnings Differences in Canada." *Journal of Human Resources* 29(2): 504–534.

Dove, F. 1993. "Affirming Women in the Workplace." *South African Labour Bulletin* 17(2): 70 72.

Dulude, Louise. 1995, October. *Seniority and Employment Equity for Women*. Kingston, Ontario: IRC Press.

Faaland, J., Parkinson, J., and Saniman, R. 1990. *Growth and Ethnic Inequality:* London: Hurst.

Filita, T. 1997. "COSATU—Marching Forward." *South African Labour Bulletin* 21(1): 40–41.

Gunderson, M. 1975, November. "Male-Female Wage Differentials and the Impact of Equal Pay Legislation." *Review of Economics and Statistics* 57: 467–458.

Horn, P. 1995. "Self-Employed Women's Union": Taking the Class-Gender Intersection." *South African Labour Bulletin* 19(6): 33–37.

Horwitz, F.M. 1998. "The Employment Equity Bill." *South African Labour Bulletin* 22(3): 80–83.

Horwitz, F., Brosnan, P., and Walsh, P. 1998. "Workplace Flexibility and Labour Cost Reduction." *South African Journal of Labour Relations* 22(2 & 3): 26–43.

Jain, H., and Ratnam, C. 1994. "Affirmative Action in Employment for Scheduled Castes and Tribes in India." *International Journal of Manpower* 15(7): 6–25.

Jain, H., and Verma, A. 1998. "Workforce Diversity, Employment Equity/Affirmative

Action Programs and Public Policy in Selected Countries." Working Paper Series, McMaster University Michael G. De Groote School of Business, 4–8.

Jantjies, V., and MacQuene, A. 1998. "Shifting the Balance: Weaving Gender into Union Work." *South African Labour Bulletin* 22(5): 67–71.

Jara, M. 1996. "Workplace Rights—A Gay and Lesbian Issue." South African *Labour Bulletin* 20(6): 21–22.

Jesudason, J. 1990. *Ethnicity and the Economy: The State, Chinese Business and Multinations in Malaysia.* Oxford: Oxford University Press.

Jhabvala, R. 1995. In *Action Programmes for the Protection of Homeworkers*, ed. U. Huws. Geneva: International Labor Organization, ix, 142.

Jomo, K.S., and Todd, Patricia. 1994. *Trade Unions and the State in Peninsular Malaysia.* Kuala Lumpur: Oxford University Press.

Jones, T. 1993. *Britain's Ethnic Minoritie.* London: Policy Studies Institute.

Joshi, Heather, and Paci, Pierella. 1998. *Unequal Pay for Women and Men, Evidence from the British Cohort Studies.* Cambridge, MA: MIT Press.

Kuhn, P. 1998, November. "Unions and the Economy: What We Know, What We Should Know." *Canadian Journal of Economics* 31(5): 1033–1056.

Kumar, P., and Acri, L. 1992. "Unions' Collective Bargaining Agenda on Women's Issues: The Ontario Experience." *Relations Industrielles* 47(4): 623–653.

Lemieux, T. 1998. "Estimating the Effects of Unions on Wage Inequality in a Panel Data Model with Comparative Advantage and Non-Random Selection." *Journal of Labor Economics* 16: 261–291.

Main, B.G.D., and Reilly, B. 1992, January. "Women and the Union Wage Gap." *Economic Journal* 102(410): 49–66.

Marshall, R. 1965. *The Negro and Organised Labor.* New York: Wiley.

Masangwane, S. 1998. "Self-employed Women." *South African Labour Bulletin* 22(2): 59–60.

Moll, P.G. 1993. "Black South African Unions: Relative Wage Effects in International Perspective." *Industrial and Labor Relations Review* 46(2): 245–231.

Moore, W.J., and Raisian, J. 1980, Spring. "Cyclical Sensitivity of Union/Non-Union Relative Wage Effects." *Journal of Labor Research* 1(1): 115–132.

Mphelo, C., Grealy, P., and Trollip, T. 1991. "Discrimination and the New South Africa." *IPM Journal* 9(5): 23.

Nickell, S.J. 1977. "Trade Unions and the Position of Women in the Wage Structure." *British Journal of Industrial Relations* 15(2): 92–210.

Norgren, P.H., and Hill, S.E. 1964. *Towards Fair Employment.* New York: Columbia University Press.

Northrup, H. 1971. *Organised Labor and the Negro.* New York: Kraus Report.

Nyman, R. 1996. "The Glass Ceiling: Representation of Women in COSATU." *South African Labour Bulletin* 20(5): 30–22.

Oaxaca, R.L. 1965, Fall. "Estimation of Union/Non-Union Wage Differentials Within Occupational/Regional Sub-Groups." *Journal of Human Resources,* 527–537.

Ontario Federation of Labour. 1990. *Taking Stock and Moving Forward: Union Women in the 1990s.*

Orr, L., Daphne, J., and Horton, C. 1997. "Preserving Privilege." *South African Labour Bulletin* 21(6): 17.

Patel, E. 1994. In Collins, D. "Affirmative Action Tokenism or Transformation?" *South African Labour Bulletin* 18(4): 44.

Plant M. 1992. "Ethnic Quotas—Lessons from Malaysia." *Work in Progress* 80: 42–43.

Prugl, E., and Tinker, I. 1997, September. "Microentrepreneurs and Homeworkers: Convergent Categories." *World Development* 25(9): 1471–1482.

Rapping, R.A. 1970. "Union-Induced Racial Entry Barriers." *Journal of Human Resources* 4: 447–474.

Ratnam, C.S. Vankata, and Jain, H. 2000. Women in Trade Unions in India. Unpublished manuscript.

Rees, R. 1998. "We Want a Union—Finding a Home for Domestic Workers." *South African Labour Bulletin* 22(6): 52–56.

Reitz, J.G., and Verma, A. 1999, May. "Immigration, Ethnicity and Unionisation: Recent Evidence for Canada." University of Toronto, mimeo.

Satyanarayana, G. 1994. " Socio-cultural and Economic Position of Rural Women: A Study of Two South Indian Villages." *International Sociological Association:* 1–10.

Schultz, T.P., and Mwabu, G. 1998, July. "Labor Unions and the Distribution of Wages and Employment in South Africa." *Industrial and Labor Relations Review* 51(4): 680–708.

Sharan, R. 1986. "Socio-cultural Constraints on Trade Union Participation: A Case of Indian Women Workers." *International Sociological Association,* 1–8.

Sidiropoulos, E., et al. 1998. *South Africa Survey.* South African Institute of Race Relations. Johannesburg, 3–6.

Thompson, C. 1993. "Legislating Affirmative Action: Lessons from Developed and Developing Countries." In *Affirmative Action in a Democratic South Africa,* ed. C. Adams. Cape Town: Juta, 21–46.

U.S. Department of Labor. 1991, January. *Employment and Earnings.*

Von Holdt, K. 1993. "COSATU and the Craft Unions." *South African Labour Bulletin* 17(2): 29–34.

Von Holdt, K. 1997. "The September Commission." *South African Labour Bulletin* 21(6): 14.

Wentzel, J. 1996. "Recycling Race in the Rainbow Nation." *Frontiers of Freedom.* South African Institute of Race Relations, Fourth Quarter, 25.

Williams, W. 1997. "W.H. Hutt and the Economics of the Colour Bar." *Journal of Labour Research* 18(2): 191–203.

Wrench, J., and Virdee, S. 1995, June. *Organising the Unorganised: "Race" Poor Work and Trade Unions.* Centre for Research in Ethnic Relations, Research Paper in Ethnic Relations No 21, University of Warwick.

Chapter 7
Public Policy

Introduction

Public policy, its rationale, content, and compliance, is key to enhancing inter-group relations, valuing diversity, and workplace justice. It may also be a source of contention and conflict if certain groups believe it has an adverse impact on their interests. Public policy sets a framework and may reflect a vision of a society's values and norms. Its legal interpretation establishes jurisprudence for organizations to follow. In this chapter we discuss the constitutional, legislative, and legal interpretative features of public policy in the selected countries—South Africa, India, Malaysia, Canada, the United States, Northern Ireland, and the United Kingdom—and compare their similarities, differences, and limitations.

Systemic discrimination is evident to varying degrees in all countries. Given South Africa's legacy of systemic discrimination, for example, it is appropriate for the right to equality to be qualified by the right of the state and employers to implement affirmative action policies (Rycroft 1999). In Canada, despite human rights laws that prohibit all kinds of discrimination on the basis of color, race, ethnic origin, and various employment equity programs designed to give disadvantaged groups including racial minorities, equitable treatment, racial discrimination in employment continues at an increasing level (Al-Waqfi and Jain 2001). In addition to moral and political imperatives, an economic rationale for special employment equity measures underpins public policy. This rationale can be described as follows.

- Deepening the pool of professional and managerial talent in the private and public sectors
- Expanding an emergent middle class as a bulwark from pressure from mass constituencies and as an advocate of populist policies, for example, in South Africa and Malaysia

- Blurring the racial or ethnic isolation of business ownership and management, which makes business vulnerable to political pressure and attack
- Yielding practical benefits to business through increased diversity via black, female, and other groups representation and economic empowerment in respect of consumer power, better race relations in the workplace, and credible relations between business and government and increasing global competition
- Expanding the tax base of the economy and increasing savings given an expanded nonracial middle class
- Benefiting race relations in the wider society when an association between race and ethnicity and economic conditions becomes blurred (Bernstein 1998).

South Africa's Constitution states that an affirmative action policy is necessary to ensure equality.

Section 9(2) of the Bill of Rights in the Constitution states:

> To promote the achievement of equality, legislative and other measures designed to protect or advance persons or categories of persons, disadvantaged by unfair discrimination may be taken.

In India, the focal point has been on the caste system. The Mandal Commission Report, first announced in 1980, recommended that 27 percent of federal government jobs be reserved for the Other "Backward" Classes (OBCs) of India. This was in addition to an already guaranteed reservation of India's scheduled castes (SCs) and scheduled tribes (STs) by the Indian Constitution. In 1991, these reservations amounted to 22.5 percent of jobs in the public sector. In all, the program recommended setting aside 49.5 percent of federal government jobs and educational seats for lower-caste Hindus and other socially and educationally "backward" classes in India. In 1990, the Supreme Court of India in *Indra Sawhney v. Union of India* ruled that the decision of a former prime minister, V. P. Singh, to implement the Mandal Commission's recommendation was indeed constitutional. Government positions are highly coveted in India because they offer security, pensions, and free housing when one is promoted to upper-level positions. Quotas for the backward classes threaten the position of upper caste students who traditionally have an advantage in merit-based competitions because of their superior education. Although many Indians accept the fact that some reverse discrimination is necessary for India's SCs and STs, they oppose having half of the federal jobs decided on factors other than merit.

Other criticisms are as follows:

- Reservations reinforce and harden the legitimacy of caste distinction.
- Reservations deny qualified candidates opportunities.

- Reservations promote inefficiency in an already immense Indian bureaucracy.
- Reservations present a strong potential for fraud because lower-caste Indians who take advantage of reservations are often those who are already wealthy and have the least need of special treatment.
- Muslim and Christian Indians also make reservation claims, adding to an already complicated system of preferences.

In South Africa, labor laws have been at the forefront of the post-apartheid government's determination to remove unfair discrimination. The legislative armory against unfair discrimination is now quite formidable. For example, Chapter 2 of the Employment Equity Act (1998) prohibits unfair discrimination against designated employees. These include black people, women, and employees with disabilities. Legislative prohibitions against unfair discrimination are also intrinsic to South Africa's Constitution (1996). Chapter 2 of the Bill of Rights, as noted above, contains an equality clause, and like the Employment Equity Act specifies a number of grounds that constitute unfair discrimination. In addition, Schedule 7 of the Labour Relations Act (1995) considers unfair discrimination either directly or indirectly as a residual unfair labor practice. Grounds include race, gender, ethnic origin, sexual orientation, religion, disability, conscience, belief, language, and culture. Temporary employees are also covered by Section 57(2) of the Employment Equity Act. The employing company and temporary employment service will be considered jointly and severally liable for any act of unfair discrimination committed by the employment service on the express or implied instructions of the client. The Promotion of Equality and Prevention of Unfair Discrimination Act (2000), seeks to prohibit discrimination in both civil society and in employment practices. As with the Employment Equity Act, it also relies on the notion of 'fairness' to distinguish between permissible and impermissible discrimination (Cooper 2001).

Similarly, Section 2(2) (b) of Schedule 7 of the Labour Relations Act of 1995 stipulates that

> An employer is not prevented from adopting or implementing employment policies and practices that are designed to achieve the adequate protection and advancement of persons or groups or categories of persons disadvantaged by unfair discrimination, in order to enable their full and equal enjoyment of all rights and freedoms.

More explicitly, Section 2 of the Employment Equity Act sets out the purpose of the Act to achieve equity in the workplace by

(a) promoting equal opportunity and fair treatment in employment through the elimination of unfair discrimination; and

(b) implementing affirmative action measures to redress the disadvantages in employment experienced by designated groups, in order to ensure their equitable representation in all occupational categories and levels of the workforce.

Whereas early labor legislation was aimed at dealing with basic labor rights such as freedom of association, organizational rights, and occupational safety, employment equity legislation reflects the specific values and policy intent of the post-apartheid government (Rycroft 1999). The public policy aim is the juridification or use of the law by the state to "steer" social and economic life in a particular direction by legislative intervention (Clark 1985).

The apartheid legacy in South Africa has seen a racial segmentation of the labor market in respect of limiting access to higher level technological skills and consequent pay (Barker 1999; Isaacs 1997; Standing et al. 1996). The legacy of apartheid has resulted in structural inequalities in the acquisition of education, work skills, and access to managerial, professional, and occupational positions. Black access to trades and skilled work was legislatively prohibited by job reservation in favor of white employees, for example, in Section 66 of the then Industrial Conciliation Act (1956) and the Mines and Works Act. The latter barred black employees from obtaining blasting certificates in the mining industry. These Acts were repealed in 1980—over twenty years ago—yet black progress in skilled and managerial work has been slow.

South Africa, together with India, has one of the highest Gini Coefficients, reflected significantly in large earnings differentials, historically based on racial exclusion and gender discrimination. Although changing, designated groups still face the problem of a "glass ceiling." Research shows that, though increasing, black employees hold approximately 30 percent of managerial posts (Bowmaker-Falconer 1999). A subsequent report shows that whites hold 62 percent of all managerial and professional positions (Nxumalo 2002). Section 27 of the Employment Equity Act somewhat controversially requires designated employers, as part of a required employment equity plan, to submit to the Department of Labor a statement on the remuneration and benefits received in each occupational category and level of the employer's workforce. Where disproportionate income differentials are reflected in the statement, an employer is required to take measures to progressively reduce such differentials. Measures include collective bargaining, skills formation, compliance with other wage-regulating instruments, and benchmarks set by the Employment Conditions Commission.

Public Policy, Legislation, and Employment Practices: Case Evidence

Proving Unfair Discrimination

In South Africa, whenever unfair discrimination is alleged in terms of the Employment Equity Act, a reverse onus of proof is on the employer to establish that the practice is fair. As part of a required employment equity plan, all employers with fifty or more employees are required to review all their employment and human resources practices to remove any provisions or practices that may have a discriminatory effect. This includes recruitment and selection and remuneration. It is in these two areas, as well as in the provision of substantive benefits and conditions of employment, that pay discrimination is most likely. The notions of disproportionate effect and adverse impact are considered in this regard.

Once an employee establishes discrimination, the onus of proof (or, more properly, the evidentiary burden) shifts to the employer to show that the discrimination is not unfair. It is nonetheless very difficult for an employee to prove pay discrimination conclusively. In particular, while discrimination may occur, an employer may cogently submit that pay differences were not the result of unfair discrimination but, rather, due to factors such as differences in performance, experience, competencies, and service. Before the introduction of the Employment Equity Act, the onus of proof was a contentious issue. The South African courts have used different tests to establish what the employee needs to prove in order to establish "discrimination" before the onus shifts to the employer to show that such discrimination is not unfair.

Organized business has, however, supported the intent of the equity legislation. Relevant in this regard is the requirement in Section 20 for all designated employers (those who employ fifty or more people) to prepare and submit to the Department of Labour an employment equity plan setting out goals, targets, timetables, and measures to be taken to remove discriminatory employment practices and achieve greater representation in the workforce, especially at managerial and skilled category levels. The Employment Equity Act does not set quotas, but rather enables individual employers to develop their own plans. Criteria regarding enhanced representation include national and regional demographic information and special skills supply/availability. Section 27(1) of the Employment Equity Act requires designated employers to submit a statement of remuneration and benefits received in each occupational category and level to the Employment Conditions Commission established by Section 59 of the Basic Conditions of Employment Act (1998). Section 27(2) requires that where disproportionate income differentials are reflected in the statement, a designated employer must take measures to progressively reduce such differentials. Section

27(3) indicates that these measures may include: (a) collective bargaining; (b) compliance with sectoral pay determinations made by the minister of labor in terms of Section 51 of the Basic Conditions of Employment Act; (c) applying norms and benchmarks set by the Employment Conditions Commission; and (d) relevant measures in the Skills Development Act (1998). The Employment Conditions Commission is required to research and investigate norms and benchmarks for proportionate income differentials and to advise the minister on appropriate measures for reducing disproportional differentials. The commission is not allowed to disclose information pertaining to individual employees or employers. There is likely to be considerable public and organizational policy debate surrounding what constitutes an acceptable pay curve in respect of differentials within organizations, and indeed whether such pay structuring is possible in a market-driven global economy.

Although the Commission for Conciliation, Mediation and Arbitration (CCMA) established by the Labour Relations Act (1995) is hearing an increasing number of disputes dealing with unfair labor practices and discrimination claims, few of these have dealt with pay discrimination. Several cases have been heard in the Labour Court and at the CCMA on discrimination claims dealing with promotion and fair procedures (*George v. Liberty Life Association of Africa Ltd.* [1996]; *Van Vuuren v. Department of Correctional Services*, Labour Appeal Court 1988 Case No PA: G/980; *Public Servants Association of SA v. Minister of Justice* [1997](5) BCLR, 577; and *Public Servants Association & Another v. Provincial Administration,* Western Cape [1999] 2, BALR 184 CCMA).

There is also growing awareness in South Africa of employees' and employers' rights regarding unfair discrimination in employment and pension fund benefits. In *Leonard Dingler Employee Representative Council v. Leonard Dingler (Pty) Ltd* (1998) 19 ILJ 285 (LC), the Labour Court considered the effects of discrimination, regardless of intent. In fact, the Court held explicitly that intent was irrelevant for a finding of unfair discrimination to be proven against an employer. In this case, differentiation in access to a pension fund was made on the basis of a monthly/weekly paid staff distinction. Most of the latter were black employees who were denied membership of a staff benefit fund. The Labour Court found that black monthly-paid employees were not given membership of the fund. This was held to be direct discrimination. Weekly paid employees were discriminated against indirectly on the basis of race. The residual unfair labor practice provisions of item 2(1) (a) of Schedule 7 of the Labour Relations Act (1995) outlaw this form of unfair labor practice.

Policywise there are some distinctive similarities between South Africa and Malaysia, particularly in that policies occur to address inequalities between majority and minority groups, with the former (i.e., South Africa) being disadvantaged in the past. In Malaysia, the 1957 Constitution (Article 153) recognized the Malays and the indigenous people of Sarawak and Sabah as *Bumiputras* (sons or people of the soil) with protected rights and privileges, including university access. Similarly to the South African Constitution, Article 8(5) states that the general principle of equality does not prohibit any provision for the protection or advancement of Malays. Like South Africa, the majority population is designated for special measures. While in South Africa numerical targets must be set by employers, in Malaysia and India quotas were prescribed and have been used extensively to increase the employment and earnings of *Bumiputras,* SCs, and STs, respectively, in the public sector. Appointments in the civil service in Malaysia were made at a ratio of four Malays to one non-Malay (Jain and Bowmaker-Falconer 1997, 75).

Differing Perspectives

Various key court decisions on employment equity and affirmative action reflect a range of perspectives, from hostility to lukewarm acceptance and full endorsement (Hodges-Aeberhard 1999, 249). They reflect on the usefulness of special measures to overcome discrimination. Recent cases in South Africa show that even in an environment where affirmative action to overcome past discrimination has been legislated as an appropriate method to achieve equity, there are differing interpretations by the business sector and government about its aims and effects (Horwitz, Jain, and Steenkamp 2000). Rycroft (1999) identifies policy issues that have dispute potential. These include failure to implement an employment equity policy and plan, challenges to interpretation of such a policy or plan, grievances dealing with recruitment and selection, promotion and pay policies, appointment of an outside person over internal job candidates, and retrenchment of white employees to make way for an employee appointed in terms of affirmative action policy. Given the racial sensitivities and periodic challenges through constitutional court actions, the above aspects of employment equity reflect on ongoing need to insure that public policy is sensitive to both the need for visible results in respect of employment equity and simultaneously maintaining and building inter-racial and cross cultural harmony.

In India in *Balaji v. State of Mysore* (1961), the Supreme Court dealt with the question of whether caste could be used as the sole test to determine "backwardness." The Supreme Court did not object to the use of caste as a criterion for backwardness. The Court held, however, that caste could not be the sole criterion for the identification of backwardness. Other factors such as occupation and place of living also had to be considered in addition to caste.

In 1963, the Court was confronted with a similar case arising from Article 16 (4) in *Devadassan v. Union of India.* In this case, the issue was whether the amount of unfilled reserved positions in government employment could be carried forward and added to reserved positions for the following two years if that amount exceeded 50 percent. Here, after carrying forward unfilled reservations from the previous year, the total amount of reserved positions came to 64 percent. This was above the 50 percent limit announced in *Balaji*. The Supreme Court declined to make such an exception and affirmed the 50 percent principle set forth in *Balalji*.

Other cases decided by the Supreme Court were: *Rajendran v. State of Madras, Kerala v. Thomas,* and finally, *Vasanth Kumar v. State of Karnataka* before the 1992 *Indra Sawhney* decision. In *Indra Sawhney*, the Court decided that backwardness had to be both social and educational and must not be determined solely on the basis of caste status. However, the type of backwardness was mainly social backwardness, according to the Court. To eliminate the possibility of advanced backward class members from profiting from the reservation schemes, the Court ordered the government to adopt an economic means test. This means test allows for the exclusion of the "creamy layer"—those members of the backward classes who do not need government assistance because they have adequate economic means to promote themselves. In *Sawhney*, the Supreme Court continued to follow the *Balaji* 50 percent rule. Only in exceptional circumstances would reservations be permitted to exceed 50 percent. The Court declined to extend reservations to promotions once a member of a backward class was employed. The Court observed that, once hired, members of the backward classes could compete and earn promotions on merit as do other public employees.

It has been suggested that the percentage of reservations for OBCs be lowered to 15 percent, plus 22.5 percent for SCs and STs, amounting to a total of 37.5 percent. Government agencies and universities should also follow the program of the compensatory education scheme whereby those members of the backward classes who fail the entrance exam by slim margins are accepted and given special training or appropriate coursework to bolster their technical skills, as used in the case of the Indian Institute of Technology (IIT) in New Delhi. Compensatory education should also be implemented at the grade school level and needs to be expanded to the private sector with incentives from the government. Labor unions, community and social organizations, and other civic bodies should also put pressure on the private sector. There needs to periodic evaluations—such as every five years—as in the case of the EE Act in Canada.

In Britain, the Sex Discrimination Act (SDA) came into force with the Equal Pay Act in 1975 and the Race Relations Act (RRA), replacing the earlier Acts of 1968 and 1975 in 2000. Each of these Acts has been amended several times. Each has a separate commission—the Equal Opportunities Commission (EOC) and the Commission for Racial Equality (CRE), respectively, with responsibility for enforcing each Act. There are differences between the two Acts and between the powers of the two commissions For instance, the RRA places a duty on local authorities to promote racial equality—to be extended to all public authorities as per the proposed amendments to the RRA—while there is no similar duty in respect of the SDA.

The Treaty of Amsterdam has inserted a new Article 13 into the European Community (EC) Treaty, empowering the Council to "take appropriate action to combat discrimination based on sex, racial or ethnic origin, religion or belief, disability, age, or sexual orientation." The UK legislation will have to be brought in line with the EU legislation (Hepple 1997). Devolution in the UK—one of the constitutional changes—can also have a significant effect on equality issues in Scotland, Wales, and Northern Ireland.

Another major constitutional change is the Human Rights Act (HRA) of 1998. The Act binds Scotland, Wales, and Northern Ireland as well and came into force in England in October 2000. The HRA provides for the enforcement in the UK courts and tribunals of rights secured by the European Community Human Rights (ECHR). Article 14 of the ECHR requires nondiscrimination on grounds "such as sex, race, colour, language, religion, political or other opinion, national or social origin, association with a national minority, property, birth or other status." The underlined grounds are not covered by the UK legislation except for religion and political opinion in Northern Ireland (Hepple 1997). Many discriminatory acts that fall outside the scope of current antidiscrimination legislation are likely to be challenged under the HRA. The HRA applies only to public authorities, including courts and tribunals (Hepple 1997).

In Britain, the EOC and the CRE have the power to request information from employers and other organizations, to undertake "formal investigations" and to issue "nondiscrimination notices." Both agencies have the authority to issue Codes of Practice. Although adherence to such codes is voluntary on the part of employers, such noncompliance may be taken into account in legal proceedings.

Although there is no general provision for affirmative action (AA) in the above-mentioned legislation, AA is permissible in recruitment and training where there have been fewer or no members of one race or sex in particular work in the previous twelve months. Northern Ireland has its own Sex Discrimination Order, 1976, and Equal Opportunities Commission (now the Equality Commission), but legislation covering racial discrimination was enacted recently. Religion, not covered by legislation in Britain, has the most extensive legislative coverage in Northern Ireland, with provisions for both AA and contract compliance.

In the United States, there are a number of legislative acts such as the Civil Rights Acts of 1964 and 1991; and the Presidential Executive Orders dating back to 1965. The United States has had Uniform Employee Selection Guidelines since 1978. These guidelines apply to selection, promotion, training, transfer, and other staffing practices. They are subscribed to by all federal government agencies in the country, such as the Equal Opportunity Commission (EEOC), the Civil Service Commission, the Office of the Federal Contract Compliance Programs (OFCCP), and the Justice Department (Jain and Bowmaker-Falconer 1999). The U.S. government has several agencies that administer various legislative acts and Presidential Executive Orders. The EEOC protects the private rights of individuals through its administration of Civil Rights Acts, for example. The OFCCP protects the employment laws and rights of the federal government and its contracts with private sector organizations. The balance of federal agencies enforces affirmative action at federally conducted and federally funded programs, where the primary purpose of the funding is employment. The federal guidelines in the United States offer sound policy advice and practices. These include alternative selection procedures which avoid an adverse impact on designated groups covered by the legislation. Specific guidelines cover job advertising, use of psychometric test selection procedures and ratios of disparate treatment in interviews, sexual discrimination guidelines, discriminatory wages, job performance measures, effective recordkeeping, and measures on enforcement and monitoring.

Affirmative action remains a highly controversial policy issue in the United States. Recent court decisions (such as *Adarand v. Pena*, U.S. Supreme Court) and state-level referenda (such as Proposition 209 in California) are likely to influence the use of affirmative action in employment at the state level. Other actions by courts and legislatures are pending in this regard (Holzer and Neumark 2000). In the *Adarand* case, the Court invalidated minority set-asides that fail to meet strict new standards, with a call for mending, though not ending, affirmative action. There has been mounting pressure at both the federal and state level to either reform or eliminate affirmative action programs (National Planning Association 1996). Affirmative action admissions to universities in some jurisdictions such as Texas have been invalidated. However, affirmative action measures have contributed to gains made by African Americans and other minorities (Holzer and Neumark 2000; Leonard 1987). It has been an effective policy tool for increasing opportunity in all countries in our analysis.

Employment equity in South Africa, unlike employment in the United States, is at an emergent stage of development as a policy measure. Although it, too, has attracted criticism, there is general agreement that special measures are necessary to redress past injustice and inequalities arising from unfair discrimination.

In South Africa, the Constitution, as well as the prohibitions contained in the various Acts mentioned elsewhere, distinguishes permissible discrimination from impermissible discrimination. (See *Leonard Dingler Employee Representative Council v. Leonard Dingler (Pty) Ltd* (1998) 19 ILJ 285 (LC) at 294 F-H). In the employment context, permisable discrimination is based on the inherent requirements of the job test. The reverse onus of proof in these statutes, whereby an employer is required to prove that discrimination is not unfair, has been criticized by employer organizations such as Business South Africa and non-govermental organizations such as the South African Institute of Race Relations (Jeffery 2000). Organized business has, however, supported the intent of the equity legislation. Relevant in this regard is the requirement in Section 20 for all designated employers (those who employ fifty or more people) to prepare and submit to the Department of Labour an employment equity plan. The plan must set out goals, targets, timetables, accommodation, and other measures to be taken to remove discriminatory employment practices and achieve greater representation in the workforce, especially at managerial and skilled category levels.

In the *Leonard Dingler* case in South Africa, the judge argued that even if the monthly/weekly criterion for membership of a staff benefit fund was valid, it was applied inconsistently on racial grounds. Indirect discrimination also occurred where criteria, conditions, or policies are applied which appear to be neutral but which adversely impact a disproportionate number of a certain racial group and where these criteria are not justifiable. Here, the reverse onus of proof becomes relevant, as the employer has to give a convincing response as to why the discrimination is not unfair in effect, particularly as an adverse and disparate impact occurred. The onus rests on the employer to show that the object of the discriminatory practice or policy is legitimate and that the means used to achieve it are rational and proportional. South African labor law allows discrimination on the basis of inherent job requirements. But the object of an employer's conduct must be fair, and the means rational.

In *NUTESA v. M L Sultan Technikon* (1997), the issue centered on whether an employer is obliged to interview all candidates who meet the requirements set out in the advertisement. In this case, only three candidates for each of the five executive positions were short-listed. The union's submission, in this arbitration case, was that all applicants who met the requirements set out in the advertisement should be interviewed. The technikon (technical college) argued that all parties had agreed that there would be a ranking of the three most suitable applicants. The time involved in each interview (about three hours) meant that it would be very time consuming and costly to bring the large number of applicants in for the interview; eighty-five had applied for the five positions. The technikon's submissions were held to be sound. It was held that as long as the selection was not discriminatory, short-listing in the manner adopted by the technikon was fair and appropriate.

The case of *Guenbaum v. SA Revenue Service (Customs and Excise)* (November 1998) provides an example of inadequate interviewing procedure. In this case, the applicant was interviewed in Pretoria by the three-person panel. Since the successful candidate was unavailable on that day, one member of the interviewing panel interviewed him alone in Richards Bay, reporting back to the other members of the panel on the interview. It was agreed that the interviews were not conducted along the lines of "targeted selection." It was held that the failure of the panel to interview the applicant in the same way as the successful candidate was irregular, since it gave rise to the perception of bias. Another important issue in the interview process is what information can legitimately be taken into account by the selection panel. In the *Rafferty v. Department of the Premier* (1998) case, subjective views of individuals on the selection panel which lead to undue suasion of the panel, based on one member's subjective preference, was considered an unfair labor practice.

Regarding interpretation and implementation of affirmative action, in *Public Servants Association of SA and Another v. Minister of Justice and Provincial Administration* (1996), the case dealt with the filling of thirty positions in the offices of the state attorney in various cities. The applicants were all white males already employed by the Department of Justice. None of them was invited to an interview for the positions for which they applied, and the Court found that their applications for the positions were never considered since their race and gender did not meet with the preference established for these positions. The applicants alleged that only women were invited for interviews for the deputy state attorney jobs. All of them had considerably less experience for the positions. The Court found that the applicants had proved discrimination since they had been treated on a differential basis because they were white and males. The judge held that merely to label certain measures as falling within the affirmative action provisions of the Constitution was insufficient and that the policy had to be designed, rather than haphazard or random, and that this had to achieve something definite. A causal link between measures and objectives had to exist (Rycroft 1999).

Systemic Discrimination and Organizational Policy

In *O'Malley v. Simpson-Sears* (1985), the Supreme Court of Canada unanimously decided that a company policy adversely affected an employee (O'Malley) because of her religion. She could not work on Saturday because she was a Seventh Day Adventist. The employer was required to show that it tried to accommodate her religious needs on to the point of undue hardship.

In Canada, human rights laws were enacted beginning in the 1960s. Since then, there have been at least three stages in the development of such legislation in Canada. In the early stage, beginning in the 1960s and early 1970s, the courts were of the view that human rights legislation was meant to deal with intentional or direct discrimination such as denying employment based on race, sex and religion.

The next stage in the development of human rights in Canada in the early 1980s was equality of treatment. This was consistent with the view that equality meant that everybody should be treated in the same way—for instance, hiring requirements such as height and weight for a police constable's job. These requirements, though neutral on their face, created adverse effect discrimination for females and minorities and had a disproportionate impact on these groups relative to majority men (Jain 2000).

The third development, called systemic discrimination, occurred when the courts recognized that many barriers can be integral to employment systems and that equality is about removing barriers (Jain 2000). Al-Waqfi and Jain (2001) analyzed 119 legal cases adjudicated by tribunals in Canada over the decade 1980–1999. They found that the percentage of complaints of racial discrimination involving public administration organizations rose from 16.3 percent of the total number of complaints during the 1980s to 42.2 percent during the 1990s. Complaints of racial and harassment doubled from 24 percent of total complaints to 41.5 percent during the 1990s.

In *Action Travail des Femmes v. Canadian National Railway* (1987), referred as the *CN* case, the Supreme Court of Canada decided that employment systems affecting a large number of employees, as reflected in the staffing systems at CN such as recruitment, selection, and promotion, resulted in inequality against a whole group of women. This form of discrimination, embedded in an employer's systems, became known as systemic discrimination. Systemic discrimination has been well established in the law since the mid-1980s (Jain 2000).

Similarly, in a case in September 1999 in British Columbia *(Public Service Employee Relations Commission v. British Columbia Government and Service Employees' Union)*, the Supreme Court determined that an aerobic standard that kept many women out of a forest fire fighter's job was discriminatory; thereby the Court removed a systemic barrier that would otherwise be a bar to women entering the workplace. In this decision, the Supreme Court came up with a new case law. The Court ruled that direct and adverse impact discrimination should be treated similarly and that the appropriate outcome for a discriminatory rule was not simply that the complainant should be accommodated to the point of undue hardship, but that the rule itself should be struck down.

The human rights statutes across Canada have not kept pace with these legal developments. Most statutes focus on individual rather than systemic complaints. For instance, in 1998, the auditor general of Canada conducted a comprehensive review of the Canadian Human Rights Commission (CHRC) and found that the CHRC, on average, took two years to make a decision on a complaint; dismissed 67 percent of the complaints filed; and had a vast backlog of complaints (from 62 to 72 percent of the total number of claims from 1991 to 1995). In essence, the Auditor General Report found the human rights system to be "cumbersome, time consuming and expensive." Delays are not uncommon to other human rights commissions. In the case of the CHRC, the CHRC's 1999 annual report revealed that about half of the commission's budget is directed to the complaints process, which is largely driven by individuals' complaints which the commission must investigate as per the Canadian Human Rights Act (Jain 2002).

In *Whitehead v Woolworths (Pty) Ltd.* (1999) 20 ILJ 2133 (LC) at 2139, the Labor Court of South Africa accepted that with racial discrimination there was a causal link, on the basis of the facts, between race and other impermissible grounds and pay disparity. The Labor Court was of the opinion that "fairness or unfairness of the discrimination cannot be measured against the profitability or efficiency of a business enterprise" and held that there was no objectively justifiable reason why the requirement of continuity of employment should be imposed on a pregnant job applicant. This was controversially overturned by the Labor Appeal Court in a widely debated judgment revolving around whether the pregnant job applicant could provide continuity of service in a managerial position. Judge Willis accepted that the operational requirements of a business or profitability could be taken into account in determining fairness. With the exception of the *Whitehead* case, most of the above cases refer to post-employment discrimination, which in the Canadian context accounts for 68 percent of all cases (Al-Waqfi and Jain 2001, 20). In South Africa and and other countries, this figure is potentially higher.

In South Africa, as in Canada, decisions based on race or gender, unless they relate to a genuine occupational requirement, can be found to be arbitrary and unfair labor practices (*Van Vuuren* and *Liberty Life* cases). In *Leonard Dingler,* the Labour Court was not willing to accept the employer's argument that the willingness to right past wrongs makes discrimination fair. Affirmative action, however, is not regarded as unfair discrimination in South African labor law. The policy context in which the dispute arises is pertinent. In *Golden Arrow*, the Court found that because it had not been determined in an objective valuation that the jobs were of equal value, racial discrimination in pay had not been established (Christie 2000, 72). The Court noted, however, that this "does not mean that the difference is not attributable to race discrimination, it does mean that racial discrimination has not been proven." Given the allegation of unfair discrimination, the Court did not consider whether there was a causal link, on the facts, between race or other impermissible grounds, and the wage disparity (Christie 2000, 75). Christie argues that an unsettling aspect of the *Golden Arrow* case is whether the real issue was that Louw and Beneke had been treated differently as employees and that despite a 61 percent pay differential, the jobs were not sufficiently similar to necessitate an inquiry into the link, if any, of pay and job grade. Adding to this concern is the ex post facto job grading that occurs only because a dispute was declared. The applicants in this case argued in the alternative that the 61 percent difference in salaries was disproportionate to the difference in value of the two jobs. Yet the Court accepted the employer's expert testimony that there can be up to 105 percent difference between a job two grades apart, and that large disparities are "normal." Yet, here the pay system and criteria for pay setting were neither systematic nor transparent, and starting pay rates were not linked to an objective reference. The employer should have been required to point to some reliable factor(s) other than race. Customary disparities are not a justification for continuing discrimination (Christie 2000, 73). A generalized reliance on labor demand and subjective criteria such as attitude may in a historically discriminatory labor market have the effect of entrenching imbalances that the law intended to remove. This is especially pertinent in light of the expert evidence led by the Company in *Golden Arrow* that entry level "pegs" the employee's salary for years to come—in that case, both Louw and Beneke continued to earn the salaries they earned in 1990, coupled with similar incremental annual increases, despite Beneke's "promotion" in 1994. That must be seen against the background of a racially distorted market in 1990—conceded by the expert witness—which would ensure a racially discriminatory entry level salary in the first place. It can therefore be argued that the current pay disparity is simply the perpetuation of past discrimination.

Conclusion

Government and other agencies in most of the countries surveyed in this work have special awards to encourage voluntary compliance by employers. But a real challenge is for organizations to move from a compliance mindset to one of commitment to the spirit of valuing a diverse workforce and respect for the individual. The intent of public policies shows considerable similarity in different countries. However, the beneficiaries, or designated groups, vary. In India, for example, the focus is on the caste system, whereas in the United States and Canada it is on racial minorities and gender issues and in South Africa and Malaysia it is on majority groups. Public policy is rooted in the historical and ethnic makeup and complexity of each society. Cross-cultural and comparative analyses are important in helping us learn how and why policies are introduced and how to assess their effectiveness. Policy choices should, however, be sensitive and directly relevant to the unique context of a particular society. But we can learn from policy and best practice elsewhere.

In South Africa, for example, apartheid employment policies resulted in distortions in the labor market, creating artificial racially-based skills shortages. As a result, white employees occupied the more senior positions and were paid more than black employees doing work of equal value, or in the same grades. The cost of a quick, short-term remedy of the "apartheid wage gap," is seen as prohibitive, especially in large organizations. A more appropriate remedy is to review relevant discriminatory practices, anomalies, and distortions resulting from past discrimination, and to develop a plan to systematically address the matter by a defined time. Even when employers explicitly espouse these policies, the consequences of years of systematic discrimination continue to skew both internal and external labor markets. This is almost universally true in the other countries analyzed here, but especially so in emergent economies such as India, Malaysia, and South Africa.

In the external labor market, skills shortages remain in several of the countries in this book, requiring employers to continue to adjust remuneration policies to attract employees who have the skills, even though they may have been beneficiaries of discriminatory labor market policies. In the internal labor market, as previously discussed, an "apartheid premium" tends to persist in South Africa. A pay premium, if based on an objective economic/business need to attract a specialized scarce skill, is not necessarily unfair discrimination. From a public policy and legislative view, a premium can be appropriate to meet a legitimate business need and as such is not necessarily unfair discrimination. (See *Woolworths (Pty) Ltd. v Beverley Whitehead* [Case No. CA 06/99, L.A.C.], where the Labour Appeal Court in South Africa in a majority ruling gave a commercial rationale of uninterrupted job continuity/availability, primacy over fair labor practices in discarding a pregnancy claim for unfair discrimination in not appointing the applicant to the position of human resource manager.) In *Food & Allied Workers' Union v. Pets Products (Pty) Ltd.* (Case No. C283/99. LC), the employer was prohibited from paying nonstriking workers a R200 Pick 'n Pay shopping voucher as compensation over and above overtime payment for continuing work during a two-week protected strike. The applicants argued that this was an act of discrimination in that it involved "unfairness." The practice of making such a payment was held to be an infringement of Sections 5(1) and (3) of the Labour Relations Act (1995). Judge Arendse concluded that there "can be no justification for giving rewards to non-strikers because they refrained from exercising their statutory right to strike" (p.24). Although the employer claimed that it had no intention to unfairly discriminate, the impact/effect of its action was held to be unfair. There were no terms of employment or practice in the company to compensate employees beyond their contractual obligations, which included overtime pay. The Court held that in the context of a legal strike, payment of any award, incentive, or bonus should be prohibited, as it fueled an adversarial approach. Employment policies and remuneration practices were not therefore used in a "neutral" or unbiased public and organizational context.

We agree with Hodges-Aeberhard (1999, 249), that major court decisions on discrimination variously reflect a range of interpretations rather than a coherent jurisprudence. This is especially so of pay discrimination. Despite the constitutional and legislative assault on unfair discrimination and a reverse onus of proof, it is difficult to prove that some forms of discrimination such as pay are due to race or gender. Courts faced with similar facts arrive at different results. Hodges-Aeberhard (1999, 269) rightly asks: "Why should affirmative action be struck down, where the conditions for such measures exist?" Of relevance here is the story of how Mao Tse Tung was once asked his opinion on the value of the

French Revolution. His response was "it is too early to tell." This may well be so in South Africa. Post-apartheid employment equity legislation is just over six years old. Its jurisprudence on employment discrimination will evolve. Unlike Canada and the United States which have had policy far longer, legislation in South Africa required designated employers to submit employment equity plans to the Department of Labour in 2000 for the first time. These plans require evidence of a review of any discriminatory employment practices and measures to address them. Some 20 percent (over 2,500 organizations) of eligible firms have been issued compliance notices for failing to adhere to the reporting requirements of the Employment Equity Act (Nxumalo 2002).

A more comprehensive black economic empowerment (BEE) strategy has been formulated by the BEE Commission in South Africa, which proposes further legislation, specifically, a Black Economic Empowerment Act to increase organizational ownership and control of both companies and productive land (at least 30 percent of the latter should be in black hands). Targets with a ten-year time-frame are proposed; for example, at least 30 percent of private sector procurement should be to black-owned companies, including SMEs and collective enterprises; at least 50 percent of borrowers (by value) on the loan books of national development finance institutions should be black-owned companies; black people should hold at least 25 percent of shares of companies listed on the Johannesburg stock exchange; and a national human resource development strategy should be developed. A proposed National Empowerment Funding Agency (NEFA) located in the Department of Trade and Industry, would be established to provide oversight and ensure coordination of financial and other support for facilitating black ownership. Of the countries reviewed, only Malaysia (where, like South Africa, the designated group is a majority one) has had comparable empowerment objectives.

Policy recommendations to combat racial discrimination in employment may include the following:

- First, antidiscrimination legislation and policies should be updated and strictly enforced, particularly as a short-term measure.
- Second, the cost of unfair discrimination should be made high enough for employers to induce them to adopt staffing and managerial policies, and procedures should be instituted to prevent such behaviors from occurring. Increasing punitive damage payments for victims of racial and gender discrimination and holding employers liable are suggested. A policy of zero tolerance for hurtful, intolerant racially and gender-offensive behavior is important, for example, in using derogatory language such as "nigger" or "boy" (*Naraine v Ford Motor Company Canada* (1996). Organizational policies and the managerial will to enforce them are vital in order to prevent intolerance, workplace conflict, and potential spreading of unacceptable at-

titudes and behavior at work. Erosion of trust and morale occur if there is a gap between policy and practice.

- Third, in the long run, education and training could be a more effective way to eliminate prejudice and misconceptions that lead to racial intolerance and discrimination (Al-Waqfi and Jain 2001). Organizations can achieve equity through the use of reward and performance management systems that recognize positive behavior and progress in both eliminating unfair discrimination and development of people from minority or majority designated groups. These measures, together with educative interventions such as diversity training and effective communication, will enhance policy performance.

Although a significant and valid attack on employment discrimination is enabled by public policy and legislation, the law at best may achieve compliance to its objectives. It cannot guarantee internal commitment and managerial support for broader transformation of organizations, or indeed institutional capacity building. A new culture of learning and integration rather than reliance only on "access and legitimacy and discrimination and fairness" perspectives has become necessary to ensure cohesive and productive work group relations in diverse settings (Ely and Thomas 2001). Public policy and its legal instruments have clear limits. Where they end, employers can make strategic choices about employment equity, affirmative action, and skills development. Organizational prerequisites for moving from compliance to a commitment model in respect of employment equity and capacity building are vital.

References

Al-Waqfi, M., and Jain, H. 2001. Racial Inequality in Employment in Canada: Theories and Empirical Evidence. Manuscript, McMaster University, Hamilton Ontario, Canada, 1–46.

Barker, F. 1999. *The South African Labor Market*. Pretoria: J.L. van Schaik, 23–25.

Bernstein, A. 1998. "Employment Equity and Empowerment: Necessities, Risks and Opportunities." Policy Making in the New Democracy, Center for Development and Enterprise, Johannesburg, 128.

Bhorat, H. 1999, December. Quoted in *Quarterly Trends—National Business Initiative,* 3.

Bowmaker–Falconer, A., ed. 1999. *Breakwater Monitor Report on Employment Equity*. University of Cape Town, 1–80.

Commission for Conciliation, Mediation and Arbitration (CCMA) publication. 1998. Vol. 7, 6.9–7.

Christie, S. 2000. "Litigating the Apartheid Wage Gap." *Contemporary Labor Law* 9(8): 71–75.

Clark, J. 1985. "The Juridification of Industrial Relations: A Review Article." *Industrial Law Journal (UK)*, 69.

Cooper, C. 2001, July. "The Application of the Promotion of Equality Act and Prevention of Unfair Discrimination Act and the Employment Equity Act." *Industrial Law Journal* 22: 1532–1544.

Ely, R.J., and Thomas, D.A. 2001. "Cultural Diversity at Work: The Effects of Diversity Perspectives on Work Group Processes and Outcomes." *Administrative Sciences Quarterly* 46: 229–272.

FAWU & Others v. Rainbow Chicken Farms. 2000. 1 BLLR 70 (LC).

FAWU, Colin Abrahams & Others v. Pets products (Pty) Ltd. 2000, March. Case No. C283/99, LC 1–26.

Fogey, H., et al. 1999/2000. *South African Survey 1999/2000–South African Institute of Race Relations*. Johannesburg: Census Statistics (1996): 295–296.

Freeman, R. 1997. *When Earnings Diverge*. Washington, DC: National Policy Association, 39–42.

George v. Liberty Life Association of Africa Ltd. 1996. Industrial Labor Journal 17(3): 571–601.

Hepple, R. 1997. "The Crisis in the EEC Labour Law." *Industrial Law Journal (UK)* 15: 77.

Hodges-Aeberhard, J. 1999. "Affirmative Action in Employment: Recent Court Approaches." International Labor Review 138(3): 247–272.

Holzer, H. J., and Neumark, D. 2000. "What Does Affirmative Action Do?" *Industrial and Labor Relations Review* 53(2): 240–245.

Horwitz, F., Jain, H., and Steenkamp, A. 2000. Pay Discrimination in South Africa: Overcoming the Apartheid Legacy. Paper presented to the Study group on Pay and Employment Equity at the 12th World Congress of the International Industrial Relations Association (IIRA), Tokyo, May 29–June 2, 1–20.

Isaacs, S. 1997. *South Africa in the Global Economy*. Durban: Trade Union Research Project (TURP).

Jain, Harish C. 2002. "The Challenge of Equality in Employment in South Africa." In the proceedings of the 54th Annual Meeting of the Industrial Relations Research Association (IRRA). Champaign, IL: IRRA, 137–145.

Jain, H., and Bowmaker-Falconer, A. 1997. "Employment Equity/Affirmative Action Codes of Practices and Best Practices." Research and Working Paper Series, McMaster University Michael G. de Groote School of Business, Working Paper # 436. 1–76.

Jeffery, A. 2000. "The Equality Bill." *Fast Facts: South African Institute of Race Relations,* No. 1: 2–3.

Juhn, C. 1999. "Wage Inequality and Demand for Skill." *Industrial and Labor Relations Review* 52(3): 424–425.

Leonard, D.K. 1997. "The Political Realities of African Management." *World Development* 15(7): 899–910.

Leonard Dingler Employee Representative Council & Others v. Leonard Dingler (Pty) Ltd. 1997. Industrial Law Journal 1438 (LC).

Louw v. Golden Arrow Bus Services (Pty) Ltd. 2000. 21 ILJ 188 (LC).

National Planning Association. 1996, August. "Affirmative Action: A Course for the Future." 38(2): 7–8.

Nxumalo, F. 2002. "Labor Department Cracks the Whip on Firms'" (Report deals with research findings by the labor consultancy NMG-Levy reported in the Sunday *Argus*, February 3, 1).

Prior, E.J. 1996, Winter. "Constitutional Fairness or Fraud on the Constitution? Compensatory Discrimination in India." *Case Western Reserve Journal of International Law*. Vol. 2

Public Servants Association of SA & Another v. Provincial Administration, Western Cape. 1999. BALR 184 (2), CCMA.

Public Servants Association of SA v. Minister of Justice. 1997. (5) BCLR, 577–656.

Rycroft, A. 1999, July. "Obstacles to Employment Equity? The Role of Judges and Arbitrators in the Interpretation and Implementation of Affirmative Action Policies." *Industrial Law Journal* 20: 1411–1429.

Standing, G., Sender, J., and Weeks, J. 1996. *Restructuring the Labor Market: The South African Challenge.* Geneva: International Labor Office, 1–11, 185–228.

*TGWU & Another v. Bayette Security Holdings.*1999. Labor Court. BLLR 4: 401–420.

Van Vuuren v. Department of Correctional Services. 1998. Case No: PA 6/98, Labor Appeal Court.

Whitehead v. Woolworths (Pty) Ltd. 1999. *Industrial Law Journal* 20: 2133 (LC): 2139.

Woolworths (Pty) Ltd. v. Whitehead, CA 06/99, Labor Appeal Court.

Chapter 8

Conclusions and Policy Implications

In this final chapter, we provide a brief review of the previous chapters, followed by an integrating framework. In chapter 1, we reviewed the experiences of six countries in dealing with employment equity/affirmative action and antidiscrimination policies relating to women and racial groups. As we noted, we deliberately chose six countries to indicate their varying responses to the equity challenge. There is no universal panacea or prescription for resolving the employment problems of disadvantaged groups in each of the countries. Cultural constraints and unique features of the policies and the groups covered have an impact on the success of such programs. For instance, constitutional provisions resulting in quotas for the disadvantaged groups in India and Malaysia, based on the cultural imperatives in these countries, have achieved mixed success. In the United States and Canada, consistent with a free market and liberal philosophy, reliance is placed on organizations to develop their own goals and time-tables consistent with their business/strategic plans. Some of the minority groups and women in these two countries have achieved a great deal of progress, but much remains to be done. In these two countries, the policies do not mandate quotas, and yet, perhaps due to better enforcement relative to India, some groups have seen their earnings and occupational status enhanced. In Britain, owing to its voluntarist tradition, little evidence of progress in the economic status of racial minorities is evident; however, not all racial minorities have fared equally badly there. Thus, the Chinese and Indians fare much better than the Bangladeshis or Pakistanis. Though it may be too early to make conclusive statements on the South African experience, improved representation of a previously disadvantaged majority is occurring incrementally.

As chapter 2 indicates, discrimination may arise from various sources, including not only employers, but also co-workers and customers. Differences in employment distribution may also occur because of preferences in tastes for particular types of work; this is most clearly seen in the very different occupational distributions of men and women. For these reasons, it is hardly surprising that views differ on the extent to which differences in the earnings distribution are taken to indicate the presence of discrimination.

Chapter 3 shows that equity policies may range over a continuum of required legislated compliance, with the Indian private sector and Britain relying more on a voluntarist approach and the Indian public sector and Malaysia having strict requirements, including quotas. In this book, we have emphasized the productivity-enhancing properties of employment equity policies, but the use of quotas may operate in the opposite direction if there are relatively few members of minority groups with the requisite skills to undertake particular tasks. Here the policy focus should be on education and training programs to enhance the skills of minority group members.

In chapter 4, at the firm level, we suggest that organizations may wish to examine the "best practice" approach in order to customize it for their own purposes. However, this is not an ultimate solution. An employment equity (EE) index is presented and analyzed in this chapter. Although this index has been successfully attempted in Canada and South Africa, more replication in other settings is needed to verify its generality. A sample methodology is presented in this chapter to measure the effectiveness of EE/AA programs at both micro and macro levels—that is, at both qualitative and quantitative levels.

In attempting to adapt the "best practice" approach to their organizations, the first step is for management to fully understand and explore the competitive advantage that may lie in workforce diversity. There is also a cost to not recognizing the diversity potential. This cost is borne by the firm if the competition discovers the advantage before the firm does. The second step is to adopt policies that would promote diversity. Firms can target diverse groups as potential new markets. Firms can likely attract and retain better talent if they adopt a pro-diversity initiative.

In chapter 5, it is clear that as far as pay equity is concerned equal pay for equal work is relatively controversial. Particularly in relation to gender, very few comparisons can be made where work really is equal. The principles of equal pay for work of equal value in Canada and comparable worth in the United States raise a whole host of issues, which job evaluation can deal with only to a limited extent because it is essentially an objective procedure based on subjective values. These concepts raise even more complex issues of how the discriminatory component of labor market forces, as reflected in different wage rates for male- and female-dominated jobs, can be addressed.

Chapter 6, which focuses on unions, indicates that labor unions are one means by which minority group workers may be protected against discriminatory actions by employers, though there is evidence in the past that they have viewed minority workers as a threat to their majority group members. Unionization varies considerably across our six countries, with unionization being low in India. Malaysia, and the United States and higher, but average by international standards, in Britain, Canada, and South Africa. To the extent that unions raise wages, while at the same time compressing the wage structure, both minority workers and women will be helped, assuming that they manage to gain employment. However, the empirical evidence does not give a clear picture of the impact of unions on employment equity across the various countries.

Chapter 7, which deals with the role of public policy, shows that legislation appears to be a necessary but not a sufficient condition for removing discriminatory practices and creating an organizational culture that values diversity. The precise form in which it is implemented remains a matter for debate, and nowhere is this more true than in the case of affirmative action. In the following, we present an analytical framework based in part on the book by Friedman (2000) and Ely and Thomas (2001).

Global Equity—Toward Convergence?

The metaphor of the Lexus and the olive tree developed in his book of the same title by Friedman (2000) is instructive in concluding our analysis. The Lexus represents a luxury motor vehicle as a symbol of modernity and globalization. The olive tree represents the deep roots of enduring traditions that may be ethnocultural, tribal, and religious and that essentially reflect local contexts. The Lexus metaphor posits that globalization is associated with increased cross-cultural diffusion of attributes of Western culture, especially that of the United States, and results in a convergence of business and management practices. The olive tree metaphor posits that local context, especially where institutions, cultural values, and associated traditions are "thick" or "high context" are less permeable to the convergence and diffusion of externally derived or imposed influences. The primacy of the local context may be region, country, and culturally specific and may even be associated with defiant reactions to modernity and perceived hegemonic American political-cultural and value systems. This latter world view prefers to see a divergence and a distancing by these societies from the ostensible cross-cultural diffusion of business and managerial practices considered ethically questionable and a threat to local interests.

Increased ethnocentrism may occur as the diffusion of cultural diversity models with particular values alien to some cultures become more pervasive globally and societally penetrative. Globalized diversity arguably results in an increase in the pluralistic relations of diverse groups and interests in an open global market and individual organizations and is inimical to the interests of groups or countries seeking to exclusively preserve some kind of isolated and distinctive, or divergent identity. However, societies that seek to preserve their cultural identities may be diverse or homogeneous in character and may simultaneously modernize. Examples include Malaysia and Singapore. The metaphors of the Lexus and the olive tree may not therefore be mutually exclusive. India, for example, has one of the most sophisticated information technology (IT) industries in the world, and also has multicultural diversity with centuries-old traditions and identity roots that run deep.

In the context of our work, we conclude that the "politics of difference" remains important in many parts of the world. Our analysis of patterns in employment equity and equal opportunity regimes shows that diffusion, convergence, and borrowing of best practices occur, especially regarding desirable legislative systems (e.g., the South African Employment Equity Act, 1998, containing several features from the Canadian jurisdiction). There are also forces, however, based on specific cultural attributes of a particular society, which enhance systemic and structural distinctiveness. In India, for example, the caste system is an important mediating variable in endeavoring to address discriminatory issues.

Both immediately prior to and after the September 11 tragedy, ethnocentrism has increased in several parts of the world, with an adverse impact on race and ethnic relations. This has not been confined to poorer emergent economies or religiously fundamentalist societies but also reflects the ebb and flow of regiocentric cross-cultural tensions in modern countries in Europe such as France. With forces of convergence associated with globalization, there is evidence of diffusion of aspects of international public policy and practice that country legislative regimes and institutions adopt. These are associated with creating fair and equitable systems of equity, affirmation, and equal opportunity for minority or previously discriminated against majority groups. Local legislative regimes are nonetheless quite carefully designed to address a specific legacy and current discriminatory practices in a particular country's labor market given its sociopolitical and cultural context.

Global Equity—The Outcomes?

Ely and Thomas (2001) identify three different perspectives on workforce diversity: the integration-and-learning perspective, the access-and-legitimacy perspective, and the discrimination-and-fairness perspective. All three may be successful in motivating managers to diversify their staffs, but they argue that only the integration-and-learning perspective provides the rationale and guidance needed for achieving sustained benefits from diversity. The access-and-legitimacy perspective is based on a recognition that an organization's markets and constituencies are culturally diverse. It therefore behooves the organization to reflect that diversity in its workforce profile in order to gain legitimacy with those constituencies and markets. This perspective underlines a business case for diversity. Progress is measured by whether there is sufficient representation in core and boundary positions.

The discrimination-and-fairness perspective is characterized by a belief in a culturally diverse workforce as a moral imperative to ensure justice and fair treatment. It focuses for example, on providing fair and equal treatment in recruitment and selection, promotion, addressing prejudice and stereotypes in the workplace, and eliminating unfair discrimination. A culturally diverse work group would therefore be evidence of just and fair labor practices and treatment. The emphasis is on distributive justice and the institutions, public and organizational policies, and procedures needed to give effect to it. From this perspective, diversity is an end in itself and may not have a direct association with the work or work outcomes of the group itself.

The integration and learning perspective holds that the insights, knowledge and skills, and experiences employees have as members of various cultural identity groups are potentially valuable resources for a work group and organization. Diversity is seen as a benefit in enhancing creativity, innovation, work practices, and group relations, whereby members learn from each other in order to achieve internal outcomes of better group cohesion and external outcomes of rethinking primary markets, business strategies, and practices.

Our analysis has focused on comparative and cross-cultural trends and country experiences in employment discrimination, affirmative action, and employment equity. It has also taken a thematic look at specific issues such as fair pay, employment, and staffing. Public policy debates tend to focus on the discrimination- and- fairness and access-and-legitimacy perspectives. They tend to require a set of rules and guidelines set legislatively by government, sometimes in consultation or negotiation with social partners, such as trade union and employer organizations in countries like Canada and South Africa. Measures of their effectiveness can be defined by:

- the extent of organizational and managerial compliance
- the institutional legitimacy of particular policies and systemic support
- the measurable quantitative improvements or progress in the diversity and representation of designated groups in organizations and industry sectors
- the successful dispute resolution of unfair discrimination claims
- the establishment of a jurisprudence in employment discrimination law, serving as a guide to policymakers and stakeholders such as government, organizational managers, employee representatives, and trade unions.

The access and legitimacy and discrimination and fairness approaches are largely focused on a macro policy framework analysis level. Although this has been the intent of our study, the micro organizational and work group dynamics of moving from a compliance and often legalistic model to a commitment model poses an enormous challenge in all jurisdictions. The-integration-and-learning perspective is most instructive in this regard. In most of the countries discussed, there is anecdotal evidence of this approach. In the cases of Canada, the United

States, and South Africa, for example, where in some, albeit a minority, of organizations, policy and strategic imperatives of diversity seek to achieve organizational transformation in a much more qualitative way. Measurement outputs differ from the access-and-legitimacy and discrimination-and-fairness perspectives. These would include:

- Quality of interpersonal relations, such as trust and cooperation
- Effectiveness of within- and between-workgroup relations
- Mutual understanding of individual and diverse group needs
- Mutual learning from work team and interpersonal cooperation and collaboration
- Organizational learning and effective knowledge management arising from increased innovation and creativity which may be associated with diversity
- Intergroup tolerance and lower levels of ethnocentric prejudice and stereotyping

These may also be associated with performance improvement and higher productivity levels. Importantly, they enable a "different" type of organizational culture to develop, one that reflects a valuing and not just management of diversity, which extends beyond the compliance model with its emphasis on procedural and distributive justice. However, the integration-and-learning perspective, which does not have the institutional safeguards of the other frameworks, will probably only work in a minority of organizations which have the leadership purpose, vision, and processes strongly committed to the integration-and-learning model as an organizational belief system or indeed culture. Arguably, for most organizations the carrot-and-stick methods and procedures of statutory and associated dispute resolution institutions will remain necessary to ensure both increased diversity and fair treatment at work.

The Benefits and Limitations of Policy

An important question arising from the above analysis is the extent to which both public and organizational policies have been effective, and how such effectiveness is to be defined. The three approaches discussed make different assumptions about what constitutes effectiveness and how it is to be measured. The access-and-legitimacy and discrimination-and-fairness perspectives offer more readily measurable factors. These include progress in respect of targets and timetables, changes in the internal labor market profile of the firm, and associated shifts in representation of minority and designated majority groups. From the access-and-legitimacy view, macro changes in the increased middle class of a society would also be an important outcome, where the middle and upper classes become increasingly diverse and multicultural in their representation. The integration-and-learning perspective is more qualitative in nature and advocates measures to establish a supportive organizational culture, leadership, and behavioral changes as noted below. All three perspectives are needed in order to accomplish meaningful progress in achieving EE/AA.

Although a comparative assessment of outcomes may be less valid than evaluating them in terms of a particular society's objectives, in most countries in our study, including Malaysia, India, Canada, South Africa, the United States, and Northern Ireland in the constitutional and/or statutory policies have had positive impacts regarding increased diversity through access to especially middle-class echelons of society with increased diversity of this growing group. In some countries such as South Africa, policy interventions have also been associated with a closing of the racial earnings gap, though this is not necessarily a universal finding. An organizational conundrum is the goal of enhancing diversity simultaneously with having to restructure and downsize through reducing staffing levels and flattening organizational structures, thereby restricting opportunities for the promotion of both historically advantaged and disadvantaged groups. Thus, the relative position of minority groups is likely to be influenced, for example, by the business cycle. In periods of expansion, labor shortages may emerge, which may make it easier for members of disadvantaged groups to find employment. In a recession, some workers will be laid off and relatively low levels of tenure for members of minorities may make them vulnerable to job loss, particularly where seniority provisions such as "last-in-first-out" operate. In general, strong economies are beneficial to members of minority groups.

In developing countries where majority designated groups have the advantage of legislated and constitutionally sanctioned affirmative action /employment equity policies and programs, the actual operationalizing of espoused policy goals and actual gains is hampered by cost-efficiency drives, which put a break on equity goal attainment. This ostensible tension between efficiency and equity imperatives is an important one, which perhaps limits the full realization of the notion that employment equity/affirmative action is good business. Ideally, these imperatives should be complementary and mutually beneficial—equity, fair employment, and nondiscriminatory practices should be good for business. These perspectives are necessary but not sufficient for institutionalizing a culture of attaining and valuing diversity in the workplace. Integration-and-learning and transforming the culture of an organization is indispensable for what we call sustainable equity in employment. The other two approaches offer the necessary procedural, systemic, and legal guidelines for compliance, but on their own are insufficient to guarantee organizational, work group, and individual commitment. Our goal has been to evaluate developments and to consider the effectiveness of employment equity measures in a global context through a country, comparative trend and thematic assessment. With Ely and Thomas (2001), Cox (1993), and Nkomo (1992), we believe that organizational and work group-level studies are also key to understanding contextual factors in managing change. Effective and sustainable change is inherent to addressing the more difficult terrain of organizational behavior issues such as:

- Appropriate leadership styles
- Values, attitudes, identity, and individuation
- Power relations and resistance to change
- Decision making, creativity, and innovation
- Conflict management issues
- Organizational culture
- Motivational and reward systems
- Support, coaching, and mentoring
- Work group dynamics, outcomes, and relations

There are limits to which constitutional and legislative enactment can change behavior, attitudes, and values. They remain critical, however, in reflecting the values, norms, and behavioral expectations that a society aspires to and that it seeks to implement through legal institutions and statutory and fair practice adherence. As noted above, the law may achieve compliance, but it cannot guarantee leadership, motivation, and commitment vital to fostering a culture that values and celebrates diversity. It is for this reason that all three approaches are necessary for achieving sustainable employment equity and fairness at work.

References

Cox, T. 1993. *Cultural Diversity in Organizations.* San Francisco: Berrett-Koehler.
Ely, R., and Thomas, D. 2001. "Cultural Diversity at Work." *Administrative Sciences Quarterly* 46: 229–273.
Friedman, T. 2000. *The Lexus and the Olive Tree.* London: HarperCollins
Nkomo, S. 1992. "The Emperor Has No Clothes: Rewriting 'Race' in Organizations." *Academy of Management Review* 17: 487–513.

Index

Abella, Rosalie Silberman, 2
Abella Commission Report, 21
access-and-legitimacy, 217–18, 219
accountability, 109, 111–12
Action Travail des Femmes v. Canadian National Railway (*CN* case), 206
Adarand v. Pena, 203
adverse impact, 80, 86, 106, 203, 205–6
affirmative action (AA): benefits of, 14–15, 18, 19–20, 84–85, 159; defined, 1–2; effect of policy on, 219–21; negative consequences of, 17–18; plans for, 73. *See also* employment equity
American Federation of Labor (AFL), 171, 181
Andrews v. Treasury Board and Department of Transportation, 81
apartheid, 157, 178, 197, 208–9
assessment centers, 86–88
assimilation effect, 57–58

back pay, 147
backwardness, determining, 200–201
Balaji v. State of Mysore, 200–201
BEE Commission (SA), 210
Belfast Agreement, 29
best practices, 111–13, 215
bias: perception of, 79, 205; in reporting, 89–90, 144; in selection, 94, 105–7, 128
B.L. Mears v. Ontario Hydro, 84
British Columbia v. BCGSEU, 84

Canada: affirmative action in, 20–27, 73–74, 78–79, 84, 86, 208; career development in, 93; collective agreements in, 21–22; legislation in, 4, 71, 79, 108, 160; pay equity in, 143–45; recruitment in, 76; targeted groups in, 6, 20–21; testing in, 81, 90, 95; unionization in, 176–77, 181; workforce in, 20, 23–25, 141–42
Canadian Employment Equity Act (EEA), 113
Canadian Federal Contractors Compliance Program, 73–74
Canadian Human Rights Commission (CHRC), 109, 142, 206
Centre for Indian Trade Unions (CITU), 154
Chamber of Mines v. Mineworkers' Union, 179
Chemical Workers' Industrial Union, 183
Civil Rights Act (USA), 18–19, 72–73, 159, 171–72, 181, 202–3, 203. *See also* Title VII
Codes of Practice, 30, 32
Commission for Racial Equality (Britain), 28, 29–30, 31–32, 109, 201–2
communication, 110, 112
compensation systems, 162
complaint-based systems, 142, 145–46
Congress of SA Trade Union (COSATU), 178–80, 182–84, 186–88, 189
Contractors Program, Canada, 22
Convention 100, 129, 145
Convention 111, 129
convergence, 2, 216–17

coordination of EE programs, 110–11
cronyism, 17
crowding hypothesis, 61, 64

Datuk Shahrizat Abdul Jalil, 156
designated employers, 197, 198–99, 210
designated groups: affirmative action
    for, 34, 42, 74–75; status of, 21, 37–
    39
Devadassan v. Union of India, 200–201
differences, allowable, 143, 147
disabilities, 73, 76–77, 90
discrimination: consumer-based, 59, 64;
    employee, 59; employer, 58, 138; and
    equity, 184, 204, 205, 210–11, 214;
    estimating, 63; positive, 72, 157; sex,
    60–61; for sexual orientation, 21; sta-
    tistical, 61–62, 64; systemic, 142,
    194, 206
discrimination-and-fairness, 217–18, 219
discriminators, 56, 58–60
diversity, 1–2, 217–18
dual labor markets, 61

economic empowerment, 113–14
economic growth, 14, 16–17, 41, 175
Economics of Discrimination (Becker),
    56
economy, effect of, 220
education and training: compensatory,
    60, 201; effect of, 65–66, 136, 148;
    elementary, 48 n.7; to eliminate prej-
    udice, 210–11; of labor force, 6, 12,
    78, 182–83; in Malaysia, 17; neces-
    sity for, 14, 47, 197; quality, 136; for
    targeted groups, 13, 48–49 n.10, 85,
    164 n.19, 215; of women, 149
EE Tribunal, Canada, 23
effectiveness, 108, 218–19
80 percent rule, 80
employer obligations, 36–37
employers: definition of, 142, 146
Employment Act (Malaysia), 155–56
Employment Conditions Commission
    (SA), 198–99
employment effects, 145, 148
Employment Equity Act (South Africa):
    compliance with, 36–39; goals of, 34,
    50 n.15, 51 n.19, 163, 173; provi-
    sions of, 74–75, 156, 179, 196–97,

198; and testing, 81; and wages, 138,
    158
employment equity (EE): benefits of, 39–
    40, 42, 194–95; disadvantages of, 40–
    41; goals for, 1–2, 109; measuring
    and analysis of, 122–25; policies, 21,
    70–71
Employment Equity Index (EEIC), 108–
    11
employment practice reviews, 110
enclave hypothesis, 57–58
Enderby v. Frenchay Health Authority,
    164 n.18
Equal Employment Opportunities Act
    (US), 172
Equal Employment Opportunities Com-
    mission (EEOC) United States, 64,
    109, 203
Equality Commission (N. Ireland), 6, 29–
    31, 202
Equal Opportunities Commission (Brit-
    ain), 18–19, 28, 109, 201–2
equal pay, 146–47
Equal Pay Act (United Kingdom), 145,
    146–47, 164 n.13, 201–2; effective-
    ness of, 147–49
equal pay for equal work/value: and al-
    lowable differences, 143; and gender
    equity, 127–28, 138, 154–55, 162,
    164 n.14; legislation, 150–52; and
    pay equity, 215
Equal Remuneration Act (India), 153–
    55
Equal Value Regulations (United King-
    dom), 145–46
ethnocentrism, 216

Fair Employment Commission (N. Ire-
    land), 6, 30–32, 109
fairness: perception of, 41–42, 79, 86,
    90, 94, 107; in the selection process,
    76, 82–83, 98, 112; as social con-
    struct, 126; in testing, 91
Fair Pay Act (United States), 151–52,
    160
Fair Paycheck Act (United States), 160
federal contractors, 72, 151
*Food & Allied Workers' Union v. Pets
    Products (Pty) Ltd.,* 209

gender composition effect, 66–67
George v. Liberty Life Association of Africa Ltd, 199
glass ceiling , 51 n.18, 197
Gompers, Samuel, 171
groups, identification of, 57
Guenbaum v. SA Revenue Service, 204–5
Guidelines on Test Use (Psychological Testing: A User's Guide), 76

Hennessey v. Coastal Eagle Point Oil Company, 95–96
home-based workers, 188–89
Human Resources Development Canada (HRDC), 109, 124
Human Resources Management (HRM), 70, 71–72, 80
Human Rights Act (Canada), 73
Human Rights Act (UK), 202

immigrants, 57, 59, 160–61, 177
India: affirmative action in, 6, 12–15, 75, 174–75, 208; caste system in, 47–48 n.1, 161, 195, 200–201, 208, 217; equity legislation in, 70–71; other backward classes (OBCs), 13–14, 48 n.5, 75, 195, 201; private sector employment in, 77–78; public sector employees, 98–99; targeted populations in, 4–6; untouchables in, 14, 48 n.1, 75; work force in, 6, 12, 153
indigenous people: Aboriginals, Canadian, 161; *Bumiputras,* Malasia, 15, 16, 18, 48–49 n.10, 75–76, 99, 199–200; Malays, 16
Indra Sawhney v. Union of India, 195, 201
Industrial and Commercial Workers' Union of Africa (ICU), 179
integration-and-learning, 217, 218–19, 219, 220
interviews, 204–5

job barriers, 111
job evaluations (JE): and fairness, 71–72, 142–43; use of, 78, 128, 146, 152, 154–55, 164 n.16; and wages, 163 n.3

job performance, 37, 39, 65, 74, 87, 105–7
jobs: analysis of, 65, 79, 83–84; designation of, 60, 127; federally contracted, 19, 22; gender predominance in, 142, 146; public sector, 13–14, 15, 17; satisfaction in, 93
Johnson, Lyndon, 19, 165 n.23

Labor Code (Canada), 172
Labour Relations Act (South Africa), 50 n.15, 74–75, 173, 178
language, 47, 48 n.2, 57–58, 62, 64
legislation: Britain, 28; Canadian, 21, 27; employment equity, 71–72, 151–52, 162–63, 163 n.8; labor, 34–35; racial pay gaps, 156; recommended, 210; South Africa, 203–5
Leonard Dingler Employee Representative Council v. Leonard Dingler, 199, 203, 204
Lexus and the olive tree, 216–17
litigation: in Canada, 84, 205–8, 210–11; and HR practices, 79, 94; in India, 201; in South Africa, 199, 207–8, 209; in the US, 65, 154, 203
Louw v. Golden Arrow Bus Services, 158, 207–8

Mahathir, Mohamad, 16
Malaysia: affirmative action in, 15–18, 75–76, 208; designated groups in, 47; equity legislation in, 70, 199–200; inequalities in, 189–90; public sector employees, 98–99; target populations of, 3, 4; unionization in, 174, 180, 184; workforce in, 155
Mao Tse Tung, 209–10
meta-analysis of validity, 83, 87
minimum wages, 138, 149, 150, 153–54, 156, 162
minorities, 58, 90
monitoring employment equity programs, 110
monopolistic exploitation, 60–61
multinational corporations (MNCs), 1, 3, 65
multiple measurements, importance of, 92–93

Naraine v. Ford Motor Company Canada, 210
National Council of Unions (NACTU), 179–80, 183
National Human Rights Commission (India), 48 n.4
National Labor Relations Act (US), 172
New Economic Policy (NEP), Malaysia, 15–16, 49 n.10
non-targeted groups, 13, 17
Northern Ireland: equity legislation in, 4, 202; experience in, 28–31; role of religion in, 47, 49–50 n.14; targeted groups, 6; targeted groups in, 29
NUTESA v. M L Sultan Technikon, 204

occupational distributions, 214–15
occupational requirements, 86, 88
occupational segregation: decline of, 159; horizontal, 127–28; in India, 161–62; reasons for, 158; and wages, 137–38, 141–42, 145, 153; for women, 150, 155
Office of Federal Contract Compliance (OFCCP), 109, 151, 159–60, 202–3
O'Malley v. Simpson-Sears, 205
organizations, and affirmative action, 124, 125, 126, 128
Outline Perspective Plans (Malaysia), 16

part time work, 28, 164 n.17
Paycheck Fairness Act (United States), 151–52
pay disparity, 207–8
pay equity plans, 144, 152
pay systems, 126–27, 207–8
peer evaluations, 97
penalties, 23
pensions, 127, 199, 204
performance appraisals, 96–97, 127
politics of difference, 216
predictor-criterion relationships, 105–7
predictor variables, 124–25
PSAC (No. 2) v. Canada (Treasury Board), 143
public sector employment: as an example, 183; in India, 75, 195; in Malaysia, 17–18; in N. Ireland, 30; unions in, 162, 180; wages in, 158, 159; for women, 153
Public Servants Association of SA and Another v. Minister of Justice and Provincial Administration, 205
Public Service Employee Relations Commission v. British Columbia Government and Service Employees Union, 206

quotas and reservations: and fairness, 112; legislated, 214–15; negative effects of, 195–96; in the public sector, 12–14, 48 n.7, 75, 99, 200–201; and targets, 74, 198; use of, 2, 13, 15–16, 36, 71, 75–76, 174, 175

race, effect of, 56, 63–64, 96, 158–59
Race Relations Act (Britain), 32–34, 49 n.13, 72, 160–61, 172, 201–2
Race Relations Order (N. Ireland), 29
Race Relations Order (Northern Ireland), 31
Racial Equality Commission (CRE), 32–33
Rafferty v. Department of the Premier, 205
recruitment of designated groups, 39, 40, 76, 77–78, 84–86, 110
religion, protection of , 28–29, 30–31, 205
Report on the Future of Multi-Ethnic Britain (Parekh), 33–34
Royal Commission on Equality in Employment (Canada), 2

SA Chemical Workers Union v. Sentrachem Industrial Court, 173–74
salary surveys, 128
scheduled casts (SCs) and tribes (STs): quotas for, 13, 75, 195, 201; as targeted groups, 4–6, 12, 47–48; in unions, 175
segregation, 59, 180
Self-Employed Women's Association (SEWA), 188–89
self-rating, 89, 92, 97
seniority, 172, 181, 220
Sex Discrimination Act (Britain), 172, 201–2

Sex Discrimination Order (N. Ireland), 202
sex *vs.* gender, 50 n.16
Skills Development Act (South Africa), 41, 183
South Africa: affirmative action in, 78–79, 208; designated groups in, 47; employment equity in, 203–5; experience in, 34–47; gender equality, 36; job opportunities in, 50–51 n.17; labor law in, 198; legislation in, 4, 50 n.15, 71, 74–75, 108–9, 195–96; policy interventions in, 220; recruitment in, 76; salary structure in, 60; target populations of, 3, 4; testing in, 81; unionization of, 178–80, 182–83; wage discrimination in, 62–63, 185–86; workforce composition of, 35–36, 37–39; workforce in, 149, 157, 197
South African Clothing and Textile Workers Union, 183
South African Department of Labour (SADOL), 108

targeted selection, 204–5
temporary employment, 196
testing: for ability, 76–77, 86–87, 90–91; behavior and personality, 88–90, 91–92, 96–97; for discrimination, 33; drug and alcohol, 95–96; employment interviews, 93–95; false results from, 92; in India, 77–78; perceived fairness of, 107; placement, 92–93; score banding, 97–98; use of, 80; validity of, 81–83
Title VII (United States), 151, 159, 171–72, 181. *See also* Civil Rights Act (USA)
trading cards, 64–65
Treaty of Amsterdam, 202
turnover, 95, 99

Uniform Guidelines on Employee Selection Procedures (Canada), 79–81
unions: certification of, 172, 174; effect of, 153, 159, 162, 163 n.7, 171, 184–85; as employers, 190; and employment equity, 110–11, 172; and immigrants, 177, 181–82; and minorities, 175–76, 177–79, 180–81, 186;

racially exclusive, 173; role of, 176, 215–16; and wage inequality, 186; and women, 175–76, 177–78, 180, 181, 186, 188–89
United Kingdom: designated groups in, 47; legislation in, 4, 70, 72; studies in, 76–77; unionization of, 177–78, 181–82; workforce in, 27–28, 65–66, 145
United Nations Convention on the Elimination of all Forms of Discrimination Against Women, 129, 150–51, 155–56
United Nations Convention on the Elimination of all Forms of Racial Discrimination, 29, 129
United Nations Development Program, 6
United States: affirmative action in, 2, 18–20, 78–79, 84–85, 208; designated groups in, 47; discrimination in, 64–65; federal contractors for, 3–4; gender discrimination in, 66; and international conventions, 129, 138, 150; large firms in, 61; legislation in, 71, 72–73, 108, 156; recruitment in, 76; studies in, 49 n.11, 105–7, 123; targeted groups in, 6; testing in, 81, 90, 95–96; unionization in, 175–76, 180–81, 184–85; validation in, 84; wage gap in, 63–64; workforce in, 18, 150
United Steelworkers v. Weber, 73

validity, 83–84, 86, 89, 105, 107; of tests, 91–92
Van Vuuren v. Department of Correctional Services, 199
visible minorities (VM), 23–24, 113, 122–23, 125, 174
voluntary actions: and HR practices, 72, 76–78; use of, 2, 148, 173, 208

wage discrimination, 126–27, 128–29, 136, 138, 156
wage gap: apartheid, 173–74, 208–9; gendered, 60–61, 66–67, 77, 147–50, 152, 153; in India, 197; organizational, 144; racial, 59, 63–64, 156, 157–58, 159, 197, 220; in South

Africa, 35, 36, 41, 197; in the UK, 164 n.11; and unions, 185–86; in the US, 18, 152–53, 158–59
wage ratios, 129, 136, 137
wage structure, 215–16
Whitehead v. Woolworths (Pty) Ltd., 207

women: in the informal economy, 153; lower pay for, 66, 129, 136; status of, 6, 12, 40; in unions, 185, 186–88, 188–89; in the workforce, 15, 23–24, 35–36, 38, 47, 56, 214
Woolworths (Pty) Ltd. v. Beverley Whitehead, 209

About the Authors

Frank M. Horwitz is Professor in Business Administration, Graduate School of Business, University of Cape Town. He specializes in human capital management, organization change and industrial relations, with some ten years executive experience in these fields with ICI in England and AECI.

Harish C. Jain is a Professor Emeritus of Human Resources and Labor Relations in the MGD School of Business at McMaster University in Hamilton, Canada. His research interests include diversity management and employment equity/affirmative action; comparative human resource and industrial relations policies of multinations; and labor relations policy.

Peter J. Sloane is a professor at the University of Wales and Director of the Welsh Economy Labour Market Evaluation and Research Centre (WELMERC) located in the Department of Economics, University of Wales Swansea. He is also Professor Emeritus of the University of Aberdeen, where he held the Jaffrey Chair of Political Economy between 1984 and 2002.

Simon Taggar is an Associate Professor of Human Resources Management at Wilfred Laurier University and has published research on leadership, employment equity, creativity, and teamwork. In addition, Simon is presently vice president of Human Resources Solutions Inc.

Nan Weiner works in Canada on workplace equity—employment equity, diversity, pay equity, and human rights and harassment-prevention. She has over 30 years of human resources experience including working within organizations, teaching at the university level, and consulting. She is author, along with Morley Gunderson, of *Pay Equity: Issues, Options and Experiences* (1990).